Watching the Match

Watching the Match

the

BRIAN BARWICK

ANDRE
DEUTSCH

Text copyright © Brian Barwick 2013
Design copyright © André Deutsch Limited 2013

First published in 2013 by André Deutsch
an imprint of the Carlton Publishing Group
20 Mortimer Street, London W1T 3JW

Updated paperback edition 2014

A CIP catalogue record for this book is available from the British Library

10 9 8 7 6 5 4 3 2 1

ISBN: 978-0-233-00432-7

Printed and bound by CPI Group (UK) Ltd, Croydon, CR0 4YY

The publishers would like to thank the following sources for their kind permission to reproduce the pictures in this book. The page numbers for each of the photographs are listed below, giving the page on which they appear in the book and any location indicator (BW=Black & White Plate Section, COL=Colour Plate Section, T=top, B=bottom, L=left, R=right, C=centre).

Courtesy of BT Sport: COL8B. **Corbis.** /BBC: BW5TL, BW4TR, BW4BL; /Colorsport: BW5L, BW5R; /Hulton-Deutsch Collection: BW3B. **Getty Images:** /Paul Bergen/Redferns: COL3T; /Central Press: BW1T; /Mike Hewitt: COL5B; /Alex Livesey: COL2B /Popperfoto: BW2B; /Reg Speller/Fox Photos: BW3T; /Bob Thomas: COL1B. **IPC & Syndication:** COL1TR. **Immediate Media:** COL1TL. **Tony Lloyd:** BW8T. **Mirrorpix:** BW6T, BW6B, BW8B, COL3B, COL4B, COL5T. **Photoshot:** / Talking Sport: BW7T; /UPPA: COL6T. **Press Association Images:** BW4TL, BW5B; /Matthew Ashton: COL2TL; /Eamonn & James Clarke: COL7B; /Owen Humphreys: COL4TL; /Paul Marriott: COL2C; /Tony Marshall: COL6B; /S&G and Barratts: BW7B; /Topham Picturepoint: BW4BR. **Rex Features:** /Colorsport: BW1B; /John Londei: COL4TR; /Daily Mail: BW2T; /ITV: BW4L, COL1C, COL7T. **Courtesy of Sky Sports:** COL8T

Every effort has been made to acknowledge correctly and contact the source and/or copyright holder of each picture and Carlton Books Limited apologises for any unintentional errors or omissions that will be corrected in future editions of this book.

CONTENTS

FOREWORD BY JOHN MOTSON

My first experience of televised football came on Saturday, April 29th 1950, when my father took me as a four-year-old to a music shop in Woolwich, south-east London, to watch the Arsenal vs. Liverpool FA Cup Final on a nine-inch black-and-white set in an upstairs room.

I can just remember the grainy black and white pictures – this was three years before most people bought their first television set for the Coronation – as Reg Lewis scored the two goals which won the Cup for Arsenal.

Little did I realise then, but the greater part of my working life was to be consumed by football on television. From my debut on BBC *Match of the Day* in October 1971 through to the end of the 2012/2013 season (and maybe beyond) I spent every Saturday and many midweek evenings seated in the commentary position.

Brian Barwick's book traces the development of our national game on the living room "box" throughout those years, and goes back further to the origins of television coverage before the war.

As a producer and editor at the forefront of the sweeping changes that have occurred over the last 80 years, Barwick is perfectly positioned to consider and analyse football's sometimes fractious relationship with television – to the point where the two became comfortable bedfellows and largely dependent on each other.

When I started in the broadcasting business, there was virtually no "live" football other than the FA Cup Final. Forty years later, it was difficult to avoid it, with matches from all over the world available almost every night of the week.

So much so, televised football became an industry in itself. Not just in showing the games, but in becoming an employment agency for presenters, pundits, analysts, producers, engineers and, of course, commentators and co-commentators.

I have been privileged to be among the chosen flock. Barwick's meticulous research has uncovered things even I was unaware of, especially in the early days when nobody had heard of action replays, studio panels, or satellite television.

The millions who have had so much pleasure from watching the game "on the box" should find a feast of information as to how it got there.

John Motson, Hertfordshire, March 2013

Above: One of Motty's legendary commentary sheets.

INTRODUCTION

I am writing these words having just spent the past weekend in late March 2014 watching an extraordinary sequence of televised football, further confirming its unopposed position as "the best in class" of small-screen sport.

Saturday lunchtime had given us Chelsea's 6–0 drubbing of Arsenal, meaning joy for Jose Mourinho but despair for Arsene Wenger in his 1,000th game as Gunners' boss and also a red face for Premier League referee Andre Marriner, who inexplicably contrived to send off the wrong Arsenal player in the heat of this important London derby.

While BT Sport were broadcasting the action from Stamford Bridge, over on Sky Sports, Derby County were drilling five goals past near neighbours Nottingham Forest in a live Championship promotion clash.

Sky Sports then went into overdrive with a run of three live Premier League matches over the next 24 hours. Saturday's tea-time treat included Manchester United's Wayne Rooney scoring a spectacular Beckham-style long-range goal against West Ham while the following afternoon, Spurs rallied to beat Southampton 3–2 and Stoke had an unlikely 4–1 win at Aston Villa.

Forty-two goals were scored in the Premier League on this mad March weekend, including a hat-trick for eventual champions, Manchester City's Yaya Toure in a 5–0 demolition of Fulham and another three-goal strike from Footballer of the Year, Luis Suarez, in a remarkable 6–3 win for Liverpool at Cardiff.

BBC's hardy perennials, *Match of the Day* and *Match of the Day 2*, were able to bathe in the screening of all of those goals while over on Sky, perhaps the best was kept until last with live coverage of an unforgettable "El Clasico" from the Bernabeu as Real Madrid took on Barcelona. This peak-time Sunday evening epic turned out to be a seven-goal thriller with Lionel Messi grabbing the match-winner, among a hat-trick of goals.

It was an absolutely stunning weekend of top-class football brought to the armchair fan with style and energy and was an exceptional example of how far football has developed from its early days, and how the broadcasting business has come along with it. It has been a fantastic journey for both.

*   *   *   *   *

It is now over 75 years since the first slice of football action was relayed to a small collection of fledging television sets; black and white shaky images broadcast on unreliable tiny screens housed in oversized polished wooden cabinets, the exclusive property of the well-to-do – and only the London well-to-do at that, because the pictures could only travel a few miles across the capital from the BBC's first TV transmission centre at Alexandra Palace.

Arsenal played Arsenal Reserves in a practice match held at the Gunners' famous Highbury Stadium in September 1937 and the short game was featured on the BBC's brand new television service – a momentous event.

A year earlier, in 1936, pictures from Arsenal's First Division home match against Everton were showcased at a Radio Exhibition in London's Olympia, and by 1938 things had significantly progressed with that year's FA Cup Final between Preston North End and Huddersfield Town covered on three cameras and broadcast live from Wembley Stadium. Televised football was off and running. And it has never looked back.

Spin forwards nearly eight decades and these days live big-time football is one of the great "must-haves" for broadcast organisations the world over. It has become a sporting currency with a value in the marketplace that just grows and grows – from millions to billions.

And there is an increasingly wide range of reasons for major international media conglomerates to invest in top-class football. Some use it as key content or an expensive marketing tool to launch a major new broadcast service, some to introduce and sell innovative new technological applications off its back, some buy it to keep it away from their competitors, some want to stack up huge commercial and subscription revenues through it, and then free-to-air broadcasters like the BBC televise football to help reflect the life of the nation.

What football on the small-screen really means to the *viewer* is absolutely top-drawer television – best watched live, a never-ending drama with a different ending every time. It is a long-running series that straddles the seasons – like a book you just can't put down.

Heroes and villains, classic goals and controversial characters, legends, great teams, great players, sharp tackles, sharp words, triumph and tragedy, memorable moments, long-lasting images, accompanied with commentary lines almost as famous as the pictures themselves.

And in every era of the television industry's remarkable development, the broadcasting of football and sport in general has often been the vanguard for technological change – a testing ground for new equipment and a launch pad for innovation and invention.

All delivered by a set of talented producers, directors, cameramen and engineers who make up the vital engine-room of an outside broadcast or studio operation that, in turn, provides the stage on which presenters, commentators and pundits can then cast their own magic spell in describing and analysing the action.

The real stars are, of course, the footballers and football matches themselves, and every game starts afresh with a sense of anticipation and excitement. Throw into the mix controversial managers stalking the touch-line, and you have all the ingredients for a smash-hit. And one that comes at a hefty price.

The summer of 2014 will have seen a World Cup staged in football-crazy Brazil, with every match transmitted to billions of viewers all over the globe, while back home, autumn 2014 marks the 50th anniversary of the first edition of a football programme that has gone on to become a national institution, BBC's *Match of the Day*.

A simple idea of featuring one match, in highlights form, began as an early evening opener for the newly launched BBC2 on August 22nd 1964. Liverpool vs. Arsenal was the first game featured on the new show, Liverpool and England's Roger Hunt was the first scorer and that afternoon, the first, and last, black cat to run onto a pitch on *Match of the Day* proved a lucky omen for the long-running programme.

The first Controller of BBC2 Michael Peacock acknowledged that putting football on his new channel was a way of bringing a wider public's attention to the new venture, as well as a way to try and sell more TV sets and aerials.

Match of the Day will feature heavily in this book and the concluding chapter will go back in time and give a detailed account of the programme's journey from just an idea to becoming an iconic piece of television.

In the 2015/16 season it will be all change for the televising of the phenomenally successful UEFA Champions League. Live match coverage of this competition is to find a new home at BT Sport after ITV, and latterly Sky Sports, have been for years the viewers' midweek destination for watching the best teams in Europe do battle.

Mind you, BT Sport have paid the small matter of £900 million "transfer fee" for three-year rights for the world's best club competition – as much a statement of intent as a matter of worth.

Of course, Sky Sports have been as much a part of the phenomenal Premier League story as the clubs and players that have graced it. This has become a mutually beneficial relationship that has seen a broadcast empire flourish and English football's top domestic league become a worldwide best-seller and market leader.

The next round of domestic rights negotiations is nearly upon us –last time around Sky splashed out an extraordinary £2.3 *billion* – and BT Sports made their debut in the soccer sales process with a cool £748 million of their own. All "quite remarkable" as the late, great BBC commentator David Coleman might have said.

* * * * *

Ah, money, football and television – always interesting bedfellows, and a subject this book will try and explore. For example let's briefly go back 60 years to 1954.

In December of that year, England hosted an international match at Wembley against West Germany, winners of that summer's World Cup. It was the first time the two countries' football teams had met in an international since the onset of World War II.

BBC covered the game live, a full house was attracted to Wembley for the midweek afternoon kick-off, including 12,000 travelling German supporters. England had Stanley Matthews on the right wing and Tom Finney on the left wing and won the match 3–1.

And the rights fee paid to the Football Association to broadcast this very special match live on the BBC? A princely £350! Another £250 was paid by the BBC for the right to relay the match live to Germany and five other European countries, as well as eight cinemas throughout England.

A fortnight later, Wolverhampton Wanderers hosted Honved in one of a series of famous friendly matches played under floodlights at Molineux. Floodlit football gave the BBC a chance to show live action in the middle of the evening and so viewers were able to watch second-half action as England's best club side at the time beat Honved, essentially the Hungarian national side, by three goals to two.

One interested viewer was a young Belfast lad called George Best who would repeatedly knock a ball against the wall of his neighbour, a Mr Harrison, about ten minutes before the kick-off of Wolves' latest floodlit friendly, in an effort to persuade him to let the future football legend watch the match on the only TV in the vicinity.

Best later attributed a key part of his love for the game to those famous series of televised friendlies. "It was the floodlights that made them magical for me." Best, of course, would become a small screen hero himself.

Watching the Match takes the reader on football's broadcasting journey from black and white to colour, from 405 lines to 625 lines, from 4 x 3 to widescreen, and from HD to 3D; from sitting in your armchair to watching the action on mobile devices.

I hope the book has the right mix of real substance and some rocking good stories from the television trenches. I spent 18 years working on both the BBC and ITV's football output and met many great professionals en route, many of whom have generously given their time to relay their own experiences of what has been an incredible sporting and broadcasting journey. The moments it all worked ... and the moments it didn't. There were plenty of both.

Special thanks must go to Lisa Seabrook, who worked with me on *Match of the Day*, and who has helped me research both the book's written content and the terrific photographic sections. I must thank Martin Corteel at Carlton Books and also the team at the BBC Written Archive at Caversham. Lisa and I unearthed some absolute gems there.

And thanks to my good friend, John Motson. "Motty", part of the very fabric of televised football over the past 40 years, has provided the foreword for the book.

And finally, a very big thank you to my wife, Gerry, for letting me "borrow" the TV remote control on many an evening and in an instant turn a "whodunnit" into a "who scored it"!

Enjoy the book!

Brian Barwick
May 2014

CHAPTER 1

ANYONE FOR BICYCLE POLO?

Back in 1936, *Monday Night Football* would have been a non-starter. No decent floodlights you see.

The towering pylons that would magically light up those stunning green rectangles of turf were still a couple of decades away from regular use, but football itself was in the vanguard of a whole new broadcast revolution.

Television had started to take its baby footsteps into British life in the early 1930s.

I say British life but in fact the early days of the "box in the corner of the room" were confined to London and also to families who could afford to buy one.

There was little early confidence in television – radio, still in its own early days, was the dominant player and would be for some time to come. It housed all the key programmes, performers and presenters – and people had developed a huge loyalty to it.

Listeners were counted in their millions; the stars of radio then would be as famous as the stars of *Coronation Street*, *X Factor* and *Downton Abbey* now – even if the reality of fame was a little gentler then.

Still, there was a young upstart in town ... well, London town. Around 12,000 television sets were out there, in residential homes, restaurants and bars, as people got used to this new-fangled machine.

One beneficiary of the restricted broadcasting range of the fledgling television industry was Arsenal Football Club. They were involved in early experiments with outside broadcasts, including having coverage of their match against Everton in August 1936 used at a radio exhibition at Olympia in London. Later, in September 1937, they appeared in their own programme, the prosaically titled "Football at the Arsenal – a demonstration by members of the Arsenal team at the Arsenal Stadium Highbury".

Introduced by manager George F. Allison, it featured the Arsenal playing staff going through their paces, with the Reds playing the Whites – and there was more of the same 24 hours later.

The Daily Herald's reporter Douglas Walters had enjoyed a sneak preview of the historic Reds vs. Whites programme that the BBC had rehearsed the day before transmission. "Seated in the GEC television theatre in the heart of London I watched members of the Arsenal football team practising at Highbury. The BBC had three cameras connected to a mobile unit.

"Even at 6pm when the light was failing, one could clearly see the farthest touchline and not once did I lose sight of the ball. The players were distinct."

Walters predicted that it wouldn't be long before we would all be watching football by the fireside.

Football on television was up and running. The 1937 FA Cup Final between Preston and Sunderland had been shown in part and more big games were to follow.

In April 1938, the international match between England and Scotland was transmitted live from Wembley Stadium. A narrow 1–0 win for Scotland was watched only in London but I'm sure the news of Scotland's victory travelled with the speed of light up to a delighted population north of the border.

The game was covered on three cameras and was just twenty-nine hours after the BBC had used its one and only mobile television unit, and those self-same cameras, to cover the much-anticipated British Light-Heavyweight clash between Jock McAvoy and Len Harvey at the Harringay Arena.

As the popular Harvey enjoyed his points success, the BBC engineers were on the move. Setting up the next outside broadcast was the task, nine miles down the road at Wembley, and it was done in double-quick time – a 48-hour job turned around in half the time.

A magazine article at the time described the hive of activity and wryly observed, "As yet there has been no rehearsal by the production side." Not the last time you hear that comment either, but possibly one of the first!

Three weeks later the BBC cameras were back at Wembley to cover the 1938 FA Cup Final.

The BBC were actually getting more excited about covering the Derby at Epsom the following month but two mobile unit vans – one for scanning, the other for transmitting – were set up for another of the nation's showpiece occasions: the FA Cup Final. That year's match was being contested between two cocks of the north, Preston North End and Huddersfield Town, and was the first to be televised in its entirety.

The *Radio Times* stated that television coverage from Wembley would start at precisely 2.27pm – and would be followed by a ballet of *The Three Bears*.

Obviously there was no pre-match room for Cup Final entertainment spin-offs. Those special Cup Final morning treats were still several decades away.

The match itself went to extra-time at Wembley – indeed it was won with a last-gasp penalty kick by George Mutch of Preston, by which time, Goldilocks was no doubt getting stuck into mummy bear's porridge!

Other outside broadcast sports covered on the fledgling BBC Television Service that week included Catch-As-Can Wrestling and a Saturday night's darts match between a "BBC Four" and a team from the Press Club. Venue? Probably any public house in London!

Mind you, photographs of the auspicious occasion show all the players looking very uncomfortable trussed up in their office suits, shirts and ties and not a "Walk On" girl or a spectator dressed as a super-hero in sight.

Later, in September of that year, the first part of the FA Charity Shield was scheduled to be transmitted at a Monday tea-time – conditions permitting.

Proud Preston, the FA Cup-winners, travelled to the home of the League champions, Arsenal. For the BBC, the fact that the title-winners were Arsenal was just another early lucky stroke.

Showing some of a game rather than all of it became an early television norm – often dictated by the failing light.

So on the afternoon of Wednesday, October 26th, viewers were able to see the first "part" of a match between England and the Rest of Europe from Highbury held to celebrate the 50th anniversary of the formation of the Football League.

England won the game 3–0; however, those watching on TV saw only two of those goals scored, by Willie Hall and Tommy Lawton respectively.

Len Goulden's goal – England's third – came midway through the second half, by which time viewers had turned listeners as they headed to the radio to follow the rest of the match.

Mind you, the odd one might have stuck with the television output and watched the rather sedate *Seen in the Row* featuring the design of a mural on the Hyde Park Scene as the action raged on at Highbury.

*   *   *   *   *

The 1939 FA Cup Final on television introduced a major innovation – a commentator! The previous year's coverage had run the radio commentary alongside the pictures, but a year on, Arsenal manager George Allison would describe the action.

Allison had taken the helm at Highbury after the sudden death of the legendary Herbert Chapman in 1934 and had kept the north Londoners on a steady course with a league title win in 1934/35 to complete a hat-trick of Championships for the Gunners. An FA Cup Final win in 1936 had been followed up with another title in 1937/38.

Allison, born in County Durham in 1883, had mixed a career in journalism with a life in football. Briefly secretary-manager of Middlesbrough, Allison moved to London as a sports journalist – a chance meeting with Lord Kitchener then led to him becoming London correspondent of the *New York Post* and a year later he joined the payroll of the newspaper tycoon, William Randolph Hearst.

During the First World War Allison had worked for the War Office and the Admiralty, and later went on to join the Royal Flying Corps.

On the cessation of fighting, Allison moved into broadcasting and became an early voice on BBC radio, describing such events as the Derby and the FA Cup Final.

He delivered his radio commentaries with polished tones, a rich vocabulary and some "pep".

Whilst in the USA he had studied American sports commentators and noticed how they kept their delivery "lively", probably to keep listeners on board for the advertisers. Allison copied that style and was soon tagged in some quarters as "By Jove Allison".

Listeners were provided with a grid pattern of the pitch that was printed in the *Radio Times*. Allison was joined on the airwaves by a voice in the background who would tell the listeners in which square the ball was, allowing them to better visualise the action.

The penalty area was included in square one of the grid and thus the phrase "back to square one" appeared in common parlance.

Allison had retained his football connections. He joined Arsenal and moved through the club's ranks until, by 1934, he had assumed the mantle of club manager.

Allison had also kept up his commentary work and thus was the voice heard on the televised coverage of the 1939 FA Cup Final between Portsmouth and Wolverhampton Wanderers – though minus the grid "prompts".

He had five goals to describe that day – four of them to Portsmouth.

Also that year he was immortalised for delivering a line whilst appearing in a film set at Highbury. The black-and-white whodunit *The Arsenal Stadium Mystery* starred Arsenal players amongst the film's actual cast and featured manager George Allison speaking to his players in a mock half-time team-talk. "It's one-nil to the Arsenal. That's the way we like it!"

And boy, didn't they just "like it" for many years to come.

The 1939 FA Cup Final television outside broadcast had two cameras sited above the Royal Box and one at pitch level and the match coverage also benefited from a stronger signal than the previous year.

By contrast, for the 2012 FA Cup Final between Chelsea and Liverpool, ITV's experienced match director, John Watts, had 28 cameras at his disposal and several more were used in the studio where the programme's presenter and pundits were working.

The big Wembley occasion was now part of a range of sporting events covered regularly on television and they were proving a hit with the small audience who could see them.

Other sporting events covered included the Boat Race, Test cricket from Lord's and the Oval – the West Indies were in town – tennis from Wimbledon, Championship boxing, the Calcutta Cup from Twickenham, athletics from White City, motor-racing from Crystal Palace and even a golf challenge match from Coombe Hill between Reg Whitcombe, the British Open champion, and the legendary South African, Bobby Locke.

Four holes – the sixth, seventh, eighth and ninth – were in camera range. The distances involved in covering golf meant it would be several decades and many cameras and miles of cable before the sport really took off on television.

Back in the late 1930s, there was still time in the fledgling schedules for a series of programmes showing demonstration sports. The likes of wrestling, judo, aquatics and bicycle polo grabbed their moment of glory on the new silver screen.

"Bicycle polo eh ... ahem!" Mind you, they were muttering like that about beach volleyball a few years back!

Other London-based non-sporting events like the Chelsea Flower Show, the Trooping of the Colour and the Cenotaph Ceremony were also televised.

As were some famous variety artists of the time. The master French illusionist, Horace Goldin, re-created one of his most noted stage illusions, the "sawing a woman in half" trick, this time live on television.

Magicians actually favoured appearing live on television rather than having their act recorded on film. Of course, a constant rewinding of the film spool may just reveal how they did their tricks and thus give the game away.

By summer 1939, the BBC was confident enough that television was making headway with the public that it published a survey revealing what its early viewers – and there weren't many of them – liked and disliked.

A regular television service had been operating from Alexandra Palace for more than two and a half years and more than 4,000 viewers took time out to fill in a questionnaire – and it highlighted the early hits and misses.

Viewers told the BBC that they liked the presenters, they liked full-length plays rather than short ones, and they got annoyed if their concentration was distracted by extraneous noises of scene-shifting. Viewers thought the commentaries on outside broadcasts were satisfactory (well done, George) but disliked continental films, and felt that opera and ballet had a limited appeal.

One early complaint – there were too many repeats! The survey of viewers underlined their displeasure at a show being repeated more than twice within a short period of time. The BBC said they took note of that criticism – and still seem to be "taking note of it" more than 70 years later!

Even in 1939, though, there were some early devotees of television who did find some value in a repeat – "so we can go out for a walk now and again".

Sporting outside broadcasts were well supported by the survey – garnering an appreciation score of 88%. Other non-sporting outside broadcasts gained an 89% appreciation score and outside broadcasts of plays or variety shows got a whopping 93% thumbs–up.

Studio-based programmes featuring orchestral soloists, ballet, opera and sports demonstrations scored low. Ah, bad news for the bicycle polo. Bottom of the pile came musical features with a worrying score of just 12%. How about singing while riding a bike, then they could combine the scores!

Overall, a very positive early picture was emerging, both of television and the audience reaction to it.

Gerald Cock, the BBC's new Director of Television, declared he was well pleased with the early indicators, which suggested the viewers found television to be "grand entertainment"!

I suppose these days such a positive, if restricted, public response to their early programming would have led to a tabloid headline such as "BBC Television cock up ... beat (!) about the fortunes of his new broadcast service".

Television had taken its first tiny footsteps, but things were soon put on hold as attention turned towards conflict, to a war that would engulf the world and cost the lives of many brave men and women.

Television screens suddenly went blank on September 1st 1939. Life had taken a serious turn.

CHAPTER 2

CHRYSANTHEMUMS AND CUP FINALS

When Prince William and Catherine Middleton were married in April 2011, a massive television audience of more than 26 million people watched the wedding service at Westminster Abbey and the subsequent celebrations as the happy couple made their way back to Buckingham Palace.

Such Royal occasions, whether happy or sad, always pile on the viewers. They are occasions that pull the nation together in huge numbers. They are genuine ratings gold-dust.

Prince William and Kate, now the Duke and Duchess of Cambridge, shared their special moment with millions of people up and down the country – and William driving his new bride out of Buckingham Palace and down the Mall in Prince Charles's Aston Martin Volante DB6 festooned in red, white and blue balloons, became a modern iconic Royal image captured for viewers worldwide.

In the early days of television, there had been some limited live coverage of the Coronation of King George VI in 1937 – essentially concentrating the outside broadcast on a short stretch of the processional route as the State Coach passed Hyde Park Corner. It was still chiefly a radio event.

Sixteen years later, in June 1953, William's grandmother, Queen Elizabeth II, was crowned in Westminster Abbey. This time, the Coronation provided the first international television event – it was the occasion that really launched television in the UK – and it also created a heavy demand from British households to invest their hard-earned cash in buying a television set and for the Government to invest in more nationwide transmitters.

Those who hadn't taken the plunge yet crowded into their television-owning neighbours' living rooms to watch the Coronation on the latest "must have" accessory.

One thing that was encouraging people to invest in a television set was that they were becoming much safer. Some of the early prototypes had a tendency to catch fire – so even if the programmes weren't red hot, the thing carrying them in the corner of your living room just might be!

Despite her own big date with destiny a month later, the Queen was actually in attendance at Wembley Stadium for the 1953 FA Cup Final between Blackpool and Bolton Wanderers.

The game turned into a classic. Dubbed the "Matthews Final", it saw the Seasiders, inspired by the twinkling toes of Stanley Matthews, come back from 3–1 down to win the FA Cup by four goals to three.

Matthews had provided the central story for all the pre-match build-up and was heavily featured in the match coverage. Now 38 years old – he would play first-class football until he was 50 – Matthews had been on the losing side in the 1948 and 1951 FA Cup Finals and it was generally accepted that this would be his last chance for Wembley glory.

That story alone had caught the public's imagination – and television sets were flying out of the shops. The numbers of sets and viewers watching them had been on the increase since the end of World War Two – by 1953 nearly 20% of wireless licence holders had a TV set; by 1958 the number would be nearer 50%.

As it still is with the modern idiom, it would be coverage of live events that would be the catalyst for the rapid growth and the ownership of the new television experience.

And in 1953, the winning double was a State occasion, the Coronation of Queen Elizabeth II, and an FA Cup Final in which the nation wanted Matthews crowned the King of Wembley. Those two contrasting stories were to light television's blue touch paper.

But not everybody was a fan.

Prime Minister Winston Churchill had made the point that television's intrusive nature would destroy the mystique of the monarchy – and events many years later made that view seem far-sighted.

The 1950s football authorities' early analysis of the impact of this rising star, television, also saw it as more of a threat than an opportunity.

Fifty years later television would be bankrolling the game, but back in the early 1950s the authorities, especially the Football League, were worried it could bankrupt it.

During the early part of the decade live television football coverage was chiefly based around England internationals, schoolboy internationals and amateur matches – lots of them, especially from rounds of the FA Amateur Cup, including the Final itself.

The FA Cup Final though was a whole different ball game. It was the match of the season and its attraction was proving an issue.

Trouble had started brewing after BBC Television's live coverage of the 1950 FA Cup Final between Arsenal and Liverpool was estimated to have pulled in a television audience of one million viewers. The facility fee paid by the BBC to the FA to televise the big match live was a little more than the princely sum of £262.

However, poor attendances at first-class matches played that afternoon in the London and Birmingham areas – the two regions carrying television pictures from Wembley – set a hare running.

London first-class football attendances were down by 42% and Birmingham's by 39% on the day of the FA Cup Final.

These were the days when the FA Cup Final did not have a Saturday to itself, one of the elements that ultimately set the match apart from the rest and helped create and sustain its "National Event" status. In 1950, as usual, there was a full fixture list being played alongside it. And anyway, football, live or otherwise, had no monopoly over screen-time, as one of BBC's famous continuity presenters, Mary Malcolm, eloquently underlined just an hour before the big Wembley kick-off.

"Good afternoon. Today is Cup Final Day and, of course, the weather is just about as bad as it could be. It's been raining hard all morning but in spite of everything enthusiasm is running high as ever at Wembley. We'll be taking you there to join the community singing ... but for now until 2.30 Frances Perry and Fred Streeter are going to give you some hints on gardening ... First then, here is Frances Perry to talk to you about chrysanthemums." Just your average Cup Final build-up!

Commentators Jimmy Jewell and Peter Lloyd described the action as Arsenal won 2–0 at a damp Wembley Stadium. Jewell had been the referee of the FA Cup Final televised live back in 1938.

One would-be future famous FA Cup Final commentator was no doubt taking notes. BBC's John Motson recalls that day. "My father was a Methodist minister and when I was five years old he took me to a musical instrument shop in Woolwich called Drysdales. They had a nine-inch TV in a backstairs room and that's where I watched the 1950 FA Cup Final."

In 1951, to try and stem the flow of would-be spectators turning instead into television viewers on FA Cup Final afternoon, the football authorities only allowed the second half of the 1951 Wembley game between Blackpool and Newcastle United to be broadcast live on BBC Television. Mind you, both of Jackie Milburn's Cup Final-winning goals were scored in the second 45 minutes.

In 1953, the BBC paid the Football Association an unprecedented rights fee of £1,000 to cover the whole match and from 1954 onwards FA Cup Final Saturday stood alone in the fixture list, a decision that would remain the same for more than 50 years.

On May 2nd 1953, everybody was trying to grab a seat to see Stanley Matthews's day of destiny at Wembley. One seven-year-old boy in Chester was in front of his family's new television set that day. Martin Tyler, who has gone on to have an illustrious career in modern television football commentary, watched the match with his family. "It was a big day and I chose to support Bolton Wanderers. Mind you the rest of the family and everybody else it seems were getting behind Blackpool and Stanley Matthews, of course."

Martin would go on to describe many FA Cup Finals himself but his fees would, no doubt, have been a little grander than the twenty guineas paid to Kenneth Wolstenholme for his memorable afternoon's work in 1953!

Of course, if you didn't have a television set yourself, you were about to become very friendly with somebody who lived nearby that had one.

A cartoon in a local Blackpool paper showed a man asking his neighbours if he could watch the game at their house. "I can't get near MINE for unexpected visitors!" he claimed with a smirk.

The all-Lancastrian affair between Bolton and Blackpool didn't just attract a northern audience. For example, this was the scene in a posh house in London, perfectly described by the late sports journalist John Moynihan, as Blackpool's winning goal from Bill Perry, set up by Stanley Matthews, hit the back of the net.

" ... men seized cushions and hugged them to their bellies and Miss H gave a tinkling laugh of pleasure. The room was electric, the television screen swarming with Blackpool players hugging and embracing and we were hugging and embracing and Miss H's young man was on his feet, his neck darting backward and forward like a heron's beak in flight."

Well, Miss H and her "heron in flight" were just two of an estimated 12 million people who found a television to crowd around and witness the BBC's live coverage of the game. The Corporation had three cameras trained on the action and a fourth camera had helped Peter Dimmock capture the pre-match mood as the fans marched up Wembley Way.

An old friend, Eddie Bentley, who watched television coverage of football develop in the early 1950s, told me, "It was difficult to see the pictures actually; the screen was so small, compared to the cabinet it was contained in. And once the game was over, there would be an interval before a lady dressed in full evening wear would inform the viewers of the television treats that lay ahead of them that night."

It was not herons but seagulls which flew over the famous Blackpool Tower swooping and swaying over a breezy Fylde coastline that welcomed the successful Blackpool team home. The FA Cup, the most famous trophy in sport, was lifted proudly above their heads as the traditional open-topped coach toured the packed streets of Britain's most popular seaside resort.

Stanley Matthews, who always felt embarrassed by the game being dubbed the "Matthews Final", not least because another Stan – Mortensen – had actually scored a hat-trick, had spent most of the train ride back from London in the toilets to get a bit of peace. Fame, eh!

The BBC was delighted with the match and the number of people who watched "Matthews's fairy-tale" unfold. Head of Television, Seymour de Lotbiniere ("Lobby" to his mates!), who would later mastermind the Corporation's Coronation coverage, richly complimented commentator Wolstenholme on his Cup Final performance.

"Admittedly, the game was a gift but all the more so might a commutation have obtruded or become a nuisance to viewers. Your restraint was, in fact, admirable." Not sure my own memos to commentators ever included such rich prose.

Later that year when negotiations took place between the BBC and the FA for the following year's Final, the Chairman of the Football League suggested a fee of between £7,500 and £10,000. The amateur element on the FA Cup committee saw this increase from £1,000 as ridiculous and settled on a figure of £2,000. FA Secretary Stanley Rous intervened and suggested that a 50% increase rather than 100% was more appropriate and that was where the deal was struck. Rights negotiations were up and running.

Away from football, the BBC was beginning to up its own game – making new inroads into light entertainment and current affairs in the Coronation year.

Panorama, a current affairs programme, began its life. The show, which is still going strong, would enjoy a difficult relationship with football, given its occasionally revelatory or opportunistic tilt at the game.

And awkward. In September 1993, the *Panorama* team tracked me down to a restaurant in Notting Hill where I was having lunch with an important member of our on-screen football team. We were actually about to renegotiate his contract. I took the phone call and was told that "out of courtesy" they were informing me that "against billing" a *Panorama* special was going to be broadcast that evening. The subject, the business affairs of the then former Spurs manager and BBC pundit Terry Venables.

I listened carefully to the BBC man on the end of the phone, expressed my frustration and went back to the lunch guest I was hosting on behalf of the BBC – Terry Venables! He left with his meal unfinished.

Certainly, in its time, *Panorama* was able to put the top men from FIFA on the back foot and suggested some dubious practices in the transfers of top-flight players were occurring. But all that was many years ahead when *Panorama* broadcast its first edition back in November 1953.

A piece of mock Victorian/Edwardian music hall, *The Good Old Days*, also started its television life a month after the Wembley feats of Matthews and co. This variety show ran for 30 years and saw the top stars of the day do a turn on the boards of the Leeds City Varieties.

The show was instantly recognisable with the audience dressed in period costume and its master of ceremonies, the mustachioed Leonard Sachs, complete with gavel and a voluminous vocabulary that stretched into the next century. Mind you, even he would have been lost for words to describe the events at Wembley Stadium that November.

1953 had been a heady year for the country – the year of the Coronation, the Matthews Final and Edmund Hillary's ascent of Mount Everest. But English football took a tumble from its own lofty heights when in November, Hungary, with the mercurial Ferenc Puskas in their ranks, came to Wembley and on a murky afternoon with a 2.15pm kick-off, set the football world alight.

BBC cameras were live as Hungary beat England, well, murdered them actually, and in so doing became the first continental side to gain a win over England on home soil.

This was the old established W-M formation meeting a Hungarian side that was unbeaten since May 1950, the reigning Olympic champions and a team of many talents.

The game was dubbed "The Match of the Century" – but it was Hungary who used the 90 minutes to make claims as a serious candidate for "Team of the Century".

Hungary simply waltzed around their English opponents. 4–2 up at half-time became 6–3 by full-time – a humiliation for England, Matthews et al.

This was a new type of football – a team with deep-lying midfield players and a deep-lying centre-forward. If the England team was struggling to come to terms with it, so was the BBC commentator, Kenneth Wolstenholme: "He may be a number 5 but he is not a centre-half," he seemed to be reminding himself.

The Hungarian captain Puskas's brilliant drag-back to bamboozle the great Billy Wright in the act of scoring Hungary's third goal was a classic moment in sports television – and would have been a YouTube sensation these days.

Kenneth Wolstenholme captured the mood and the move perfectly. "Oh ... a lovely goal. My goodness if he can call on tricks like this we ought to have him on the music hall. They're almost playing basketball this Hungarian side."

As the final whistle blew, Wolstenholme uttered a string of words that would take on a life of their own when he used them in different circumstances some 13 years later on English football's greatest day. Perhaps it was a subconscious rehearsal for that momentous occasion.

"... It's all over ..." he pronounced as referee Leo Horn brought proceedings between England and Hungary to a close at a stunned Wembley Stadium in which the crowd had just witnessed the changing of the guard in world football.

Interestingly, the final goal of the game was scored from the penalty spot by England's full-back, a certain Alf Ramsey. Wolstenholme would also play a big part in Ramsey's finest Wembley moment in 1966.

Hungary had simply outclassed England and they beat them again in a return game in Budapest six months later. This time the score was 7–1.

Although recognised as the best team in the world, Hungary lost to West Germany in the 1954 World Cup Final in Berne – like the Holland team that created new football rhythms in the 1970s, the innovators were beaten by the innovated.

Hungary, however, had shown England that their style of football belonged in the past and new television viewers watched in awe. Things were moving on – and not just on the football field.

The BBC, like the national football team, was also about to realise it was not going to have things all its own way in the future.

A new young player called ITV was stripping off its tracksuit ready to join the big match.

CHAPTER 3

SETTING THE STANDARDS

ITV came into the world on September 22nd 1955 – the same day Grace Archer left it.

The BBC's response to a new and potentially dangerous television rival was to try and scupper ITV's big opening night by sacrificing one of its most popular cast members in its hugely successful daily radio soap, *The Archers*.

You can imagine the conversation in the BBC radio rehearsal rooms a few weeks earlier. "Ah, Ysanne, how're things? Enjoying playing the part of Grace? Loved the wedding scenes in April. Oh, heard about this new-fangled ITV thing? No, it won't affect US, it may just pose a little bit of a problem for Grace ..."

And it did. On the BBC Light Programme, Grace Archer bravely fought her way into a blazing stable to save a friend's horse but was struck by a falling beam and when pulled clear of the fire was raced off to hospital only to be pronounced dead on arrival.

Dramatic stuff. And 20 million listeners thought so too. The newspapers were full of it for days on end and ITV's big night was somewhat scuppered.

Veteran broadcaster Leslie Mitchell, who remarkably had performed a similar task for the BBC back in 1936, got the new commercial channel under way with the words "This is London. Ready our friends, you citizens of London. Wish us Godspeed. Over to the Guildhall."

At London's glittering Guildhall were a group of VIPs and the Hallé

Orchestra, which gave the new channel a classical musical opening.

The real highlight of the evening though came at exactly 8.12pm when the first commercial on British television was broadcast.

Gibbs SR toothpaste was the opening advertisement, followed by those for Cadbury chocolate and Summer County margarine. The first commercial break had come and gone.

Later in the evening, there was a rather unfortunate moment when during an interval between rounds in some live Championship boxing, a commercial featured a man pouring a bottle of beer into a glass only to be followed instantly by a boxer violently spitting out some liquid into a bucket when they cut back to the action!

Mind you, fast forward 43 years to December 1998 and yours truly was in charge on the opening night of ITV's first new channel launch since 1955. ITV2 was about to start life.

The BBC seemed a lot less worried about this one – nobody took a tumble in *The Archers* and somebody even broke into a smile on *EastEnders*.

There's me hiring pop star Billie Piper and a member of Wimbledon FC's Crazy Gang, footballer turned actor Vinnie Jones, to set off fireworks across the River Thames marking the new channel's arrival, but as fewer than a couple of thousand people could actually receive ITV2 on its opening night, soap actors and actresses up and down the country slept soundly in their beds!

In 1955 though, ITV's arrival as the country's first commercial television channel was very significant and the powers-to-be at ITV very quickly hooked on to the fact that sport was a ratings winner – and football the best of the breed.

The BBC had obviously got a head start on its new rivals in many areas of broadcasting and in 1954, ahead of ITV's creation, had brought a new venture, *Sportsview*, to the screen.

Peter Dimmock, who had been an RAF officer during the war, was the Corporation's outstanding Head of Outside Broadcasts. Dimmock was a man of huge ability and foresight who would lead from the front – in-vision and in charge.

Dimmock actually presented the first edition of the new *Sportsview* programme and its midweek mix of action, features and studio interviews proved popular with the audience.

The programme won a favourable audience reaction. The 20-minute show, broadcast at 7.50pm, drew a reaction index of 67% and "the items on boxing and football were very popular". Many people were frustrated by the brevity of the programme, but that was soon put right.

Boxing and football became key ingredients for midweek sports programmes on the BBC and ITV for many decades. Certainly football matches played on the night and transmitted within an hour of the final whistle gave the programmes an extra frisson even if it nearly put the production teams responsible for getting the shows on the air into the funny farm – especially when cup ties went into extra-time.

Midweek football highlights are part of the forgotten treasure trove of the game's television history but they played a huge role in making the likes of *Sportsview*, and similar programmes on both channels, required viewing from the very start.

Peter Dimmock was a central figure in the development of BBC Sport. He had produced the coverage of the Coronation in 1953, presented *Sportsview* and the opening editions of *Grandstand* in 1958. He was a towering presence in BBC Sport; he set the standards – and set them high.

Paul Fox was the editorial guru behind the early life of both programmes. Another hugely talented man, he would enjoy a successful career at both the BBC and ITV. Later knighted for his services to television, Fox's innovative early footprint is still measured by the mile at the BBC. *Sports Review of the Year* was another of his pioneering ideas.

Sportsview itself made a vital early strike in its broadcast life, transmitting coverage of Roger Bannister's four-minute mile within an hour of it happening. The programme, with its familiar theme tune and "stop-watch" opening titles, soon became a pivotal part of the BBC midweek schedule – until 1968, when its successor, *Sportsnight with Coleman*, took its place.

So the crack sports team at the BBC were determined not to roll over and allow themselves to be holed below the water-line by the new kid on the block. But ITV was here and here to stay.

Records suggest the commercial channel first tipped its toes into live football coverage at an England vs. Spain international played at a foggy Wembley Stadium in November 1955.

Simulcasting the match with the BBC and using the Corporation's match coverage, the game was broadcast by Rediffusion but in the London area only.

The established commentary style of the BBC's Kenneth Wolstenholme was countered on ITV by the voice of Kent Walton.

Walton spoke with a slight transatlantic twang, and had been in RAF Bomber Command during the war. He would soon become a household name when describing the action from town halls and swimming baths up and down the country in the smash-hit world of All-In Wrestling.

Jackie Pallo, Mick McManus and Big Daddy were names for the future, as Ken and Kent both called home goals for John Atyeo, Tom Finney and a brace from Bill Perry as England beat Spain 4–1.

The first shared FA Cup Final was the following year as Manchester City played Birmingham City.

Earlier in the competition the new commercial channel had broadcast live coverage of the second half of the FA Cup third round replay between Bedford and Arsenal on a Thursday afternoon.

Arsenal scraped home 2–1 and ITV continued its fledgling broadcast policy with live second-half coverage of the replays in the FA Cup fourth and fifth rounds, Chelsea vs. Burnley and West Ham vs. Tottenham Hotspur respectively.

On May 5th 1956, both channels covered the Final and the first "battle of the build-up" took place.

Fittingly, Manchester City's appearance in the Final coincided with the first weekend of commercial television in the north of England, broadcast from a converted cinema, the Capitol in Didsbury.

The ITV Friday-night news bulletin included interviews with Manchester City fans making an early departure for Wembley.

These were still pre-*Grandstand* and -*World of Sport* days when the rivalries between the broadcasters became intense and occasionally out of control – but in 1956, ITV went to air at 2.30pm with a *Road to Wembley* feature and the BBC matched that on-air time with its own build-up.

A bit of motor-racing and a link to a pleasure boat with two of the stars of the day Anne Shelton and Jimmy James provided the BBC with their half-time entertainment. ITV no doubt got some adverts away.

The BBC promised interviews with the winning team in its *Today's Sport* programme whilst Granada proudly announced that its first ever live outside broadcast would be the return of the victorious winning team.

Manchester City won 3–1 and future Leeds manager Don Revie was outstanding. German goalkeeper Bert Trautmann carved a place in FA Cup Final history by playing the latter stages of the match with a broken neck.

On the evening of the homecoming, the jubilant City players were running late and commentator Gerry Loftus found himself filling for some 45 minutes rather than the pre-arranged quarter of an hour.

Still, ITV was up and running.

Over at the BBC, a new Saturday-evening sports show had been created to complement its mid-week *Sportsview*.

Sports Special, later to be renamed *Saturday Sport*, went to air on September 10th 1955. The programme was introduced by Kenneth

Wolstenholme and included brief highlights of matches, in a maximum of five minutes.

The first games featured on the programme were Luton Town vs. Newcastle United and Charlton Athletic vs. Everton. Wolstenholme and Cliff Michelmore were the commentators.

All in a day's work for Wolstenholme, but for Michelmore it was a stroll off the beaten track. He would become a massive early star of the BBC's peak-time television, fronting the ground-breaking *Tonight Programme*, forerunner to the BBC's *Nationwide* and current early-evening magazine, *The One Show*.

Michelmore would generally be at the front of anything that needed his classy but welcoming style. He could be serious ... and less serious.

In the early days of television, everybody seemed to do everything – these were pioneering days – and there was no time to be choosy or self-conscious, as Michelmore reflected.

"It was no good hiding behind a screen of shyness when it came to being a commentator at a football match. Crowds loved to see us struggling up vertical ladders to the tops of grandstands. We did it all on film with the commentator telling the cameraman when to roll. And then doing the commentary simultaneously.

"At the end of the first half of the match the film would be rushed by despatch riders to laboratories for processing, then to the cutting room for editing. As the match finished we would belt to the waiting aircraft or car and leg it hot foot to the (London) studio."

Michelmore accepted his place in the commentary pecking order. "Ken was the number-one commentator but I remember covering memorable matches like Bournemouth's little FA Cup run against Spurs and Manchester United and the first game young Denis Law ever played in the league for Huddersfield."

As *Sports Special* morphed into *Saturday Sport* so filming techniques improved, not least with film now being processed in provincial centres like Birmingham, Bristol and Manchester as well as London.

And filming became continuous, thankfully eradicating the possibility of missing a goal or vital incident as the rolls of film were being loaded or unloaded.

Weather was also a problem. Film cameras were more sensitive to changes in light than their more sturdy electronic equivalents. And on a winter's Saturday afternoon the cameraman could be wrestling with four different light conditions in the space of 90 minutes. From sunshine to darkness with a bit of fog and mist thrown in for good measure. Out came the light meter on frequent occasions.

The audience was already on the broadcaster's case on selection of matches – whatever the conditions. The late Kennneth Wolstenholme recalled those early days.

"... One camera unit was in the north of England going from town to town to find a match that could be played. It failed. Every northern match except one was postponed. Another unit was in the south, but London too was fog-bound. Match after match fell out until just one was left – Tottenham Hotspur vs. Chelsea. Yet some viewers wrote to complain that a London 'derby' was chosen for coverage!"

The horrendous winter of 1963 posed particular problems to commentators and film crews alike.

"On January 5th only three third round ties were played, but *Saturday Sport* covered all three ... even though I did have to travel overnight to Leeds and race over the snowbound Pennines and across Lancashire into Cheshire to cover the Tranmere Rovers vs. Chelsea match."

Tough, but even at this distance you can sense both the pride and excitement of getting the show on the air whatever the problems.

The BBC's big push into more regular sports programming was enhanced with the launch of a Saturday-afternoon show, *Grandstand*, on October 11th 1958.

The BBC's flagship sports programme was developed by Paul Fox and another strong off-screen personality, Bryan Cowgill.

A no-nonsense northerner, Cowgill, like Fox and Dimmock, demanded high standards and his "hair-dryer" moments, when staff came up short, were both legendary and frequent, and most definitely of their time. Cowgill would go on to become a power-house in both the BBC and ITV but his expertise in television sport gave the BBC Television Sport's Department a huge push in its formative years. Later, senior executives like Alan Hart and Jonathan Martin would build on those foundations and carry the organisation forward.

The BBC's vision of putting together an afternoon of action, interviews, news and results was ground-breaking in its concept and magnificent in its delivery.

Grandstand became part of the social culture of the country and every big sporting event and every big sporting star featured in *Grandstand* during its lifespan of more than 40 years.

The Cup Final editions, like those that presented marvellous domestic events like the Grand National, the Boat Race, the Rugby League Challenge Cup Final, the Open Golf Championship, Wimbledon and international events like the Summer and Winter Olympics, were precision-television, building on the brilliant presentation and commentary skills the BBC had harnessed and the top-class producers, directors, cameramen and technicians it had fostered and trained.

Only when Sky Sports moved the goal-posts irrevocably by claiming so much sporting "real estate" was the BBC forced to wave the white flag and take its flagship programme off the air. Whilst I probably supported the decision at the time I still feel the BBC, in general, and BBC Sport, in particular, have never really recovered from its removal.

After Peter Dimmock had fronted the first few editions of the programme, a 32-year-old Cheshire-born broadcast journalist took over the programme and all but made it his own for the next decade or so.

David Coleman had worked on local northern newspapers before joining the BBC in Birmingham in 1954. He worked across regional news programming, sport, radio and television. Then down to London and his big break, *Grandstand*.

Coleman was a natural – a brilliant incisive professional, in front of the camera and behind the microphone. A talented athlete himself, he had an empathy with sportsmen and sportswomen and the keenest news sense.

Perhaps the sequence in *Grandstand* he is best remembered for is the teleprinter segment that filled the back-end of each *Grandstand* during the football season. As the results chugged along the screen to the soundtrack of a news service printer there was a real sense of drama.

And Coleman, like Jeff Stelling on its modern equivalent, Sky Sport's *Soccer Saturday*, would have a mercurial grasp of the nuances behind any result.

"... Rochdale ... 1 ... Tranmere Rovers ... 1

"And that's Tranmere's sixth away draw this season and their tenth in the past 11 months – five of them 1–1. Rochdale's fifth home game without a win."

"... Tottenham Hotspur ... 8 (eight) ... Sunderland ... 2

"Spurs in top form today, two from Greaves, a brace from Jones and even Maurice Norman got in on the act ... Sunderland's fourth defeat in five. Drop two places."

And so on, and so forth. We all particularly liked the high-scoring matches because the score would come up in both figures and words – but they were rare.

There was real drama in the teleprinter sequence. Most of us didn't know how our team had done – information and information technology was much scarcer back then – and the pure theatre of watching the results being revealed one at a time in a completely random order, accompanied by an informative live commentary and the sound of a tickertape, was compelling television.

Coleman, who died in late December 2013, had earlier recalled how he had come up with the inspired idea of his famous teleprinter sequence.

"I was due to present *Grandstand* from its third-ever programme and went to the studio to watch the second edition and get a feel for it. One thing I did notice was how slow the football results came along in the teleprinter sequence. I then had the idea to fill in the gaps with relevant information on the day's games and how the results would affect the league tables, etc. I had a good memory, did the homework the day before and I tried it out on my first Saturday on the programme – and it worked. And everybody was amazed ... amazed. But really it was designed merely to fill in the gaps between the scores coming along on the teleprinter."

Every other programme that does the same or similar job these days owes its presence to that little piece of television gold.

Plus, of course, there was one extra ingredient. Back then, *everybody* did the football pools. It was a national phenomenon – the original X factor.

Celebrating the 90th anniversary of football pools starting, current pools operator Sportech's chief executive Ian Penrose recalls: "People had an opportunity to win enormous amounts of money, instantly ... there weren't many ways of doing it at that time.

"It was through skill, putting their football knowledge to the test, something we all like to think we're good at.

"Listening to results on the radio or watching them being read out on TV became a Saturday afternoon ritual."

Indeed we lived around the corner from where Vernon's Pools coupons were sent to be checked and for many years, my mum would leave our house about 3pm every Saturday afternoon to become one of the army of people doing the checking.

I don't think my mum ever made anybody an overnight millionaire but if she did, she never told us.

CHAPTER 4

FORGETTABLE

In August 2001, ITV tried something different. Having won the rights
to cover the glossy and glamorous Premier League the previous year, it
decided to put its new highlights programme, *The Premiership*, on air at
7pm on a Saturday evening – slap bang in the middle of ITV's weekend
peak-time landscape, usually the preserve of Cilla Black's *Blind Date*
and Matthew Kelly's *Stars in Their Eyes*.

Now they were going to get Des Lynam's *Premiership*.

Having paid a small fortune for the rights and a decent whack for
Des, it seemed a risk worth taking. After all, we sensed *Match of the Day*
at "sometime after 10 o'clock" was getting old hat and perhaps this was
the right moment to break that mould.

Having been responsible for helping to win the rights for ITV, I
was totally up for taking on the challenge of the early slot. We were
confident that the technology we would be using to construct the
programme would also be sufficiently capable of turning around the
action in such a short time from the final whistles being blown up and
down the country to going to air just two hours later.

Indeed, if we'd been contractually allowed, we'd have pitched for a
6pm start time but that move was blocked by the Premier League and
Sky, the latter claiming that our highlights would become "near-live" if
we went that early.

Starting a football programme in the heart of the Saturday-
evening schedule did have its issues. I went around the country

and took a straw poll of Premier League chairmen on the new start time.

They seemed broadly in favour of the idea – mind you, I think they thought we'd "over-paid" for the privilege of putting it anywhere anyhow. One man, however, took the contrary view when Jeff Farmer, ITV's Head of Football, and I went to see him at his Hertfordshire company base.

Lord Sugar, or mere Alan Sugar, Tottenham chairman, as he was then, heard us out and then offered this thought.

"It is an interesting idea but you may find it throws up a few problems. I don't know how it works in your house, but in mine the women in the house own the TV controller on a Saturday night. It is their night of the week to choose what to watch. So be careful what you wish for, chaps."

Jeff and I nodded in Sugar's direction, got out of the room without being FIRED ... and then completely ignored his advice – the consequences of which I will return to later.

Mind you, if we'd have looked back into the annals of ITV history we may have found an episode that would have put us on red alert.

Before the start of the 1960/61 season, ITV, now recognising the primacy of football on its channel, did a deal with the Football League for live coverage of 26 games – 19 on a Saturday and seven on a Friday evening.

The Football League made sure the games didn't clash with the afternoon fixture list and hoped the sport would benefit from peak-time exposure. ITV thought the games would bring home the advertising bacon.

Their idea was to have the games kick off at 6.50pm, and start a programme at 7.30pm with the closing moments of the first half and the second half live.

The Big Game, as it was called, and ITV's *Saturday Spectacular* would share the peak-time slot for the rest of the season.

However, just the title of their big light entertainment show alone set the bar high for the football – and my, did it live down to expectations in the first week.

The first match of the series was at Bloomfield Road on September 10th 1960, where Blackpool played host to Bolton Wanderers. But this was to be no repeat of their famous 1953 FA Cup Final classic.

The Soccer by the Fireside plan began with a damp squib.

With clubs up and down the country still worried that the television matches weren't all scheduled for Friday night to keep Saturday clear of counter-attractions that might prevent people actually going to the games, there was a sense of unease about the whole project.

A full-scale camera rehearsal under the floodlights at Blackpool the night before had gone well but on the evening itself the game was poor and the coverage poorer.

The three cameras had all been sited BEHIND the goal and at the corner flag in Bloomfield Road's Spion Kop rather than more conventionally half-way along the main stand. That bizarre decision; a commentary team of Peter Lloyd and former Wolves and England captain, Billy Wright, both criticised for being too "pallsy" in their descriptions of the action; and the news that the game's star attraction, Stanley Matthews, had been declared unfit to play, set ITV up for a nasty fall.

And, noticeably, the crowd itself in Bloomfield Road was down on the usual numbers and the atmosphere flat as a fluke. Oh, and there was only one goal, scored late in the second half for the visitors by Freddie Hill. Other than all that, everything was hunky-dory!

The next scheduled slot of *The Big Game* featured Cole – no, not Cole as in Andy, Ashley or Joe but as in Nat ... *The Nat King Cole Show* was hurriedly rushed off the shelf and on the air to replace the football.

Arsenal had refused to allow ITV's cameras into Highbury for their match against Newcastle United, the next on ITV's list, and Spurs and Aston Villa followed suit with other clubs falling into line to help kill off this counter-attraction to their own Saturday-afternoon fixtures.

The Football League–ITV deal collapsed, as did another one that the BBC had worked through for the FA Cup.

The 1960/61 FA Cup Final, between Tottenham Hotspur and Leicester City, was transmitted by both broadcasters as had become the norm.

BBC went on the air at 11.15am with *Grandstand* and David Coleman presented the programme from within the bowels of the magnificent Wembley Stadium.

Regular features like "How They Got There" and "Meet the Finalists" were peppered with live golf inserts from the Martini International and action from the G.B. International Swimming Trials in Walsall. Then it was live to the Community Singing and into the match itself.

ITV countered the BBC's build-up with a later on-air time and an "All Star Afternoon" which combined looking ahead to the afternoon's big match with a chunk of wrestling. Whatever the merits of the grappling game, it was developing a huge following and delivered big audiences for ITV for many years to come.

Spurs ended the afternoon as the first winners of the League and Cup Double since Proud Preston back in the late 1880s.

Well done, Spurs, and lap of honour over, David Coleman signed off *Grandstand* and the BBC was gone and away for a bit of *Mr. Pastry*, *Juke Box Jury* and *Perry Mason*.

ITV's Saturday evening wrapped *Candid Camera* and two big American cop shows, *Highway Patrol* and *77 Sunset Strip* (all readers of a certain age will now be singing the catchy theme ...) around a big entertainment special, *Big Night Out*. Oh, happy days.

*   *   *   *   *

The 1962 World Cup Finals in Chile presented the BBC and all other European broadcasters with huge problems of how to cover the tournament and get the pictures out of South America and on to our screens seven thousand miles away.

These were still quite primitive times in television. Previous World Cups in Switzerland in 1954 and Sweden in 1958 had been limited in the number of matches covered. And despite strong representations no doubt made, there was no guarantee one of our nation's matches would be the Eurovision "pool" match on any particular day.

Indeed in 1958, while England were playing their opening group game against the Soviet Union, BBC viewers were watching West Germany begin their defence of their title against Argentina. England's later crucial game against Austria was also missed as Eurovision picked the Germans again against Northern Ireland.

In Chile four years later the issue was time and distance. The matches were covered live locally but transatlantic satellite broadcasting was still at an experimental stage.

This time, ITV opted out of broadcasting the tournament while the BBC covered every England game, whether a pooled match or not. And they also sent commentators to other games that attracted attention. Which is how David Coleman found himself at a Group 2 match between hosts, Chile, and Italy later dubbed "The Battle of Santiago".

The Italians had two men sent off for violent conduct in the first half and fights were breaking out between the two sides all over the field.

Seemingly an element of the bad blood between the teams had been created because some Italian journalists had been critical of Chile as the host country.

The South American republic was indeed recovering from the after effects of the massive Valdivia earthquake which had rocked Chile in 1960 but did not prevent it from staging the World Cup.

The game became infamous and English referee, Ken Aston, struggled to keep order. He later went on to invent yellow and red cards. Given the number of times he could have used them on this particular day, he would have ended it as an expert shuffler on the popular TV western, *Maverick*, without any problem.

Chile won the game 2–0 but it went down in the chamber of horrors of World Cup moments.

This is how a young David Coleman memorably opened his report on the game.

"Good evening, the game you are about to see is the most stupid, appalling, disgusting and disgraceful exhibition of football possibly in the history of the game.

"You, at home, may well think that teams that play in this manner ought to be expelled immediately from the competition. See what *you* think?"

Nobody was going to be turning the television off or over after an introduction like that!

And that game remains one of my own personal earliest memories of watching football on the telly.

That report from David Coleman got on to our screens like all the other game and feature coverage. By air.

All the BBC's World Cup coverage was air-freighted. Film cans were flown out of Chile into New York and after a three-hour wait sent on to London. That time in New York wasn't wasted though; they processed the film there before placing it on a transatlantic flight that would arrive in London in time to show the action a couple of days after the match had finished.

England's opening match, a 2–1 defeat against Hungary, was played in Rancagua on Thursday, May 31st, and shown in full two days later at 10.30am on Saturday evening. There were similar two-day delays for the other group games against Argentina, a 3–1 win, and a 0–0 draw against Bulgaria.

Even a showpiece quarter-final, against Brazil and an inspired Garrincha, was played on a Sunday evening UK time and transmitted on the BBC the following Tuesday.

And there wsa no difference for the Final itself, played on a Sunday evening UK time with a full recording shown at 9.25pm two days later.

The stars of that trip were not the presenters or commentators but the logistics guys who, ahead of the tournament, had worked out how they were going to get their valuable cargo back to London safe and sound.

Every route and airline schedule was pressed into action in an early example of the determination that existed at the BBC to super-serve their sports fans.

The next World Cup would involve a different set of logistics but long-distance travel wasn't one of them. After all the 1966 World Cup was being staged in England.

CHAPTER 5

"NOW, HAVE I GOT A GOOD IDEA"

"Welcome to *Match of the Day*, the first of a weekly series coming to you every Saturday on BBC Two. As you can hear we are in Beatleville for this Liverpool versus Arsenal match."

Those words from Kenneth Wolstenholme, on August 22nd 1964, kicked off the life of a new television programme that has since gone on to become a national institution.

In 2014, the programme will celebrate the 50th anniversary of its very first show, and perhaps it was always destined to be a smash hit, especially having based its first programme in the city that was also sending out the Beatles to conquer the pop music world.

And, perhaps the black cat that ran across the pitch at Anfield on that sunny August afternoon back in the 1960s was just adding its own stroke of luck on the debut of a legendary title that has gone on to become a much-loved part of the British television landscape. "Treasured" is how one senior BBC executive described it to me recently.

I have had a near half-century relationship with the programme – both personal and professional. Whether it be as a young viewer allowed to stay up past my bedtime to watch it; or recruited as a starry-eyed assistant producer a decade or so later; being made the actual Editor of the programme; then at its chief broadcast rival ITV, a rights negotiator for and against it; and having some pride in being the person who discovered and nurtured some of the on-screen talent that now present the programme.

These days I'm back in the armchair watching it and, in the not too distant past, I found myself deciding whether my own boys could stay up to watch it!

It is simply impossible to calculate the impact of *Match of the Day* on the sporting life of this country but the fact that its famous upbeat opening music was voted television's all-time favourite theme tune gives a clue to the programme's place in people's hearts and minds.

After all, the same piece of music has also sent newly-weds down the aisle and football-lovers to their graves, such has been its impact and the affection there is for it, and the programme it heralds.

It is worth remembering that it wasn't even the original theme music. That piece of music was "Drum Majorette", written by Major Leslie Statham, the bandleader of the Welsh Guards, under a pseudonym, Arnold Steck.

A rousing tune, it was later replaced in 1970 with the theme that has become synonymous with televised football. The imaginatively named "Match of the Day" theme was written by Barry Stoller. And the rest is history.

Every famous footballer since the mid-1960s has seen himself pop up on *Match of the Day* – that's 50 years' worth of top talent – and the odd one has scored on the programme and gone on to present the show!

Match of the Day now represents the BBC's statement on football. Essentially priced out of regular live football by big spenders elsewhere, the channel's diet of Premier League highlights each Saturday and Sunday evening throughout the season has retained for it a significant foothold in the national sport. The BBC obviously no longer has its their own way in football, far from it, but it does own one of British television's iconic shows.

After all, you can buy the rights, but you can't buy the brand and all that goes with it. I know – I tried and failed.

Not every programme is a "Rembrandt" and sometimes it could do with a healthy size 12 up its occasionally smug backside, but essentially it regularly turns up like an old friend that you are happy to make a date with.

This is how the BBC's Head of Football, Phil Bernie, sees it.

"Amidst all the live games available, it retains its value as a one-stop shop for Saturday's best football. In 90 minutes you can absorb the key moments of all the 90 minutes played in the Premier League that day – as well as hear from the key participants and see the major incidents analysed. For most of those watching it provides the first view of the day's action and it is free.

"*MOTD 2* was set up to extend the success of *MOTD*, where more games were now being played. We wanted it to be clearly related to *MOTD*, but to have its own distinct identity."

The story of how the programme came into being is a fascinating one and reflects the caution that existed at the Football League about letting television encroach on the game.

An early exchange of correspondence between Bryan Cowgill, the BBC's Head of Sports Programmes, and the Football League's Secretary, Alan Hardaker, in 1964 set the discussion in train.

Hardaker had not been a fan of televising the game as he felt, like many of his member clubs, that the television organisations were trying to get the game on the cheap and that over-exposure would ultimately affect attendances. The BBC, however, persisted with their idea of *The Match of the Day* programme and over the summer months persuaded the League Secretary and his Management Committee of the merit of this new venture.

An agreement for the programme was finally drawn up in July 1964 that allowed the BBC to "film" a selected Football League match every Saturday. The film was to be used in the form of an edited report to be called *Match of the Day* (the "The" prefix had gone) for up to a maximum length of 55 minutes. Transmission of the programme was to be at, or any time after, 6.30 pm.

For the above access the BBC paid the Football League a total sum of £20,000 and agreed they could not release their choice of the match to be covered until 4.00pm on each respective Saturday. The BBC had hoped to be able to reveal the match in the programme's weekly *Radio Times* billing.

Match of the Day was born and Cowgill looked forward to "wetting the new baby's head" with Hardaker and Senior Producer, Alan Chivers, in the opening weeks of the programme.

And, of course, for those old enough to claim it, we all say we saw the first edition of the show which went out on the air on August 22nd at 6.30pm on BBC Two.

But only if you lived in London, could you. That was the limit of where the BBC's new channel, which had been launched that April, could be seen at that point. And, indeed, there were more than twice as many people at Anfield that afternoon than watched an iconic show being born a couple of hours later.

Technological advances in both electronic cameras and videotape meant that the pictures directed by Alan Chivers were instantly sent from the stadium to the videotape area in Television Centre, edited swiftly and then put on air.

Roger Hunt, Liverpool's goal-scoring machine, later a World Cup-winner with England, scored the first-ever goal on *Match of the Day*, a volley from a cross by fellow England man, Ian Callaghan.

The game ended 3–2 to the Reds with a late goal from Gordon Wallace, his second of the match. Injury dictated that Wallace would have at fitful career at Anfield, while over the years *Match of the Day* would return time and time again to a stadium, and an atmosphere, that added an extra layer to the action on the pitch.

Of course getting the opening show on the air was a triumph in itself but the late Alec Weeks, who was *Match of the Day's* Executive Producer from 1965 to 1980, and directed matches for the programme for 22 years, remembered that hectic first day in his autobiography, *Under Auntie's Skirts*.

"I use the word 'editing'. 'Butchering' would be more appropriate. We were due on the air at 6.30pm for this first *Match of the Day*. The match finished at 4.50pm.

"We found an 'out' point on a piece of activity in the first half – a throw-in taken by Ron Yeats. Just as the ball left his big hands, snip went the scissors, and we spooled off the next ten minutes of play and picked up with the ball in midfield. A bit of glue, a bit of tape and off we spooled, looking for another editing point.

"On transmission, when that particular edit came up not only was it a world-record throw-in, the ball being thrown by Ron Yeats from the near side to the far side, but it also landed at the feet of ... Ron Yeats!"

Hey, we've all done it, Alec!

One interested London viewer on that early Saturday evening was somebody who has become completely synonymous with *Match of the Day* and who still continues to work on the programme more than 40 years since he made his commentary debut back in 1971. John Motson, "Motty", typically spent that late-summer afternoon back in 1964 at a football match.

"In August 1964, I was working for the *Barnet Press* and on Saturday afternoon I was covering a match in Finchley. After I'd finished, one of my work-mates, Jonathan Lang, invited me back to his house to watch the first programme in a new series called *Match of the Day*."

Match of the Day was off and running, but with a later on-air time, 7pm on the second week, 7.30pm the two subsequent weeks and then never before 10pm for the rest of the season.

With only one match covered each week, the BBC were careful not to feature the same teams each week. Indeed, Liverpool were seen only twice more that season while that season's champions, Manchester United, were covered on eight occasions.

The team of the early 1960s, Tottenham Hotspur, actually chalked up nine appearances, and West Ham, Bobby Moore et al., seven appearances.

But not everybody was a fan of television – and its growing encroachment into the game. For example, there were widely contrasting views on Merseyside where ebullient Liverpool manager, Bill Shankly, loved the exposure the new BBC enterprise gave his club and would remain a loyal advocate of it. The programme would be a regular visitor to the club in its early years. Indeed when the BBC filmed its first colour edition of *Match of the Day* in November 1969 it chose Anfield to host the occasion.

His opposite number at Everton, the highly successful if less populist Harry Catterick, actually requested his club be omitted from selection for coverage as he believed it gave his fellow managers and opponents an opportunity to check out the current form of his players and his team's latest tactics. Indeed Everton did not feature in a home league game on *Match of the Day* until the opening game of the 1967/68 season, three years after the start of the show.

In its debut season the occasional dip into the Second Division saw *Match of the Day* debuts for the likes of Leyton Orient and Northampton Town and a solo visit to Division Four witnessed Oxford United's 1–0 win over Tranmere Rovers.

Overall, around 30 teams helped *Match of the Day* get its first season under way. And Manchester United's Denis Law was undoubtedly the first year's star turn, scoring nine goals in eight games – including four double strikes.

The BBC stretched the broadcast range of BBC Two during the season, but the funeral of a national hero from another walk of life, Sir Winston Churchill, rightly halted the programme for one Saturday in early 1965.

The programme had been a success in its first season but with the football authorities still at odds about whether televising the sport was for good or ill, they chipped away at *Match of the Day*'s running time, and negotiations delayed its return until early October. The Football League also made sure the identity of the match to be shown was still kept under wraps until at least the end of half-time when *Grandstand* could then reveal its identity.

In its second season, *Match of the Day*'s reputation continued to grow and among its second-year treats were a pair of classic matches between Tottenham Hotspur and Manchester United. Just a couple of months apart they both remarkably ended 5–1 to the home team. In October's White Hart Lane clash, Spurs' brilliant striker, Jimmy Greaves, scored a wonderful individual goal that has been rerun a million times since. While Bobby Charlton crashed home United's consolation from 30 yards.

In their return fixture in December, United won with a similar scoreline and with similar panache. Their Scottish brave heart Denis Law scored a brace and Bobby Charlton thundered home a volley.

This was rich fare for BBC Two and its new controller, a young man with a big BBC future of his own ... David Attenborough!

Match of the Day was making its mark and soon discussions were afoot as to whether to take the programme over to BBC One for the 1966/67 season and that argument was helped, of course, by the nation's consciousness of football being at an all-time high because the impending 1966 World Cup was to be hosted in England.

Match of the Day had been in part created to help hone the skills of cameramen and technicians ahead of the World Cup that was looming large on the broadcast horizon for both the BBC and ITV.

The two organisations would work together as a consortium to produce pictures for the waiting world in 1966 and ITV, like the BBC, was putting their people through their paces.

ITV could actually lay claim to having been the first to broadcast the "edited highlights" format.

Two of its regional broadcasters almost breasted the tape together in getting the first programme of that type on the air.

Back in September 1962, Tyne Tees had produced the first edition of its Saturday-night regional show *Shoot!* with George Taylor at the helm.

The diet of football was based on matches played at Newcastle, Sunderland, Middlesbrough, Hartlepool United and Darlington. Money was tight and challenged production standards, but they were on the air.

Meanwhile, down at Anglia Television, the interest that followed Ipswich Town's unlikely League Championship win the previous season had got them thinking.

What followed was *Match of the Week*, a series of highlight programmes built around the region's four football clubs, Ipswich Town, Norwich City, Peterborough United and Colchester United.

The series, regularly broadcast on a Sunday evening, went ahead despite protestations from Ipswich manager, Alf Ramsey, who was cautious about the growing influence of television. But the Anglia team persuaded the Ipswich chairman, John Cobbold, that the exposure would be good for the club. And he agreed.

John Camkin commentated on the games and added his own analysis later. In the scanner directing the outside broadcast cameras was a young Bob Gardam, who went on to become one of ITV's star directors. A wonderfully creative and dynamic professional, Gardam would throw all his energy and enthusiasm behind his work and come up trumps time and again.

Away from league football, the FA Cup Final continued to give both broadcasters a chance to shine.

In 1965, after David Coleman's introduction to FA Cup Final day on *Grandstand*, it was followed by a tour of the empty Wembley dressing rooms with Danny Blanchflower, who was twice an FA Cup Final-winner in the early 1960s.

The *Radio Times* front cover was adorned with rosettes of the two finalists, Leeds United and Liverpool, and the programme had the traditional "How They Got There" and "Meet the Teams" features as well as a look back at the midweek action from Sir Stanley Matthews's Testimonial.

Being *Grandstand*, there was still time to squeeze in some rugby from Twickenham, golf from Sandwich, racing from Ascot and swimming from Coventry before getting back to Wembley and the Community Singing.

ITV countered with its own new Saturday programme, *World of Sport*, which began in January of that year.

"From 'A' for ankle-hold in wrestling to 'X' for draws in soccer there's a whole *World of Sport*."

The publicity blurb in the *TV Times* above could have added 'C' for cliff-diving, 'L' for log-rolling and 'T' for truck racing – but those sporting delights lay in years ahead.

World of Sport ran for 20 years, often in *Grandstand*'s shade in terms of heavyweight content, but with a perky and bright style of its own – its early editions would be fronted by Eamonn Andrews and later by Southern Television's Richard Davies, who took Jimmy Hill's suggestion and gave his name a tweak, and as Dickie Davies, would be the programme's popular host for many years.

During this period, book-ended by football previews, horse racing, the ever-popular All-In Wrestling and with the classified football results bringing up the rear, *World of Sport* gave Grandstand a decent run for its money.

On FA Cup Final day in 1965, *World of Sport* began at 12.50pm. Only a spell of wrestling, from 1.20pm, kept it away from Wembley and the football matters of the day. Gerry Loftus would provide the ITV match commentary.

The match itself went into extra-time but Liverpool finally won their first FA Cup Final. Three days later they met European and World Club champions Inter Milan at Anfield in the first leg of the European Cup semi-final tie.

Liverpool famously beat Inter 3–1 but controversially went down 3–0 in the second leg.

What underlines the fact that this was still sports television from a different era is that neither of these two semi-final matches was live, and neither was the Final itself. Only highlights of the matches were shown in the BBC's *Sportsview*. Indeed none of the English champion's games in Europe that season was live.

It all seems a long way from the UEFA Champions League of today and Sky Sports' "8-match" live choice on *Matchday 5* or whatever. As well, of course, as ITV's live pick on Tuesday nights.

Anyway, Liverpool had come up short in that European Cup, while West Ham had won the Cup Winners' Cup Final against TSV Munich at Wembley. In 1964, Bobby Moore had lifted the FA Cup there. Now, a year later, he was lifting European club football's second prize. People began asking a leading question. Would Bobby Moore, as England captain, land a glorious hat-trick by lifting the World Cup at Wembley the following season?

Another hat-trick would provide the answer.

CHAPTER 6

BLACK-AND-WHITE ... BUT PURE GOLD

One of the more pleasant duties bestowed on me during my time at the Football Association was to be a member of an Advisory Board set up to help the acclaimed sculptor, Philip Jackson, in delivering the statue of the great Bobby Moore that now stands so proudly outside the new Wembley Stadium.

Other more significant members of the panel included three footballing knights – Sir Bobby Charlton, Sir Geoff Hurst and Sir Trevor Brooking.

Our role was to help the master-sculptor understand how Moore walked, ran, thought and looked. He then brought all those aspects and others together in a stunning impression of England's World Cup-winning captain that still stops people in their tracks today.

Bobby Moore himself never was knighted but he remains England's favourite footballing son and whenever I visit Wembley and see the statue I always have two thoughts.

First, what a great player and a great man Bobby Moore was – and second I think 1966!!!

2012 saw the nation galvanised by London's hosting of a magnificent Olympic Games. Everybody suddenly seemed to have a touch of gold fever – and Team GB blew everybody away with their quality, class and courage.

Television viewing figures for the Games went absolutely through the roof – as the BBC used every conceivable technical gizmo to capture the breadth and beauty of the Olympic sports, including streaming non-stop action on a 24-hour digital channel service as well as a comprehensive service on BBC One and BBC Two. It was a triumph!

*   *   *   *   *

Forty-six years earlier, it was coverage of the 1966 World Cup that took the country by storm.

At that time the World Cup tournament's final stages were only a 16-team, eight-venue, 32-match competition. But for 19 days in July 1966 the country was at fever pitch as England set out to win the World Cup for the first time – and on home soil.

When I was at the Football Association we were always advised to be guarded and cautious when asked by the media about the prospect of winning a World Cup or European Championship. "Hostage to fortune stuff" I was told.

No such problem for Alf Ramsey when beginning his reign as England manager after being appointed in September 1962. He showed both a clear determination and supreme confidence. His message was clear.

"Most certainly, we will win the World Cup in 1966."

We were off and running. Mind you, his first match as manager ended in a 5–2 defeat against France in Paris in February 1963.

Over three years later, only the two Bobbies survived from that Parisian mauling to go on and play in the World Cup Final – Charlton and Moore were, of course, in Ramsey's most important line-up.

Dagenham-born, Ramsey had a clipped style of delivery softened, it was thought, by having taken some elocution lessons. In the end, it didn't matter all that much; his team did his talking for him.

When the whistle blew to end the 1966 World Cup Final, Wembley exploded, the England players and fans alike were delirious with joy, but Ramsey sat stock-still on the trainer's bench – a model of cool, calm leadership.

Born in 1920, Ramsey's post-war playing career, following a spell in the army, had been largely spent at White Hart Lane and he became part of Tottenham Hotspur's famous push-and-run team that won the League Championship in 1951.

An England international who won 32 caps, full-back Ramsey subsequently went into football management and took unfashionable Ipswich Town out of the Third Division to League Division One Championship glory in 1961/62.

The Football Association took notice and came knocking. Ramsey would join them and be the first England manager to actually pick the team – that had been the stuff of an all-powerful selection committee up until then.

Ramsey had publicly set an ambitious target. And, he would famously go on to achieve it and, in so doing, inadvertently help immortalise another man synonymous with the English football scene of the 1950s and 1960s.

Kenneth Wolstenholme, who coincidentally was also born in 1920, also found July 30th 1966 and the World Cup to be the high-water mark of his illustrious BBC broadcasting career.

His famous commentary lines, as Geoff Hurst crashed in England's fourth and final goal against West Germany at Wembley on that famous Saturday afternoon, has guaranteed his place in broadcasting immortality. In a BBC career that straddled 23 years "the voice of football" never topped those special words he found to describe the closing moments of the 1966 World Cup Final.

"There's people on the pitch … they think it's all over – it is NOW!"

Like Ramsey, Wolstenholme provided a similar show of coolness under pressure even at the very height of the action; perhaps his wartime exploits kept things in perspective.

Between 1942 and the end of the war, the would-be football commentator flew exactly 100 missions as a pilot with the RAF's bomber command over Germany. This was a remarkable total in a conflict that would take airmen out of the sky at a tragically frequent rate.

Many wartime pilots' bombing missions never reached double figures before they were brutally shot out of the sky.

Defying those odds, Wolstenholme subsequently went on to win the Distinguished Flying Cross and Bar, and that doyen of sportswriters, Ian Wooldridge, would later write of the BBC commentator's style of delivery:

"Wolstenholme didn't much bother about players' birthdays, their wives' names or whether they had some aunt who had once played in *Coronation Street*. He criticised but didn't denigrate and I never once heard him patronise. I guess it is something you learn over places like Dortmund and Berlin in the dead of night."

Wolstenholme's World Cup Final commentary was the soundtrack to the immaculate camera coverage of the historic match directed on the BBC by Alec Weeks.

Seven months shy of his 40th birthday, Weeks had put together a crack team to deliver the best football coverage possible at Wembley in the nine World Cup games that would be played underneath the famous Twin Towers.

Weeks had joined the BBC as a 14-year-old office junior in 1941. He soon graduated to junior programme engineer, with jobs like adding spot effects (essentially sound effects) on wartime programmes like *ITMA*.

In 1944, he was called up to the RAF, and, in truth, the Germans had to be on the look-out – Weeks was a man who could handle himself!

A boxing enthusiast, he sparred with future world middleweight champion, Randolph Turpin, while in the forces, and carried that aggressive competitive edge into peacetime and a remarkable career in broadcasting.

And, boy could he give out a volley! On one occasion a senior BBC man, on a "state" visit to an outside broadcast, was talking rather loudly in the back of the television scanner while Weeks was trying to direct a match.

"Listen, cocker," said Weeks, "either pipe down or you'll be in the car park." He piped down.

Many years later, while working as a young producer for the BBC at my first World Cup in 1982, I too was on the end of one of Weeks's raging furies.

Unfortunately, I had been under the rather mistaken impression that I had been called into his Madrid office for a pat on the back. For a pat on the back, read a serious and memorable kick up the arse. I still shudder at the memory of it more than 30 years later.

Seemingly my over-enthusiastic efforts to deliver top stuff for the BBC in another part of Spain had been costing a fortune in overtime for the film crews involved and Weeksy's budget had now come under heavy artillery fire. As a consequence he let me have both barrels.

Equally, typically, a couple of days later he called me back into the office and gave me a ticket so I could go to my first World Cup Final.

"Enjoy it, cocker!" he said and smiled.

So three men, Ramsey, Wolstenholme and Weeks, all had a key part in the passion play that would develop over 19 days in July 1966.

In many ways it was this super-concentrated fix of live World Cup action on both the BBC and ITV that set me, a 12-year-old football fanatic in Liverpool, on the road to my future career in journalism, broadcasting and football itself.

Four World Cups with the BBC, two with ITV, and one, 40 years on from those glory days of 1966, with the Football Association itself are amongst my own professional landmarks, along with another six World Cups wrapped around them spent glued to the television watching the destiny of another tournament unravel. 1966 got me hooked.

Two things may surprise younger readers. First, the tournament was shown in black-and-white. This frustrated both the BBC and ITV, who wanted to show off their ability to cover the matches in colour.

Unfortunately for both broadcasters, the television manufacturers were able to persuade the government to hold off granting a licence for the introduction of colour television for another 12 months.

Also, despite there being 32 matches in the competition, only 12 were actually shown live because games often kicked off at the same time. Indeed on the Saturday of the World Cup quarter-finals, BBC and ITV both broadcast the action from the England vs. Argentina match at Wembley, while the other three quarter-finals that started at the same time as England's were all shown in highlights form later.

Obviously, these days every game from what is now a 32-team, multi-venue, 64-match competition is shown live and in colour (!) – including across two channels when the final group games are played simultaneously.

Both viewers' and broadcasters' mutual demands, and the huge fees paid to FIFA to buy the rights to televise the World Cup, define the scale of blanket coverage that now swamps the schedules these days.

Back in 1966, both BBC and ITV recruited from the good and great of the football business to augment their established commentary teams.

On the BBC, Kenneth Wolstenholme, Walley Barnes, David Coleman, Frank Bough and Alan Weeks were joined in the commentary box and studios by Billy Wright and former and future England bosses Walter Winterbottom, Don Revie and Ron Greenwood.

Also on parade were Joe Mercer, Tommy Docherty, Johnny Haynes, Danny Blanchflower, referee Ken Aston and a man who would become synonymous with televised football, the one and only Jimmy Hill.

Over on ITV there was also a formidable line-up: presenter Eamonn Andrews and commentators Hugh Johns, Gerry Loftus, John Camkin and a young Barry Davies had the likes of Bill Shankly, Jock Stein, Phil Woosnam and Dave Bowen alongside them.

The BBC–ITV consortium, which had come together to service the demands of 500 visiting broadcasters from their base at BBC Television Centre, split responsibilities for match coverage by venue.

The BBC covered matches at Goodison Park, Hillsborough and Ayresome Park while ITV were responsible for the pictures from White City (one match), Old Trafford, Villa Park and Roker Park.

Each broadcaster had its own cameras at Wembley and both had a new piece of kit – the slow-motion-stop-action machine. The action-replay machine was now in play but was still at a rudimentary stage in terms of its use.

And so on Monday, July 11th, the World Cup began as the Queen, this time without James Bond in tow, got proceedings under way with a short speech ahead of the opening match at Wembley.

The BBC, as has traditionally been its style down the years, got on the air first, at 6.50pm, following that night's edition of the twice-weekly football soap, *United!*

People who say football is a soap opera these days may not realise that there was a programme which ran for a couple of years that was just that.

As that night's programme's billing suggested: "Holiday time is over ... it's back to work for Brentwich United."

And that was certainly the case for the England team. ITV joined the World Cup "party" shortly before kick-off at 7.25pm after Ena Sharples, Annie Walker and Hilda Ogden had done their stint in *Coronation Street*.

What followed was a dull goalless draw between England and Uruguay. A real anti-climax if ever there was one.

No problem, the next live match the following night on the BBC set the tournament off on the right rails. World champions Brazil beat Bulgaria 2–0 with goals from football legends, Pele and Garrincha – both stunning free-kicks.

A pattern of live coverage on the BBC and highlights on ITV developed, although both broadcasters were live as England, and Bobby Charlton, ignited the Wembley evening skyline with a goal against Mexico that came straight from the footballing gods.

Possibly the game of the group stages was Portugal vs. Brazil at Goodison Park. The world champions, having lost their second group game against Hungary, in driving rain on Merseyside, needed to win to secure progress in the tournament, while Portugal, with their outstanding new star Eusebio, were on top form.

I missed this game on television, but for all the right reasons because I was actually at Goodison Park myself to see it. My father had spirited up a couple of tickets and so I was able to see Pele and Eusebio up close and personal. Not as close as my dad though, as he was one of the policemen on duty, walking around the pitch as the match got under way.

Sadly, Pele was kicked out of the match, but Eusebio who died in 2014, scored twice and was truly exceptional. Brazil were now out of the tournament. For me, who would later travel across the globe to see World Cup football, this, my first World Cup match, reached by a sixpenny bus ride, was one I've never forgotten.

England came through a tough encounter with Argentina in a famous Saturday-afternoon quarter-final at Wembley. This, on a day when the tournament's surprise package, North Korea, scared the living daylights out Eusebio and co. by taking a three-goal lead inside the first 24 minutes at their quarter-final tie in Goodison Park.

This remarkable match finished 5–3 to Portugal, but was only ever a series of score caption updates and highlights because it was played at the same time as England were toughing it out against Argentina on both BBC and ITV.

Indeed, as already explained, all four quarter-finals kicked off at 3pm on that Saturday afternoon and therefore only one match was broadcast live. A total anathema in these days of exorbitant rights fees and broadcasters' policy of "throw open the schedule" to major football competitions.

England deservedly defeated Portugal in a wonderful Wembley semi-final and the final, against a very talented West Germany team, was set up.

For Messrs Ramsey, Wolstenholme and Weeks their day of destiny had arrived.

Ramsey, in fact, did some of his most important work the day before the final. He quietly reassured Roger Hunt and Geoff Hurst they would be playing the following day and also, just as importantly, told Jimmy Greaves he wouldn't be.

Greaves got injured against France in a group-stage match but had recovered, and there was now a press clamour for Ramsey to select him ahead of Hurst or Hunt.

Hunt especially had failed to win over the southern-based journalists as they saw him as a work-horse rather than a marksman. Mind you, he had scored three goals already for England on their route to the final and it was that very work-rate that Ramsey so admired.

Anyway, Hunt and Hurst were in and on the morning of the game sat down for breakfast at England's base at the Hendon Hall Hotel knowing their number "21" and "10" red shirts would be tracked by the television cameramen later that day.

Kenneth Wolstenholme's World Cup Final day started early. He was at Wembley Stadium shortly after nine o'clock. Alec Weeks and his team were already there.

Weeks had put together a top team of cameramen and technicians, 54 in all – and everyone had been hand-picked for the job. The BBC had ten cameras located in and around Wembley Stadium plus 19 effects microphones to pick up the sounds of this historic sporting day.

His cameramen, who had honed their skills over two seasons of *Match of the Day* duties, were primed and ready for "the big one".

Weeks had insisted that they all stayed at the Wembley Hilton Hotel the night before the final, away from their wives and partners. Sex, it would seem, had been banned!

The BBC's match coverage had been chosen by the Consortium to be the one distributed worldwide – some 48 countries across the globe took the game live.

An hour before the kick-off, Wolstenholme made his way around the perimeter track inside the stadium. En route he was greeted by a policeman, who wished him luck and, nodding towards the fans behind him, said, "Don't worry, if one single person tries to get over this small wall and on to the pitch I'll have them."

Luckily for Wolstenholme, that very same policeman – or one of his colleagues nearby – momentarily got caught up in the emotion of the occasion, failing in their duty in the final moments of the match and thus setting up the BBC commentator to deliver the line of a lifetime.

Mind you, before all that, the veteran of a hundred bombing missions over Germany in the Second World War still had one aerial adventure to handle before settling down to his afternoon's work.

The way up to the gantry in the South Stand that housed the mobile studios and key camera and commentary positions was via a rickety old lift that had seen better days – and that's putting it mildly.

Indeed, I travelled up and down in that lift many times myself when working for the BBC at Wembley and was always mightily relieved when it reached its destination – at either end of its journey.

And so the 1966 World Cup Final unveiled itself to a capacity Wembley crowd and a British TV audience of some 32 million viewers.

Well, actually 32 million people and one very famous dog. Pickles, a black-and-white mongrel, had saved the Football Association, indeed the nation, from profound embarrassment earlier in the year when, while out on his daily walk with owner David Corbett, he had happened upon a package hidden in some bushes.

Astonishingly, its contents proved to be the missing Jules Rimet Trophy – the World Cup, which had been dramatically stolen from an exhibition eight days earlier.

Pickles became an overnight sensation, as newspapers and television channels fought for access to the canine crusader, and on the day of the World Cup Final itself, sure enough he was photographed watching the match in front of his owner's television set!

And Pickles had plenty to watch.

The BBC's World Cup *Grandstand* was on the air from 12 noon to 6.15pm, while ITV came on the air at 1.00pm.

Wolstenholme was joined in the commentary box by former Arsenal player and broadcaster Walley Barnes, while ITV's Hugh Johns had Wales manager Dave Bowen by his side.

Johns was an outstanding commentator in his own right and worked for many years on ITV's football output, but on this Saturday, destiny – and the natural pull of the BBC's coverage – meant his words over Geoff Hurst's World Cup-clinching goal have something of a curiosity value.

As his BBC colleague and friend Kenneth Wolstenholme was guaranteeing his place in broadcasting legend by talking of "people on the pitch", Johns went for "Here comes Hurst, he might make it three. He has! He has … so that's it. That is IT!"

And it was. England had won the World Cup. They had survived an early reverse in the game, hit back, taken a late lead, and then seen it extinguished with virtually the last kick of the game.

In extra-time, Geoff Hurst had scored the goal that still courts controversy – was it over the line? Nothing we were shown at the time, or have been shown since, was conclusive – other than the scoreboard itself, of course.

And then, we witnessed Bobby Moore's coolness under pressure and Hurst scoring his dramatic clincher. England had made it. A feat that is still revered today – and as yet, still not replicated.

The whole country went mad, including a 12-year-old lad and his family in Liverpool. It was a special day.

For Ramsey, Wolstenholme and Weeks it was a red-letter day in each of their own special professional disciplines.

Celebration followed celebration – Ramsey (later knighted) and his team attended an official function on the Saturday evening before they slipped off to join their wives and girlfriends to celebrate privately late into the night.

The following day it was a champagne lunch held at ATV Studios in Borehamwood, with Eamonn Andrews fronting a programme that looked back at the glorious events of the previous day in the company of the men who had made it possible – and were probably dying to have some time to themselves.

For me, even at this distance I still glory in Wolstenholme's words, not just when Geoff Hurst crashed England's fourth goal home to clinch victory but when Bobby Moore walked up to receive the World Cup from the Queen and then lifted it proudly aloft.

"It's 12 inches high, it's solid gold, and it means England are the WORLD CHAMPIONS."

CHAPTER 7

THE SUNDAY SERVICE

"Ooh I do hate Sundays. I'll be glad when it's over. It drives me
up the wall just sitting here looking at you lot. Every Sunday it's
the same. Nowhere to go, nothing to do. Just sit here waiting for
the next lot of grub to come up."
(*Hancock's Half Hour* – "Sunday Afternoon at Home")

As was often the case, Simpson and Galton's marvellous scripts for
the late great comedian Tony Hancock were bang on the money in
describing the somewhat drab life and times of the British people in the
1950s and early 1960s.

Post-war austerity was followed by, well, more post-war austerity
before it was declared in the late 1950s that "You've never had it
so good!"

The sceptics challenged that presumption but economic and social
progress was slowly being made and on we went into the 1960s waiting
for something to truly give us lift-off.

And sure enough it came along, both literally and metaphorically:
man was fired off into space while for us lesser mortals there was just a
little bit more of a skip in our step.

Pop music, sport, television, air travel, cars and holidays overseas –
the British people were on the move ... but still not on Sundays!

Certainly compared to these modern times of the non-stop seven-
day week, Sundays were a lot gentler when I was growing up.

Shoe-horned out of the house with my brother, David, for a morning trip to church or Sunday school – straight back home (there was no playing out on Sundays); a quick squint at my dad's *Sunday Express* with its Giles cartoons and "The Gambols", plus, of course all the league tables; a couple of hours of homework (ugh!); a slice of the BBC's Light Programme and *The Clitheroe Kid*; Sunday lunch; a quick trip round to granny's house; ITV's *Sunday Night at the London Palladium*; a bath and then bed. Another Sunday was over.

And that was it – week in, week out, year in, year out. Until November 7th 1965, that is, when a special after-lunch weekly treat hit our television screens – following the roast beef and Yorkshire pudding along came a very tasty dessert – FOOTBALL!

After "four years of complicated negotiations, a constant series of meetings, discussions and protracted arguments ... da de da de da ..." the football authorities had given a green light to a new series of regional ITV Sunday football highlights programmes.

It was a big breakthrough and it meant *Match of the Day*, which would move across from BBC Two to BBC One at the start of the 1966/67 season, now had a commercial television proposition alongside it.

Programmes popped up all over the country and in my own backyard in the north-west, ABC TV, which broadcast across the north and the Midlands, launched its weekly Sunday football show *World of Soccer*. A month earlier ATV in London had also launched its own show.

Of course this was a particularly rich period for clubs in the north-west, Yorkshire and the Midlands. The two Merseyside giants, Everton and Liverpool, the equivalent football forces in Manchester — City and United – Leeds United, under Don Revie, were all making big strides and the Midlands could throw the likes of West Bromwich Albion, Leicester City and Nottingham Forest into the pot.

Plus there were plenty of other famous football names knocking about such as Burnley, Blackburn Rovers, Bolton Wanderers, Blackpool and Aston Villa. The first match in the new *World of Soccer* series featured two teams with a wealth of football history, Preston North End and Wolverhampton Wanderers, from Deepdale.

The Second Division sides shared a point apiece in a 2–2 draw with a future Everton great, Howard Kendall, on target for Preston, as was Wolves' bright new striker, Peter Knowles.

Knowles later featured in a remarkable short film on *Sportsnight with Coleman* reflecting on his "new" life as a Jehovah's Witness. Knowles would eventually give up a lucrative career and the fame and fortune of football to follow his religious beliefs.

Back on Merseyside, we settled down to our new Sunday football feast at 2.35pm and were fascinated to know where the three-camera unit had been sent the previous day to fill the 40-minute programme.

The initial season of *World of Soccer* had Martin Locke at the microphone, but he asked to be released from his contract to take up an opportunity with the South African Broadcasting Company.

The vacancy created by his departure was good news for a young man who had made a favourable impression commentating for ITV on the north-east group in the 1966 World Cup and would go on to have a stellar career at the microphone across a range of sports at BBC Television.

"I learnt a heck of a lot while my mistakes went unnoticed up in the north-east – no live stuff. But my way of identifying looks, physique, movement was born with the North Koreans. I never was much good with numbers, and of course in the World Cup, it was 1 to 22."

An early memory of commentary life from Barry Davies. I would later select him to commentate for BBC Television at the 1994 World Cup Final.

Davies would do some of his early commentary work for Granada in the north-west.

"I used to stay up on the Saturday night to watch the editing, scissors and tape, of course, and then on the Sunday lunchtime went to the local in Cheadle Hulme of one of the directors, Geoff Hall. I got used to getting stick from the regulars there about the previous week's programme. Again I learned a lot and established a good rapport with the fans."

Within a couple of years Davies had been snapped up by the BBC, where he delivered with distinction for more than four decades.

In 1968, the ITV franchises had been redistributed and Granada became a full seven-day operation and Yorkshire TV, London Weekend Television and Thames Television were all created.

With this new franchise arrangement came new possibilities for football – Granada dropped the *World of Soccer* series and replaced it with the imaginatively titled *Football* ... which was probably followed in the schedule by some "Singing" and "Dancing"!

Star Soccer became a long-standing and popular Midlands title with Hugh Johns at the microphone, while another famous brand was about to make its entrance on LWT.

The Big Match made its debut on the London Weekend channel on Sunday, August 25th 1968 and it made an immediate impact.

Jimmy Hill, the bearded super-chinned Fulham player turned Coventry City manager, had been plucked out of football and appointed LWT's Head of Sport.

A bright man awash with ideas suddenly had an electronic canvas to paint them on. Hill, a one-off, became part of the television sporting scenery for the next 40 years. His early days at ITV were followed by a long stint at the BBC before he ended his broadcasting days at Sky Sports.

He became one of television's most famous faces, often outspoken, frequently mimicked, never ignored.

A good footballer, he had scored for Fulham in an FA Cup semi-final, and had once notched five goals in an away match at Doncaster Rovers in 1958 – a feat he regularly drew to our attention!

Jimmy Hill had become a successful football manager too, as he took Coventry City into the top league – and he developed the Sky

Blue train – a football special, and wrote the "Sky Blue Song", well, with a little help from the "Eton Boating Song".

In 1961, he had also famously led the fight for the PFA on its mission to scrap the maximum wage for its members – and won.

The kid from Balham, who as a member of the local Boys' Brigade had got used to blowing his own trumpet, took that energy and enthusiasm into everything he did.

Hill was to become a big television personality. A man of opinions, he would be admired one minute and hammered the next. And he didn't care which of those contrasting views came his way.

I had the pleasure of working with Jimmy at the BBC for nearly 20 years and found him a remarkable man to be around – a tenacious character, supremely self-confident, a man full of original thought and views, a man impossible to straitjacket and also, on occasions, impossible to keep on track and on time in the programmes he appeared on. He was a challenge, but a challenge well worth having.

I once told him the outcome of a viewers' survey on sports programmes and their on-screen teams.

"Good news, Jimmy," I said, "you've finished top of the viewers' poll for favourite sports presenter."

"Lovely," he said.

"Well, Jim, I'm afraid there's some bad news too: you've also finished top in the viewers' poll for their least favourite presenter."

"Really? That's lovely too!"

"Lovely?"

"Yes, the place you don't want to finish in those blasted surveys is in the middle."

And he was right of course.

Many years later, while on BBC duty, Desmond Lynam and I accompanied Jimmy around the perimeter track at Anfield on the way to the television studio there.

With one collective voice, the Kop hit the three of us with a super-loud chorus of "Jimmy Hill's a banker"... or something along those lines. As Des and I felt the ground swallow us up, Jimmy, chin out, shoulders back, hit back with "Well, that's fame for you!"

More of Jimmy later, much more. Alongside him at LWT was presenter and commentator Brian Moore. Fresh from BBC Radio, he was a real catch, had a broadcast voice to die for and credibility by the boatload.

He would work for ITV for 30 years and I had the privilege of sitting alongside him in the Stade de Paris when he brought the curtain down on his illustrious career describing the action at the 1998 World Cup Final.

This was serious stuff that Hill and another ITV legend, executive producer John Bromley, were setting about in building their football team at LWT.

The programme also brought director Bob Gardam on board from Anglia. His innovative and imaginative match coverage proved another star appointment and a strong committed production team completed the line-up.

The Big Match became a big show for LWT and, like its contemporary, ITV football shows up and down the country would ultimately be a mix of a main game from their region and two cut-down edits from matches that involved local teams playing away from home and covered by the other regional companies.

Being in London, however, there was an extra pressure on *The Big Match* because many of the industry's movers and shakers who lived in the capital were able to compare and contrast it to the Saturday-night juggernaut that *Match of the Day* was becoming.

After all, over in Shepherds Bush, things weren't exactly standing still at the BBC either.

Kenneth Wolstenholme had heralded *Match of the Day's* big move from BBC Two to BBC One following England's big World Cup win by introducing the first post-World Cup edition like this.

"Welcome to those who have followed us from BBC Two to BBC One, but a special welcome to those new viewers who have been won over by the World Cup. We hope you will go along and watch your local team as well as *Match of the Day*. And in response to your many requests, I will explain some of the more technical points of the game as we go along ..."

World Cup fever delivered a newer, bigger audience and plenty of women and children watched the game for the first time. They had to be catered for.

Their new interest, along with the programme's established audience, helped kick-start *Match of the Day*'s new life on BBC One. The final decision to move from BBC Two to the senior channel had been taken by one of the Corporation's luminaries, Huw Wheldon. He thanked the then Controller of BBC Two, a certain David Attenborough, who would enjoy a stellar career in broadcasting, for agreeing to the move but underlined the fact he knew that losing *Match of the Day* would seriously damage the new channel and only "agreed to it with real regret". More than 40 years later *Match of the Day 2* would return the favour.

Over the next few seasons the programme captured some wonderful moments as English football proudly puffed its chest out – like West Ham's World Cup-winning trio, Moore, Hurst and Peters, running out at Upton Park to a fantastic ovation on their first appearance since creating football history at Wembley.

There was Chelsea's Bobby Tambling scoring five goals in a 6–2 win at Villa Park, Tottenham goalkeeper Pat Jennings scoring direct from his own penalty area in the 1967 FA Charity Shield against Manchester United. The match ended 3–3 and Bobby Charlton scored two absolute belters.

In a league encounter between the sides, we saw Jimmy Greaves pick his way through the Manchester United defence before stroking the ball home; and watched Rodney Marsh's brilliant individual goal make headlines as he spearheaded Third Division's QPR beating WBA in the 1967 League Cup Final – the first at Wembley.

We marvelled as Manchester City, under the joint tutelage of Joe Mercer and Malcolm Allison, danced on ice to beat Spurs on a wintry day at Maine Road; revelled in the magic of George Best as he showed signs of his true greatness; and witnessed the Merseyside pair, Liverpool and Everton, vie for honours.

It was a vintage period for British football. England were World champions; Celtic, under the gifted Jock Stein, had become the first British team to win the European Cup with the marvellous "Lisbon Lions" team; and the following season Manchester United had beaten Benfica in the European Cup Final at Wembley, ten years on from the tragedy of Munich.

It was a very special night for Matt Busby (later Sir Matt) and Bobby Charlton, who sent United on their way to victory with a rare headed goal, before George Best dazzled us with a wonderful extra-time goal. The final score was 4–1. And it was a match broadcast on both channels.

Football was as hot as it had ever been and so was the competition building up between the two major broadcasters, each trying to get some edge over the other.

There was fierce rivalry, tough men on both sides and something had to give – and sure enough at the 1969 FA Cup Final, the game's big showpiece occasion, it did, and how!

CHAPTER 8

SECONDS AWAY! IT'S THE FINAL ROUND!

In June 1963, Henry Cooper landed his famous left hook flush on the jaw of the slick-talking Cassius Clay, knocking his backside on to the ropes.

The Wembley Stadium crowd went berserk. Was "'Enery's 'Ammer" going to turn the odds upside down and change the course of boxing history?

The bell sounded for the end of the round, and with it came a welcome chance for Clay – later, of course, the great Muhammad Ali – to clear his head, and for some quick-thinking corner-man to accentuate a tear in his glove and buy some more recovery time for the man from Louisville, Kentucky.

It worked. Clay got off his stool and battered Cooper into submission – and the rest, as they say, is history.

The next time fisticuffs were on the sporting menu at Wembley was in a rather more unseemly and unlikely episode which perhaps underlined the growing antipathy and hard-nosed rivalry that had developed between the sports broadcast teams at the BBC and ITV.

Indeed, at the end of the 1969 FA Cup Final between Manchester City and Leicester City, there would be a full-on skirmish between the two production teams as they literally fought over who would get to the winning team first for those all-important post-match interviews.

Punches were thrown, ankles kicked and insults hurled as members of the two broadcasting teams squared up to each other just yards from Wembley's hallowed turf and under the disapproving gaze of the stadium's famous Twin Towers.

It was totally unacceptable behaviour, made headline news for several days and the FA later threw the book at the two warring television teams.

The FA Cup Final itself had become the regular ring canvas on which the BBC and ITV sports presentation and production teams would metaphorically slug it out for ratings and reviews.

The only guaranteed live match of the football season, the FA Cup Final attracted huge viewing figures and had become the occasion on which both broadcasters wanted to put their best wares on show, and put their rivals out of the game.

The rivalry got fierce. And in 1969, a little too fierce it would seem. But that was all at the end of the afternoon; the earlier part of the day had seen the BBC and ITV vying for viewers in the more traditional build-up to the final itself.

Like millions of other people up and down the country, I was up early on Saturday, April 26th 1969, bagging my place in the armchair nearest the telly, some four hours before the final actually kicked off.

Curtains drawn together to keep out any unwanted daylight, breakfast rushed down, sports pages of the newspapers digested, a large bag of wine gums (loved the green ones) at my side, I was ready for a long day in front of the box.

Even the odd trip to the loo was planned so as not to miss anything significant, and to make sure my dad and my brother were preoccupied doing other things and so my precious "spec" was safe.

After all, almost military precision had to go into this special day's viewing. You built up to it all season.

Each round of the Cup threw up a big story and now, on the last Saturday of April, the 1969 FA Cup-winners would be crowned.

On the BBC, Saturday-morning television was language lessons from Spain, Italy and France. Nowadays we have their players instead.

This was followed by twenty minutes of canine cartoon capers, Deputy Dawg-style.

Then at 11.25am it was time for the opening titles of Cup Final *Grandstand.*

David Coleman was on site at Wembley welcoming viewers to the BBC's coverage of the big match ... to coin a phrase!

He set the scene in his typically assured fashion, and then led to Frank Bough and Alan Weeks, who were at the two finalists' hotels ... and so off we went.

As well as all the BBC's pre-match hardy perennials – *How They Got There, Meet the Teams, People at the Match* – there was also live cricket from Arundel, the Duke of Norfolk's XI against the West Indies, and *Fight of the Week*, World Featherweight Champion Johnnie Famechon against challenger Giovanni Girgenti.

The "Fight of the Year" would happen a little later that afternoon.

Over on ITV Richard Davies, later Dickie, of course, got things under way at midday and went straight into nearly an hour's football content, including a look back at the football action from Wembley during the 1960s, a report from that week's Footballer of the Year Dinner and a preview of that afternoon's Scottish Cup Final.

Then, as ever, it was off to the wrestling, and the local Brent Town Hall bill, which featured that loveable grappling goon, Les Kellett, and a fearsome tag-team combination of Mick McManus and Steve Logan. They would have been useful for ITV later on that afternoon! Anyway, it was all top names for a top day.

Live coverage of the day's big race, the Whitbread Gold Cup, completed their other sporting fare before, like the BBC, it was back to Wembley and the FA Cup Final.

In truth, Manchester City, league champions the previous year, and Leicester City, struggling in the relegation zone, served up a fairly tepid final at a damp Wembley Stadium.

Neil Young scored the vital winning goal for Manchester City 24 minutes into the game, but the half-time marching display of the Massed Bands of the Guards Division provided just as much colour and action as the footballers for the millions watching the Wembley output.

If it was quietish on the field, it was anything but off it, as the BBC and ITV went head to head. And one or two liberties were being taken, it seemed.

Malcolm Allison, the more flamboyant part of the successful Maine Road managerial duo with Joe Mercer, had been banned by the FA from sitting on the Manchester City bench for the match – and was sitting close by in the stand.

Alongside him was his close friend and inventive Granada TV Sport producer, Paul Doherty, who had a microphone up the sleeve of his coat.

ITV viewers were given Allison's views on the game via Doherty's microphone.

Another talented journalist, Peter Lorenzo, was apparently hidden under a carpet close to the touch-line benches and was getting insights on the game for ITV from Leicester City manager, Frank O'Farrell.

Add to that a small team of ITV "interview grabbers" dressed in Manchester City tracksuits, close to the action, ready to claim the game's headline-makers first, and the scene was set for "The Rumble in the Tunnel".

Ahead of the Cup Final, the Wembley authorities had spoken to both BBC and ITV sports executives about making sure the winning team's lap of honour was not interrupted by excessive interview demands from the two broadcasters.

They were told the interviews with the two teams had to take place in the mouth of the tunnel once the players had reached there – and out of sight of the supporters.

Sensible stuff, but on the day the television teams' mutually competitive nature meant they were still determined to outdo each other.

The BBC claimed they had signed an exclusive contract worth £1,850 with Manchester City for after-match interviews and had shared a non-exclusive contract with ITV for access to Leicester City.

But it quickly became apparent that those pieces of paper meant little or nothing as one of the ITV "Manchester City tracksuit men" got stuck into his BBC rival who was shepherding Colin Bell to the Corporation's interview cameras in the tunnel.

Also ITV, it seemed, were already in the process of interviewing some of the winning Manchester City heroes.

The BBC had been "scooped" or double-crossed or both – and they weren't having any of it.

For the ultra-competitive Alec Weeks, producing the BBC's coverage that day, enough was enough. "Move in. Stop those bastards. Use any means possible."

What followed was an unedifying spectacle as legmen, riggers, cameramen, stage managers and suchlike, on both sides of the television divide, stood their ground and got stuck in to each other.

Bemused players from both Cup Final teams dodged the flying fists and swinging boots as the two television crews took each other on.

A BBC man took a punch to the face, breaking a tooth in the process, while LWT outside broadcast manager, David Yallop, also lost a tooth, as the brawling went on.

Yallop has gone on to become an renowned author, whose book titles include *An Unholy Alliance*, which may well have fitted that day's proceedings at Wembley Stadium back in 1969 when the BBC and ITV literally came out fighting.

The newspapers loved it all, of course, and senior BBC and ITV sports executives had to explain themselves.

Bryan Cowgill, the BBC's Head of Sport, said, "We had an exclusive contract to interview the Manchester City players, which was known to all concerned, including ITV, who were beaten by the BBC in competition for these rights. Saturday's episode represents nothing more than a rather undignified attempt to break the contract which had been genuinely given to the BBC in preference to ITV."

Jimmy Hill, Head of Sport at London Weekend Television, countered: "We have our own contract with the Manchester City players, which obviously the BBC were unaware of. It was a non-exclusive contract, but the BBC always wants to buy the rights to everything. Their way of competition is to try to destroy the opposition from even getting a chance to compete.

"The BBC had as many as 20 people there. Some of them were physically interfering with and manhandling our operators – pulling out plugs and trying to grab players away from us. At no time did we do anything to stop their men working. It was the BBC who were under the misapprehension, and we have breached no contract."

So there you have it – nobody was to blame!

The Football Association took a very dim view of the free-for-all at their showpiece event and senior television executives were summoned to explain themselves.

An FA Executive Committee meeting at Lancaster Gate, on May 8th 1969, outlined the football authorities' displeasure.

Minute 52(a)

"FA CUP FINAL – TELEVISION. In response to a question from Mr A. D. McMullen (Bedfordshire FA representative), the Chairman, Dr Andrew Stephen, stated that a meeting had been arranged with the television and Wembley authorities to discuss the unseemly incidents that had occurred at the end of the Cup Final."

The FA Secretary, Sir Denis Follows, called it a "shameful exhibition".

Knuckles were rapped – bruised knuckles, no doubt – and a new policy was devised to guarantee there would never be a repeat of the "Fist-Fight Final".

Trying to repair the damage between the two television sports sides, a football match was organised, not far from Wembley itself. However, that attempt to restore some television kindred spirit was dashed when the BBC's Bryan Cowgill got wind of the match and banned his staff from taking part in it.

In due course a new interview selection system was introduced whereby on the eve of every FA Cup Final, representatives from the two television sides would meet up, each with their preferred list of interviewees. A coin was tossed and the winner picked their first choice, and then each broadcaster made alternate selections.

Sanity was restored, although it was always highly competitive down there on the Wembley pitch. And, in a way, it seemed to be fiction turning into fact. I myself became one of the BBC's "legmen" for the early FA Cup Finals of the 1980s.

I'd like to think I was being picked because of my extensive knowledge of the FA Cup's glorious history or my carefully compiled list of football contacts, but I rather think the fact I was six feet tall and nearly sixteen stone was the real reason I made the line-up.

Yes, after years of watching the FA Cup Final on the BBC from what seemed like dawn to dusk, I was now part of their Cup Final team and one of my jobs on the big day was to pluck out "our picks" as they went around Wembley Stadium on their lap of honour.

By now things between the two sides had calmed down a little. Indeed, I once actually remember the pre-Cup Final interview toss for first choice between the BBC and ITV taking place down the phone.

You call. "Heads" ... "Sorry, it's tails."

And we accepted it!

It was fun down on the Wembley pitch as a "legman" on FA Cup Final day. It was about as close as you could get to playing in the final without actually putting your boots on.

Before the match you would walk across the hallowed turf and pick out the potential star turns for their pre-match pitchside interviews.

Indeed, while I was performing that role at the 1984 FA Cup Final between Everton and Watford, the Hornets' chairman, Elton John, walked over to me on the Wembley pitch and solemnly wished me well for the afternoon. I think he had overheard my Scouse accent and thought, as I was wearing a blue suit and blue tie, that I was a member of the Goodison Park outfit!

After the pre-match ceremonials were over, I would always park myself cross-legged immediately behind the goal at the Tunnel End and watch the game from no more than a couple of yards behind the posts. And remember, I was getting paid for this!

At the end of the match, we would check our respective lists and wait to grab our selections. Oh, and I was always under one other instruction, which was on neither list.

"Brian, just make sure you get the FA Cup."

Yes, interviewing the winning players in the makeshift Wembley studio, without the famous old trophy in camera shot, just felt that something was missing, so I would always have one eye on my playing "target" and the other on the FA Cup itself.

A good afternoon's work would be getting both.

The system used by the broadcasters then was far from perfect and did throw up that infamous dust-up, but these days I am a little dismayed at how long the interviews take, from the moment the final whistle blows at the FA Cup Final or any other major domestic football occasion.

I know broadcasters believe they have paid handsomely for the privilege but they have also become part of the post-match paraphernalia rather than observers of it. The interviews can feel intrusive and players naturally want to be celebrating with their mates rather than explaining how the third goal was scored.

Just an observation from a former "legman"!

CHAPTER 9

TAKING THE MIKE TO MEXICO

Ian St John has enjoyed a marvellous career as both footballer and football pundit. His television double-act with Jimmy Greaves, Saint and Greavsie, proved to be an absolute winner.

Their combination of sharp wit and wisdom on all matters football – especially Scottish goalkeepers – kept a Saturday-lunchtime audience entertained for well over a decade.

And yet St John, a Scottish international, could have taken a completely different tilt at a sports broadcasting career – and a lot earlier.

When Watford surprisingly knocked Liverpool out of the FA Cup at the quarter-final stage in February 1970, it was time for legendary Reds manager, Bill Shankly, to ring the changes.

Out went veteran players, such as Tommy Lawrence, Ron Yeats and St John, who had been among the stalwarts of the great Scotsman's 1960s side.

St John would start only one more game for Liverpool. His long spell at Anfield, during which time he had played more than 400 games for the Reds, scoring more than 100 goals including an FA Cup Final winner, was drawing to a close.

The canny centre-forward was, however, already homing in on a new career route. And he had nearly landed it.

The 1970 World Cup in Mexico was just around the corner and during the previous year the BBC had come up with a novel way of recruiting an extra commentator for the big tournament.

They had already tempted Barry Davies to leave Granada TV and become part of the Corporation's commentary stable. Now the BBC was looking for one more voice – one more person to describe the action in Mexico. And their hunt went nationwide.

Sportsnight with Coleman held a competition called "So you want to be a commentator?" The answer seemed to be a resounding "yes!" and the BBC was simply flooded with entries and audition tapes.

Literally thousands of people from all walks of life fancied themselves as "the next Kenneth Wolstenholme" and the field included some extremely good prospects.

One or two were a little young, such as the keen 15-year-old boy from Nottingham whose mum entered him for the competition. Yes, whatever did happen to that chap called Clive Tyldesley!

Contestants were eliminated round by round – from 5,000 to 1,200; 1,200 to 400; 400 to 30; 30 to 12; and ultimately 12, including the late Tony Gubba, to the final six.

En route, the would-be commentators had been judged on home-made cassettes of their commentaries. Then auditions took place in BBC studios nationwide before the surviving entrants actually went on site at Wembley Stadium, commentating "live" on an England home international against Wales. The potential winners had been whittled down to a final six.

The competition had been a big hit, but now could the BBC actually find "The Voice"?

On May 22nd 1969, the six final contestants appeared on a special edition of *Sportsnight with Coleman*. And they were an interesting bunch.

Ed "Stewpot" Stewart, a disc jockey, children's TV presenter and Evertonian, had made the cut; as had Tony Adamson, a hospital radio broadcaster and later BBC Radio's voice of tennis; Brummie-based Scotsman Larry Canning, a former Aston Villa player; Gerry Harrison, a BBC Radio Merseyside presenter who has since enjoyed a long career in the business; Idwal Robling, a former Welsh amateur footballer and the manager of a sweet factory; and a certain Scottish football international, Ian St John, who had some early exposure to broadcasting on BBC Radio Merseyside.

The judges deciding the fates of these would-be World Cup commentators were Bryan Cowgill, BBC's Head of Sport; Sir Alf Ramsey, the England manager; Tony Book, captain of Manchester City; Peter Black, TV critic of the *Daily Mail*; and the Rt Hon. Denis Howell, Minister of Sport.

The competition was tight; the judges reviewed the contestants' performances at the microphone during the various stages of the competition. They took into account the would-be commentators' identification accuracy, their reading and analysis of the game and, of course, the quality, strength and range of their broadcast voice.

After much deliberation the judging panel reached their decision. Disc jockey Ed Stewart had finished fourth, Gerry Harrison third, Ian St John runner-up and Welshman Idwal Robling had come out top of the pile.

Robling was declared the winner, but the competition would seem to have actually finished in deadlock between him and the Liverpool and Scotland centre-forward, St John, who also had his supporters on the judging panel.

Indeed, legend has it that it was Sir Alf Ramsey who put his foot down and said he wouldn't have a Scotsman winning the competition at any price.

St John, never a man to take a step back when he felt wronged, greeted the decision by alluding to Ramsey's own tailored delivery style. "Well, it just shows you, maybe I should have had elocution lessons …"

Scotsmen and Ramsey had always had a touch of oil and water about them. After all, he once arrived at Glasgow Airport and a "Welcome to Scotland" greeting and had retorted with a sharp "You must be fuckin' joking!"

The Saint therefore always seemed destined to finish second at best, and Idwal Robling enjoyed a sweet success and was packing his sombrero and on the plane to Mexico.

Robling subsequently had his brief moment in the midday Mexican sun before settling down to a long and fruitful career with BBC Wales.

St John retired from playing in due course and then headed into football management in the early 1970s, before turning back to broadcasting and subsequently starting his marvellous partnership with Jimmy Greaves, another man who – ironically – had struggled to get the ultimate selection nod from Sir Alf.

Greaves, invited by producer Trevor East, started his early television work on Central TV alongside Gary Newbon, and later became part of a legendary Saturday-lunchtime double-act with the Saint. But that was all still many years away.

*   *   *   *   *

Having not made the World Cup Final team back in 1966, and – much more predictably – not been included in the squad for England's 1970 World Cup defence in Mexico, Jimmy Greaves set about a rather novel way of keeping involved in that tournament. Greaves joined motorsport star, Tony Fall, as his co-driver on a London to Mexico City Rally that celebrated the staging of the World Cup over there. Greaves (and Fall) actually finished a very creditable sixth.

Ian St John was eventually chosen to work as a studio expert on the BBC's World Cup coverage but like many other people had an envious eye on how ITV had set about presenting the big tournament to a highly engaged UK audience. At one point, it had seemed the commercial channel might have won the rights to the tournament to themselves via a deal with World Wide Sports, a subsidiary of ATV. The BBC was outraged and the EBU ultimately rode to their rescue.

This was a World Cup that was broadcast in colour for the first time, involved many live matches being transmitted in the late-evening television schedules, introduced a new, entertaining and controversial panel of ITV experts, gave us our Esso World Cup coins, and buggered up my 'O' levels!

However, like many others, I found the draw of this particular World Cup absolutely compelling.

England were heading to Mexico not only as world champions but also as smash-hit recording artistes. Their pre-tournament song "Back Home" stayed at number one in the pop charts for three consecutive weeks in May 1970 and the squad's appearance on BBC's *Top of the Pops* was suitably memorable.

There they all were, rather over-dressed and self-conscious in black tie and dinner jackets, but still singing their hearts out. It remains a fond memory of those times. In fact, I am humming the tune as I type these words. Come on, after three join in ... One ... two ... three ... "Back home, we'll be thinking about you, when we are far away ..."

Among the teams looking to dethrone our singing sensations were the spectacular Boys from Brazil who played football with a samba rhythm all of their own. Drawn in the same group as England and determined to put the disappointment of their early exit in 1966 behind them, they were out to win a third World Cup – and take the trophy, memorably found in a bush by Pickles, back to Brazil for good.

With Pele, now 29 and hot to trot, the Brazilians would deliver a brand of football in Mexico that kept us on the edge of our seats and won a place in our hearts for ever.

This was going to be a great World Cup. Sure, the colour television pictures from Mexico occasionally looked blurred, almost like a watercolour painting caught in a rainstorm, and the kick-off times were not always UK-viewer-friendly, but this was an EVENT. And for those of us old enough and privileged enough to have witnessed the action from the comfort of our armchairs, it had some unforgettable moments.

And as well as the match action over in Mexico there were plenty of other elements to get fired up about back home.

In the *Radio Times* published ahead of the tournament, Paul Fox, now Controller of BBC One, made a strong case in defence of duplication of coverage of major matches across both BBC and ITV. The draw had thrown up a classic group game between England and Brazil which neither broadcaster was prepared to miss out on. This despite ITV claims that the match, the second group game, was theirs exclusively via a pre-draw agreement with the BBC. There was little love lost between the two organisations – with the characters involved almost on a war footing over all things World Cup '70.

Fox's point was that audiences clearly chose the BBC over their commercial rivals for big football occasions and therefore duplication rather than alternation of matches, as was preferred by ITV, was the solution to the scheduling dilemma. With the BBC offering 70 hours of World Cup programming compared to ITV's 60 hours, he did, however, mischievously offer the view that ITV could actually provide alternative programming to the football when the big games came along.

These days the matches in major tournaments are split between the broadcasters with very little dual coverage. And when it does happen the BBC still get the lion's share of the audience.

However, the 1970 World Cup was the tournament where ITV's style of coverage made a greater impact on the public than the established BBC output. Perhaps not when it came to the actual matches themselves, which, when head-to-head, were still resounding victories for the BBC, but in the analysis and arguments around the action, in which ITV was clearly the popular choice.

Brian Moore and Jimmy Hill hosted programmes with an expert panel that consisted of Manchester United and Scotland's Paddy Crerand; Wolves and Northern Ireland's Derek Dougan, the "Doog"; the gloriously outspoken Malcolm Allison; and Bob McNab, who had been left out of Sir Alf Ramsey's final 22 in Mexico.

McNab, Arsenal's left-back and a quietly spoken Yorkshireman, made a neat counter-balance to the self-opinionated and cutting contributions from the other three.

In a neat move, McNab was given a bell to ring every time he wanted to make a point. It was a clever gimmick and he soon became the housewives' favourite.

Mind you, there were plenty of female hearts a-flutter for another of the panellists. Malcolm Allison was the guy the panel was built around. He was a big handsome man who dressed expensively, had a taste for champagne and loved to puff on a big cigar. And with his south London accent, Big Mal expounded views on everything and everybody, which made for some great television.

Allison, Dougan, Crerand and McNab, with Moore and Hill at the helm, became a television hit, and with a much wider public than just sports fans. They gave ITV an edge over their rivals at the BBC.

Three matches stand out from the World Cup in Mexico: England's group game against Brazil, their quarter-final against West Germany and the final itself when the Brazilians met Italy.

All three matches were broadcast at peak time on Sunday evenings, the perfect scheduling slot for three such massive games, and television audiences flocked to them.

England vs. Brazil was the stand-out game from the group stages and didn't disappoint. Both broadcasters transmitted the match live (the BBC winning the audience battle four to one) and witnessed a marvellous duel of champions. In a game within a game, England's captain Bobby Moore and the mercurial Pele came up against each other time and again, although it was the West Ham man's marvellous block tackle of Jairzinho that stays in the memory.

At the end of the game Moore and Pele embraced and it was clearly a gesture of mutual respect.

The game was won by a single goal laid on by Pele and scored by Jairzinho. England had chances to equalise but squandered them.

Perhaps the most memorable sequence in the game came when Gordon Banks pulled off a remarkable save from a Pele downward header destined for the net. It still stands out as one of the best saves of all time – "And Jairzinho leaves Cooper standing ... PELE! WHAT A SAVE!"

The words of David Coleman, who had prised Kenneth Wolstenholme out of the main commentary slot amid an ongoing dispute between the man synonymous with the '66 World Cup and his BBC bosses.

They were keen to promote Coleman into the top commentary job despite some contractual assurances Wolstenholme could fall back on. It was the beginning of the end for a man who would leave the BBC the following year after 23 years of sterling service. But, for now, both he and England had the mutual objective of getting to the 1970 World Cup Final.

The second Sunday saw a titanic struggle between England and West Germany in Leon. This time England took the lead and added to it. At 2–0, midway through the second half, Sir Alf Ramsey made a substitution that many feel changed the match. He took Bobby Charlton off, to keep him fresh for a potential semi-final. Unfortunately, the move freed up Germany's Franz Beckenbauer to make mischief further up the pitch.

During the tournament, the *TV Times* had run a series of features aimed at attracting both male and female viewers to the World Cup, which is how the talented Chelsea and England goalkeeper Peter Bonetti and his family were photographed kitted out in jumpers. "Knit a World Cup Woolly!" was the headline. "What a World Cup Wally!" might have been a more appropriate headline after Bonetti, a late replacement for a poorly Gordon Banks, failed to keep out two soft German goals from Beckenbauer and Uwe Seeler.

The game went into extra-time and Bonetti, and England, conceded a third and decisive goal via the killer touch of Gerd Müller.

England were out of the World Cup. It was a crushing defeat that had seemed so unlikely when they enjoyed a 2–0 lead. Ramsey was criticised for substituting Bobby Charlton but one of ITV's post-match pundits directed his barbs elsewhere.

Malcolm Allison hit out at England midfielder Alan Mullery, saying Manchester City's Colin Bell, who he believed would have had more energy in the searing heat, would have been a better option. Bell, of course, was one of Allison's men at Maine Road.

Mullery, who had actually scored in the match, returned to London and found himself the subject of heated debates based on Allison's opinion.

ITV, spotting an opportunity, invited Mullery into their Wembley studio to fight his corner. And he certainly did that, taking Allison to task about his views, before dipping his hand into a plastic bag that he was holding under the studio desk and pulling out a velvet England cap.

He had hit the uncapped Allison where it hurt most – his pride. "There you are," said Mullery. "I've got 30 of them and this one's spare. You have it because it's the only way you'll ever get one."

There was also no love lost between senior BBC and ITV sports executives. In a telegram sent to his opposite number at ITV, the BBC's Bryan Cowgill claimed to "share your regret over England's lost World Cup and regret your share of the viewing audience means ITV did likewise". Friendly stuff, eh.

The World Cup Final itself pitted Brazil against Italy. The stage was set for Pele to deliver another masterclass. In the Brazilian training camp there had been concerns about his overall fitness, and along with others he had been a member of the "fat man's table" at mealtimes but when on the pitch he had simply served up a football feast.

With England gone, Kenneth Wolstenholme was restored to the top commentary seat, despite David Coleman's name being the one all over the programme billing in the *Radio Times*.

Coleman presented the programme and Wolstenholme broadcast his fifth and final World Cup Final commentary for the BBC. A year later, Wolstenholme was gone from the Corporation.

But on June 21ˢᵗ 1970, like tens of millions of viewers around the world, he enjoyed witnessing Brazil lift the Jules Rimet trophy for the third time.

Pele scored the first, Italy equalised before Brazil hit them with a three-goal salvo – Gerson, Jairzinho, who scored in every game, and the Brazilian captain, Carlos Alberto, sweeping home a trio of wonderful goals.

On my office wall, I have a signed Brazilian shirt and photograph of Carlos Alberto's famous goal. I have it there because it remains my favourite goal of all time and Wolstenholme's commentary line of "sheer delightful football!" so beautifully sums up that goal, that game and that day.

One would-be BBC commentator was also happy. Before the tournament started in Mexico, all the members of the BBC World Cup team had been asked to pick their finalists and the potential winner of the 1970 tournament. The "Saint" had gone for Brazil and Italy with Brazil as his choice for winners. In competitions at the BBC, St John had now played two, won one, lost one!

June 21ˢᵗ 1970 was also my 16ᵗʰ birthday and I've always considered Carlos Alberto's match-clinching super-strike as the extra candle on my birthday cake.

In recent times, I acted as an ambassador for Soccerex, the internationally renowned football convention, and I was delighted to find a certain Carlos Alberto also involved with them in a similar capacity. Team-mates eh!

Carlos Alberto, Pele, Jairzinho, Gerson et al. collected the Jules Rimet trophy and it went back to Brazil for good. Or so we believe; sadly it went missing some years later and one theory is that it was stolen, melted down and has never been seen again.

What the Brazilians would have done for their own Pickles the dog!

Above: England vs Scotland, April 1938, and the BBC's three outside broadcast cameras, fresh from a big boxing night at the Harringay Arena, are at Wembley to witness the visitor's 1–0 victory.

Below: Captains Billy Wright (left) and Ferenc Puskas lead out Wolves and Honved, respectively, ahead of live BBC TV coverage of their famous floodlit match at Molineux in 1954.

Above: Mary Malcolm, one of the BBC's famous continuity announcers, gives the 1950 FA Cup Final joint top-billing with the day's gardening tips – it's the Cup Final and chrysanthemums'.

Left: "It's OK, Billy, you can turn around now … the highlights of England v Hungary have just finished. I'll make you a nice cuppa when I'm done darning these socks."

Opposite top: An FA Cup final, the Coronation or whatever? People were getting turned on to television – and watching in increasing numbers.

Opposite below: A young Peter Dimmock checks his notes while the cameraman does his stuff. Dimmock was one of the founding fathers of BBC's outside broadcasting and a huge influence on television sport as we've grown to love it.

Top left: Peter Dimmock, Paul Fox and Bryan Cowgill (pictured here) – three men that helped shape the BBC's philosophy towards sport, creating iconic programmes and setting standards.

Top right: Kenneth Wolstenholme interviews a young Bobby Charlton and Nat Lofthouse, possibly ahead of the 1958 FA Cup Final. Wolstenholme would become one of televised football's most famous names and voices.

Left: Anglia TV's *Match of the Week* commentary pairing, John Camkin (left) and Gerald Sinstadt.

Bottom left: Cliff Michelmore – an early BBC commentator.

Below: "…the most stupid, appalling, disgusting and disrespectful exhibition of football possible in the history of the game." Chile v Italy at the 1962 World Cup Finals – David Coleman with the strong words.

Left: David Coleman in action in the famous BBC Grandstand studio. His teleprinter sequence as Saturday afternoon's football results rolled in was pure television gold.

Below left: In the studio … .and out in the thick of it, David Coleman, here at Wembley at the end of the 1964 FA Cup Final with Bobby Moore and the FA Cup itself.

Below right: The lucky black cat that ran across the pitch at Anfield as Liverpool and Arsenal contested the first match ever transmitted on *Match of the Day* in August 1964. The cat was a lucky omen for Liverpool that day … and seemingly for *Match of the Day* ever since.

Bottom: The BBC TV line up for the 1966 World Cup Finals. Back row (L-R) Frank Bough, Alan Weeks, David Coleman and Walley Barnes. Front row (L-R) Ken Aston, Kenneth Wolstenholme and Arthur Ellis.

Above: Pickles, and his proud owner David Corbett, sit back and watch the 1966 World Cup Final. Pickles had become an overnight national hero when he found the missing World Cup whilst out on his daily walk. Dog biscuits all round!

Below: Rangers' captain, John Greig, talks tactics with his team-mates and the opposition Celtic, led by Billy McNeill, ahead of their *Quiz Ball* clash.

Above: Jimmy Hill puts his LWT's *Big Match* team-mates through their paces: John Bromley and Bob Gardam are far left and presenter Brian Moore is far right.

Below: "Is there a linesman in the stadium?" From business suit to tracksuit (probably via telephone box), Jimmy Hill comes to the rescue to replace an injured official. Liverpool's famous manager Bill Shankly and Arsenal's Charlie George enjoy the moment.

Left: Jimmy Hill takes movie queen and '70s sex symbol Raquel Welch to Stamford Bridge to see Chelsea in action. Over in London to promote her new film *Bedazzled*, Raquel said she had enjoyed the day, but probably not as much as Jimmy!

Below: The two Brians – Moore and Clough. They became great friends as well as top-class television colleagues. Moore was an outstanding presenter and commentator, and Clough an outspoken yet truly gifted football man.

CHAPTER 10

"RAQUEL, WE'RE OFF TO CHELSEA"

As football crashed into the 1970s it came in on a wave of huge enthusiasm for the game. Attendances were booming and television viewing figures were hitting new highs.

The midweek replay of the 1970 FA Cup Final, between eventual winners Chelsea and arch-rivals Leeds United, had attracted a staggering television audience of more than 28 million – still to this day one of the biggest-ever audiences for British television.

The game was on everybody's radar, and it was a sport blessed with real characters, both on and off the pitch.

Match of the Day was thriving and about to form part of a BBC One Saturday-evening scheduling spine that blew the opposition to bits. With Bruce Forsyth and his new family-friendly vehicle, *The Generation Game*, *The Two Ronnies* – Messrs Barker and Corbett in sparkling comedic form – and of course, a Yorkshire lad with an inquisitive brain, *Parkinson*, forming the BBC's bridgehead, *Match of the Day* was in good company.

One of Michael Parkinson's big pals was Manchester United's mercurial George Best, and although his star would ultimately wane, at his very best, George was simply the best.

No more so than in the early part of the 1971/72 season when he scored a sumptuous goal against Sheffield United at Old Trafford. The goal featured that night on *Match of the Day* and on Granada's Sunday highlights show *Football* Best was captured on camera scoring a remarkable hat-trick against West Ham United, also at Old Trafford.

Gerald Sinstadt, who had been brought in to replace the BBC-bound Barry Davies, was able to describe the goals in suitably purple prose – a header, an acrobatic left-foot shot and then a driving right-footer. It was Best at his best.

George, of course, had become more than a footballer to the British people. He was a pop star in football boots – and his fame matched his talent. And in the new commercial world that football was about to leap headlong into, he was the top attraction.

So, advertisers chased him to endorse their products. In the previous decade it had been World Cup-winners, Bobby Moore and Martin Peters, accompanied by their wives, walking into the pub and having a friendly game of darts, to extol the virtue of a trip down "the local".

Now it was an aftershave television commercial for George, wind blowing through his hair, girls left, right and centre in the background of the shot.

Mind you, George, for all his fame and infamy, was a pretty grounded guy, so it was no surprise when he also turned up between programmes on ITV, talking up the value of a decent breakfast and the humble British egg.

All together now, "E for B, and Georgie Best!"

Kevin Keegan had introduced himself to the waiting world in August 1971, when the ex-Scunthorpe man made his debut for Liverpool in front of the Kop. He scored in the 12th minute and set off a career that would reach heady heights on and off the pitch. He would soon be "splashing it all over" as well as bashing in the goals.

All this while that wonderful Tottenham Hotspur, and later Arsenal goalkeeper, Pat Jennings, brought to life the virtues of the Unipart spark plug, by dressing up as one while saving shots in a television advert filmed at Watford's ground.

Match of the Day had now become a central part of the nation's Saturday night, and people were getting into the habit of leaving the pub early to get home to see it – and it was even wryly suggested that the sex lives of British married couples were even taking a bit of a hit as blokes were putting their Saturday-night football fix ahead of doing their conjugal duty! As if.

The viewers themselves were being drawn to the late-evening programme by a whole new rhythm method as Barry Stoller's new theme music for the programme, "Match of the Day", had now replaced "Drum Majorette" as *Match of the Day*'s clarion call and was on its way to becoming the most recognisable tune on British television.

What we schoolboys were also doing was watching the top players doing their stuff on the Saturday and Sunday television football shows and attempting to replicate the best bits in the schoolyard on the following Monday.

So on Monday, October 5th 1970, I'm sure I wasn't the only would-be footballer at school trying to do the "donkey kick" as it became known. Mind you, I needed a mate to help me achieve it.

On the previous Saturday's *Match of the Day* Ernie Hunt had scored a remarkable goal against his former club and reigning champions, Everton.

Team-mate Willie Carr jumped with the ball lodged between his legs and then released it to set up Hunt's stunning volley from a free-kick outside the box. It was spectacular and would win the BBC's inaugural Goal of the Season – we left the spoilsports to decide whether it was legal or not and struggled to replicate it.

Week in, week out, we were treated to something to savour. Fourth Division Colchester United springing an FA Cup surprise by beating Don Revie's powerful Leeds United side in a fifth-round tie at Layer Road. Then the controversy that surrounded West Brom's league win at Elland Road and an "offside goal" from Jeff Astle that denied Leeds vital Championship points. "That decision, or non-decision, will be talked about for years," said Barry Davies, now firmly established in the BBC football family.

Later that year another legendary commentator made his *Match of the Day* commentary debut when John Motson was at the microphone for a goalless draw between Liverpool and Chelsea at Anfield.

"In 1970 I was at the FA Cup Final working for BBC Radio 2 and, whilst I was checking out the post-match interview position, David Coleman, who I had never met before, came up to me and said that he had mentioned my name to Sam Leitch, who was then running the BBC's football output. The following season I got my chance."

"Motty", as he is now so affectionately known, would make a substantial early contribution to the BBC football archive when he stumbled on one of the FA Cup's best-ever giant-killing stories later that season.

Southern League club Hereford United were playing host to First Division Newcastle United – Malcolm MacDonald and all – in a delayed third-round replay. The clubs had shared a 2–2 draw at St James Park, but it was still expected that the Geordie club would make short work of their non-league opposition at the second time of asking.

Fledgling television commentator Motson, and rookie match director John Shrewsbury were dispatched to Edgar Street to cover a game that was expected to make up less than five minutes of programme time in that night's *Match of the Day*. Instead, on the day of the fourth round of the FA Cup, it was the story of a third-round replay that made the day's sporting headlines – and remains one of the competition's landmark results.

Malcolm MacDonald's goal eight minutes from time had put Newcastle seemingly on their way to the next round and a home tie against West Ham. But the footballing fates were in play and, three minutes later, Hereford's Ronnie Radford played a one-two with Brian Owen, and arrowed a ball into the net from fully 30 yards.

It was an absolute belter and was later voted BBC's Goal of the Season. It is now almost on a loop when FA Cup third-round Saturday comes around each season – and, most importantly, it set up extra-time and the upset was on.

With 13 minutes played of the first half, extra-time Hereford substitute and an old mate of Motson's, Ricky George, popped up with Hereford's close-range winner. A joyous crowd invasion followed – and *Match of the Day* had a serious scoop on its hands.

The two men, Motson and George, are still in demand on the speaking circuit and the questions always get around to that game, that day, that goal and that commentary. It may have been the highlight of Ricky George's football career but it was just the start of John Motson's illustrious commentary journey that continues to this day. More of Motty later.

Over on ITV, Jimmy Hill was still in top form and was never shy of spotting an opportunity to build his personal brand and that of the programmes he worked on.

Hill's currency was high at ITV, and although he was frustrated by some of the ever-present politics between the various regional ITV companies, at LWT his influence was spreading across a wider range of their output than just sport. But it was in his favourite topic of football that he was most clearly in his element.

For example, short of a song to match Liverpool's "You'll Never Walk Alone" at the 1971 FA Cup Final, Jimmy and his LWT sports team hosted a competition to help Arsenal over this unusual hurdle.

The result: "Good Old Arsenal" to the tune of "Rule Britannia", lyrics provided by Good Old Jimmy.

The following year, he attended another Arsenal vs. Liverpool match, this time in the league, and when one of the linesmen tore a thigh muscle early in the first half the game's immediate future looked in serious doubt.

"Is there are qualified official in the stadium?" came the tannoy call. There was a delay, a further delay and the crowd were beginning to get restless.

Off with the business suit, on with the tracksuit (he was only short of the phone box to complete the picture), and up stepped Super-Jimmy to save the day and run the line at Highbury.

Despite the occasional cat-call from the crowd and a bit of needling the following day from some of the newspapers, it seemed he got the vast majority of his calls from the touch-line about right and typically, he proved it on that weekend's edition of *The Big Match* – courtesy of the odd replay or two.

So lyricist, linesman and now would-be Lothario, it would seem. Surely not, but Jimmy couldn't be blamed for spotting the publicity opportunities when Hollywood beauty Raquel Welch came to London in November 1972.

Her publicity agents thought her showing an interest in football, and particularly the Chelsea side and their star striker, Peter Osgood, would create a headline or two.

Jimmy helped set up a press conference for Ms Welch at London's Sportsman's Club. When it looked as if it would be poorly attended, the gaps were filled by staff at the club all posing as journalists without Raquel being aware of it.

That ruse over, the Hollywood superstar then asked Jimmy whether he could help organise a trip for her to visit Stamford Bridge the following day so she could see Chelsea play.

I'm sure Jimmy had plenty of other business matters to deal with but he managed to find time to organise Raquel's match-day trip to Chelsea – and accompany her too!

Leicester City were Chelsea's opposition that day, but so was the incessant wind and rain which all but looked to have ruined Raquel's (and Jimmy's!) day. She had left the Savoy looking stunning but was in danger of being more bedraggled than bedazzled before somebody came to her rescue with a sturdy umbrella.

Anyway, Jimmy and Raquel sat together during the game and he explained the rudiments of the game to her, and the following day, *The Big Match* enjoyed the showbiz and sport scoop of the week.

Jimmy was left reflecting on one final request from his new friend, Raquel. "Jim," she asked, "how would you like to handle me in Europe?"

I'm sure even the great Jimmy Hill was momentarily speechless as he pondered the dimensions of that question.

Despite enjoying a lively and largely successful time at LWT, when the BBC came a-knocking for Jimmy Hill's services in early 1973 it became clear he was ready to move on.

Hill was to move over to the Corporation, with its nationwide audience reach, and become a one-man studio team. He was both presenter and analyst, a role he performed with great chutzpah for more than 16 years before Desmond Lynam came along to take over his presenting role and leave Jimmy to retain the position as the senior expert on a team that had expanded to include his side-kick Terry Venables, and new boys Gary Lineker and Alan Hansen.

Punditry had become a new extension of studio presentation and is still now the element of the hours and hours of television football output that raises the most debate, controversy and argument. Niall Sloane, a long-time senior executive at both the BBC and ITV, who has discovered and developed many of the household names in today's football broadcasting landscape, is clear about what defines a successful pundit. "Forthright opinions backed up by credibility and accuracy."

Sloane's choice of Roy Keane, who played his club football under Brian Clough and Sir Alex Ferguson, in ITV's line-up of live football action, has given the sharpest of edges to the channel's peak-time output. His edgy "this is how it is" style makes for compelling, if occasionally uncomfortable, viewing. But it is peak-time quality, that's for sure.

What is clear is that punditry has become a second-career destination for many retiring, and less retiring footballers, and some, like Alan Hansen and Mark Lawrenson, have made it a longer and more lucrative career than the original one they fall back on when describing and detailing their analysis.

* * * * *

Some ex-professionals take to it like a duck to water. For example, Gary Neville, who came straight from a long and distinguished career at Manchester United, has moved with great alacrity into the prime expert's position at Sky Sports, vacated by the swift departure of long-serving Andy Gray.

Neville, to whom I gave an early television opportunity during the 2002 World Cup when injury forced him out of the England squad, has made the switch from pitch to pundit in a seamless fashion.

Back in the early 1970s a certain Brian Clough was doing the same – and some. As a player, he had seen a promising career as a centre-forward cut tragically short by injury, but then turned to management. After a spell at Hartlepool United, Clough proved himself something of a Svengali by taking a group of largely workmanlike players at Derby County out of the Second Division and on to winning the Football League Championship.

And he would famously repeat the adventure with unfashionable Nottingham Forest whilst adding a couple of European Cup Final wins to his remarkable managerial trophy roster.

Clough was an absolute one-off, charismatic, candid and, at times, cutting. His delivery style had television audiences hanging on his every word and provided impersonators with tons of material; they all had to have a "Cloughy" in their routine. Television and radio interviewers never knew where they stood with him, invariably, as they were, addressed as "young man" (I'm proud to say I too was addressed by him in this way) and not knowing where the subject matter of any interview would end up.

He was irreverent, awkward, self-opinionated and not short on self-confidence. But, boy was he good television, as Trevor East remembers.

"When he first started he was the hottest property there's ever been in terms of being a pundit. I asked him whether he would do a piece once a month on *ATV Today* and he said 'Yes'. He said: 'What do you want me to talk about?' 'ANYTHING!' I said. And when I asked him how much he wanted for doing it, he said, 'I want as much as you can give me, young man!'" Priceless stuff.

There is a brilliant film sequence of Clough, directed by Bob Abrahams, coaching his Derby County players and specially shot for a BBC *Sportsnight* feature. It was later part-replicated in the film *The Damned United*, which tracked Clough's career and ultimately his tumultuous brief spell at Elland Road.

For part of the sequence in the BBC film, the viewer just sees a man from knee down barking out orders to his players, who are training for a forthcoming fixture. But it is the soundtrack that accompanies it that is so special. Clough is razor-sharp, in charge, personal and to the point. It was a brilliantly original visual portrait of a man who had the power of persuasion as one of his key managerial attributes. Mind you, he'd have called it giving the players a good bollocking. Straightforward Brian Clough.

Clough didn't hold back about television on television. In a typically forthright exchange with a spirited John Motson in the late 1970s he took the *Match of the Day* presentation team to task. "You and your colleagues, John, are turning it off from being family entertainment by lecturing to us at the moment. We used to look forward to sitting in comfort and watching on a Saturday night but I think you are setting yourselves up as judge and jury and becoming too deep, going over the dividing line – dogmatic, overbearing and boring. I suggest you shut up and show more football!"

It is believed Clough often laid a towel down on the dressing-room floor before a match, placed a football on it and asked his team to gather around it. He would then implore his players to treat the ball like "your best pal" in the forthcoming 90 minutes and "the rest will be easy".

There was one game, however, when Clough called it wrong. Before England's crucial World Cup qualifying game against Poland at Wembley in October 1973, Clough, now becoming established as an ITV pundit, had criticised the Polish goalkeeper, Jan Tomaszewski, in the previous weekend's *On the Ball* programme, dubbing him a "clown".

Despite protestations from ITV's Brian Moore, Clough wouldn't retract the view and the nation then watched as Tomaszewski repelled attack after attack, and shot after shot, from the England team and denied them the vital breakthrough.

*   *   *   *   *

Tomaszewski was his nation's hero and on the night it was the "clown" who had the last laugh, while Brian Clough, who had resigned from his managerial position at Derby County two days earlier over issues that included the club's objections to his growing television commitments, went back to the Midlands to stir the hornets' nest up again before heading off to the sea breezes of Brighton.

Clough never made it to the post of England manager. He would have been a popular choice with the public but would have probably driven the "blazers" at the Football Association bonkers.

Still, Clough retained his public appeal for many years and was "great television", but his reputation suffered through the difficulties brought about by his well-known problems with alcohol.

And sadly, the compelling Brian Clough died a relatively "young man" himself at just 69 years of age.

CHAPTER 11

FERGIE GOES ROUTE ONE!

Sir Alex Ferguson's illustrious football career has been littered with cups, medals and laps of honour. Indeed his celebrated time as Manchester United's manager has made him an iconic figure in world football. He's been top of the class in so many ways.

And yet you have to go back to his more humble origins in football and a spell at Falkirk in the late 1960s to really home in on one of his more exclusive achievements.

Yes, Fergie actually scored the winning goal in an edition of BBC's *Quiz Ball* against Huddersfield Town.

Forget the European Champions League triumphs, the Premier League domination and FA Cup wins, as well as the Aberdeen era of success that stilled the twin giants of Glasgow – scoring the winner in a *Quiz Ball* round must stand out in his own personal roll of honour!

Fergie was also on target for Falkirk in a semi-final against Everton but ended up on the losing side. A brace of goals by Everton's captain and club brain-box, Brian Labone, secured victory for the Merseysiders in the same year they had won the Football League Championship. No lap of honour for this latest success though.

Quiz Ball was just one of a number of programmes that were developed off the burgeoning appeal of the national game in the wake of England's World Cup win and the weekly diet of league and cup football that was brimful of stars and stripes – well, Newcastle United and Sunderland at least.

Several series of *Quiz Ball* ran between 1966 and 1972 in an early-evening midweek slot, and the programme's format was simple. Football clubs were represented by a four-man team consisting of three players, or well-known club officials, and a guest supporter – normally a well-known television or sports celebrity.

They would "play" a knock-out match against a rival team and the winner would go through to the next round.

"Goals" were scored by answering quiz questions correctly – and the method of hitting the target gave the sport itself a new and enduring turn of phrase.

Basically, teams scored by taking an easy or difficult route to goal. From route four – four simple questions – via route three and route two, to route one, one really tough question.

Played across an imaginary pitch in the studio, route one football was born – and the term stuck.

Presenters of the programme included David Vine and Barry Davies and some footballers became better known for their success on *Quiz Ball* than out on the real pitch itself.

Take the late John Osborne, West Brom's well-respected goalkeeper and an FA Cup-winner with the Baggies in 1968. Osborne became one of the stars of the show. "I have become better known as the man who is on *Quiz Ball* ... than for keeping goal for West Bromwich Albion."

He led the Albion team of manager Alan Ashman, team-mate Doug Fraser and celebrity, motocross champion Jeff Smith to *Quiz Ball* success in early 1968.

With the "big one" behind them, West Bromwich Albion then went on to win the FA Cup!

Other bright sparks who made their mark were Ian Ure, then of Arsenal, and Jim Craig of Celtic. Indeed Celtic were particularly strong, twice taking *Quiz Ball* titles, oh, and the odd European Cup into the bargain!

Broadcaster and writer Gary Imlach, in his award-winning book, *My Father and Other Working Class Football Heroes*, tells the story of his father, Stuart, being one of the Crystal Palace team that appeared on an early edition of *Quiz Ball*. When he received his appearance fee of 25 guineas (£26.25) from the BBC, his father realised there was "more for turning up and simply being a footballer for an hour or so than he'd been able to earn sweating at the business of playing football for most weeks of his career".

Teams' guest stars included the likes of cricketer Brian Close; comedian Peter Cook; actors Sam Kydd, Gordon Jackson, Roy Kinnear and John Laurie; sports presenter Harry Carpenter; and a likely lad called James Bolam.

And it was with Sunderland-born James Bolam, as Terry Collier, and his side-kick, Rodney Bewes, playing the role of Bob Ferris, that football provided the perfect backdrop for a classic episode of *Whatever Happened to the Likely Lads?*

Trying to avoid the football scores, when you want to, is almost impossible these days, what with a myriad of television channels and radio stations geared to sport and the internet and mobile phone apps streaming information by the second.

In the early 1970s it was a little easier, such as when Bob and Terry made a £5 bet each with their mate Flint, played by Brian Glover, that the pair could not get from the lunchtime kick-off of an international between Bulgaria and England until the highlights after 10 o'clock without knowing the score, the bet sets in train a series of near-misses, including a memorable trip to an empty church, as Flint did his best to spill the beans and win the bet.

At one point, as our two likely lads are making their latest getaway from Flint, Terry thinks he sees the headline "England F ..." and the two boys go through agonies trying to work out all the variations that headline could offer, from "England Flop" to "England Fight Back After Early Setback", even "England Five ...". Just what could it be?

Bob and Terry make it through the day, despite Terry settling the bet with Flint anyway (with Bob's tenner!) and the pair are still blissfully unaware of the result as they settle down in front of the telly, with a beer apiece, to enjoy the match highlights. Only then do they learn that there is to be a change to the television schedule as that afternoon's match between Bulgaria and England had been postponed because of heavy rain ... "England FLOODED OUT!"

In October 2012, fiction turned fact, when England's World Cup qualifier against Poland in Warsaw was called off at short notice as the stadium, which had failed to close its roof, was hit by a torrential rainstorm.

As the television viewers waited to see the outcome of the hapless referee's repeated inspections of a pitch both open to the elements and now resembling a swimming pool, we watched to see how ITV presenters Adrian Chiles, who can do glum, the taciturn Roy Keane, Lee "it'll be called off" Dixon and Gareth "what about Roy's underpants?" Southgate coped with the best part of two hours' empty broadcasting space as we awaited the final decision. The honest answer is not bad and certainly better than the referee did. The match replayed the following day and ended in a 1–1 draw.

Everywhere you looked or listened in the 1970s would bring you back around to football. Even that peerless comedy duo, Morecambe and Wise, were in on the act. "Arsenaaal" Morecambe would cough nervously if he needed to cover up his or Ernie's latest faux-pas.

And, of course, Eric, a genuine football fan, would never miss an opportunity of giving his favourite team, Luton Town, a mention in plays "wot Ernie wrote". Even when cast as a Roman guard in an "Antony and Cleopatra" sketch with Glenda Jackson, he walks on to the set to the *Match of the Day* theme and the ceremonial standard he is bearing with Roman letters on its front flips into "LUTON FC" at the flick of a switch!

In another play "wot Ernie wrote", this time set in the warring Middle Ages, a concerned aristocrat implored, "Any news of Carlisle?"

"Yes," said Eric, "they won 3–1!"

If the ill-fated soap opera *United*, a pre-watershed '60s precursor for *Footballers' Wives*, lasted only a couple of years on BBC television – too female for men, too male for women– football's growing appeal still made great subject matter for drama – even the sort of football you and I were playing.

Jack Rosenthal's marvellous comedy drama, *Another Sunday and Sweet FA*, made in 1972, was a beautifully observed piece of writing around the life and times of a fictional Sunday League match in Manchester. The referee's world-weary words to the opposing captains, both staring each other out before the toss-up, are beautifully crafted.

"A few pearls of wisdom. From one who knows. What we're now about to witness is called a football match. Not the beginning of World War Three. Not the destruction of the human race. A football match. In it, each of the teams will attempt to score more goals than the other ... And that will be done by kicking the ball in the net – as opposed to kicking other people in the crutch."

I think I played in that match! Of course, the Saturday-lunchtime preview programmes were now becoming established. On *Grandstand*, their *Football Preview* with Sam Leitch would morph into *Football Focus* with ex-Arsenal goalkeeper, Bob Wilson, its long-time presenter. Over on ITV, *On the Ball* was eventually housed in the *World of Sport* studio after being filmed outside broadcasts in which presenter Brian Moore was carefully framed so as not to reveal the ground he was going to be commentating from later in the day. That would upset the football authorities even more than they already were.

At the start of the 1970s the Football League was still very wary of the growing influence of broadcasting and in its own publication, *The Football League Review*, which they inserted into many league clubs' match-day programmes, they underlined the potential threat, as they saw it, based on a survey they had commissioned.

"There are danger-signals in this survey and the most significant is surely this: whilst filmed matches on television play a major image-building role for the game, football must beware that it does not become just another television programme – and a highly popular one at that.

"Weekend television audiences of nearly 25 million on both channels, compared with live attendances of three-quarters of a million a week, suggest that a new type of football supporter is being bred. The armchair fan ...

"The main purpose behind football as an entertainment is to persuade people to pay for the privilege of watching from inside grounds ... not from a TV screen ... the fact is that football will never live by television alone ... and that is why the league must strenuously oppose live telecasting of league matches and must also insist that a proportion of filmed games come from the Second, Third and Fourth Division."

Some strident views there that would split the public even now, but the Football League's position on live football now looks implausible and, in fact, only just survived the decade before broadcasters pushed the envelope hard for live football.

Watching football, outside of the First Division, on either *Match of the Day* or in the hugely popular ITV regional highlights, was actually part of the charm of the programmes. John Helm, who was a fine commentator on Yorkshire Television's football output, pointed out that "many players at so-called lesser clubs really became celebrities through regional football coverage. The likes of Ken Wagstaff, Chris Chilton and Ken Houghton at Hull City became well known to a wider audience because we featured them regularly on YTV."

And Helm, who followed in the footsteps of Danny Blanchflower, Keith Macklin and Martin Tyler as the region's football voice, also felt match-day conditions played their part in producing exciting football.

"And, of course, the matches were played in all types of weather – snow included – and the pitches were pretty dreadful. But it was all part of the charm of it all back then."

Regional television could also get super-close to their clubs and on occasions because of that daily access pull off a scoop to match their national equivalents. Certainly, in September 1974, Yorkshire Television did just that when it broadcast a "Calendar Special" on the occasion of Brian Clough being sacked as the manager of Leeds United after just 44 days in the job. Austin Mitchell, a news presenter, who later went into politics, had a great dry run for this future life when he brought together the out-going Clough and Leeds United's previous "father-figure" at the club, the England manager, Don Revie. The pair debated Clough's departure and the state of the club and its players – and viewers witnessed two huge figures in English football verbally slug it out live on television.

As a viewer, there was the serendipity of not every league match being covered each weekend and therefore not knowing which ones would be televised. Some of the goals you saw at matches that weren't filmed stayed in your memory that bit longer because they somehow only "belonged" to those present. You "owned" the goal – and the description of it later in the pub was your own. Oops, am I getting misty-eyed? Back to the plot.

Many of the ITV regions developed very watchable Sunday-afternoon highlights shows and many were also trying to develop their own preview and sports news programmes.

Granada screened *Kick-Off*, the brainchild of innovative producer Paul Doherty. This Friday-night show was originally presented by Gerald Sinstadt and he often had Ian St John as a studio side-kick. Despite being a region rich in football clubs, Granada TV itself had a languid attitude to the game until the likes of Doherty pushed hard to develop its output.

And he did it. Doherty's programmes were editorially tight, great on access and carried some of the region's best goals, including, bizarrely, one of my own!

A little bit by way of explanation. Manchester United's talented winger, Steve Coppell, and I had been at the same school and our paths had crossed again when he chose the same Economics course that I was struggling with at the University of Liverpool.

Steve was still in the middle of his studies when he was transferred from Tranmere Rovers to Tommy Docherty's Manchester United. The Scottish boss encouraged him to complete his degree whilst playing at Old Trafford, which is why both Granada TV's *Kick-Off* and BBC's *Football Focus* bowled up at the university to film a feature on Scouse student Steve Coppell, who with United was facing a trip to Anfield that weekend. Steve, himself, was a big Liverpool supporter.

Cameras were set up in our university lecture rooms as Steve pulled together a few mates to help "fill the shot" as we were filmed earnestly listening to a lecture on the velocity of circulation or some such thing. Then *Kick-Off*'s reporter was dispatched to the university sports ground at Cronton where every Wednesday afternoon, Steve would come along and "manage" our department side from the touch-line. He did so again on this particular day and as the camera crew filmed a brief sequence of the game to fill the story out, I scored. A bit of a fluke, sure, but it made the final edit of the Steve Coppell feature *Kick-Off* transmitted that Friday evening and then the following day up we popped up again on *Football Focus*. Such notoriety kept us in beer at the university all the following week.

That was way back in 1975, and within seven years I was actually the producer of the self-same *Football Focus*, and was fiercely going head-to-head with ITV's Paul Doherty while on BBC duty at the 1982 World Cup in Spain. In a further coincidence, I would later co-author a book on the Merseyside derby with *Kick-Off* presenter Gerald Sinstadt. Bizarre.

Sinstadt, himself, has cause to remember one particular edition of *Kick-Off* in 1978, which was transmitted two days after Liverpool had been knocked out of the European Cup by Nottingham Forest, having, of course, won the trophy in the previous two seasons.

There were no goals in the second leg at Anfield, which had been on ITV – Forest's 2–0 first-leg win had been on the BBC. So *Kick-Off* decided to go off the air instead with a moody set of black-and-white stills of disappointed Liverpool players taken at the end of the game. Nice idea – but the music track to the sequence was laid very late in the day and Sinstadt hadn't heard it himself as he led to the pictures with a closing link along the lines of "Goodnight, in what has been a very sad week for Liverpool Football Club."

Up came the still photographs to the sound of Johnny Mathis singing, "The party's over. It's time to call it a day. They've burst your pretty balloon ..."

The Granada switchboard went into meltdown. I think most of the calls were coming from Merseyside. I remember being enraged myself at the time. And for years to come when Sinstadt went to Anfield to cover a game and Liverpool, in their pomp, were ramming the fourth or fifth goal into some unfortunate opponents' net, the Kop would serve up a lusty rendition of "Gerald Sinstadt, Gerald Sinstadt. How's the party going NOW?"

As for the young researcher who laid down the music track to the pictures, I don't think it held him back. Paul Greengrass later won a BAFTA and an Oscar nomination for his work on *United 93*, the compelling film about the 9/11 hijacking of United Airlines Flight 93. He also has *The Bourne Supremacy*, *The Bourne Ultimatum*, *The Green Zone* and the acclaimed *Captain Phillips* on his personal filmography.

It would seem the party's still going strong for Paul.

The weekend standard setter for ITV was London Weekend Television's *The Big Match*. It was able to deliver high-quality programmes week in, week out, not least because of the number of big clubs in its patch, but also because its presenter and chief commentator Brian Moore – who was recognised as a top-class sports broadcaster– was as keen as mustard on how the programme looked and felt.

One of the members of its production team in those days who went on to become executive producer of ITV's live football coverage in the late 1980s, and will head up BT's live coverage in August 2013, was the vastly experienced Jeff Foulser.

"I think a lot of the type of qualities that *The Big Match* came to be recognised for was a product of having Brian Moore as its presenter and commentator. He was a stickler for high standards.

"As a young guy growing up in the business it was a great place to be. It was a buzzy environment – and we felt we were taking on the establishment, as in the BBC – and it was true that good competition brought up the standards everywhere.

"We also had a boss in the late John Bromley who encouraged us to try a few things and told us not to be scared of doing things a little differently. We tried to make things a bit more fun."

CHAPTER 12

WELCOME TO THE VIDEO DISC!

I joined BBC Television Sport in October 1979. One week I was watching *Match of the Day* in my armchair, a week later I was actually working on the famous programme.

I'd followed up my university life with a three-year spell working as a journalist on the *North Western Evening Mail* in Barrow-in-Furness.

Then owned by Westminster Press, the *Evening Mail* gave me a great grounding in the rudiments of a journalist's life and I soaked it all up. It was to be my chosen profession and I found every day on the local paper an exciting and challenging experience.

Working across both news and sport, I was given opportunities to develop my editorial thinking and style while also doing all the other bread-and-butter stuff that was demanded by the paper's local readership.

Like many journalists before and since, I learnt that a bit of "give and take" was the sure foundation from which to build a story on yet another Golden Wedding Anniversary. Football and rugby league were the two leading sports on my patch and an occasional rising star of the entertainment world would fleetingly pass through our region. One such stellar-bound performer was a young Scottish comedian called Billy Connolly, whom I interviewed while sharing a post-concert crate of lager. Whatever happened to him?

In the summer of 1979, I decided it was time to move on from the *Mail* and scoured the UK *Press Gazette* for new opportunities. I had interviews for jobs in both Newcastle and Sunderland and also hopped down to London to pursue a potential opportunity for a six-month contract with the "world-famous BBC Television Sports Department". After two interviews with them it seemed I'd convinced them I was worth a shot – and when I left 18 years later as the BBC's Head of Sport, I had probably proved to them that I had been a reasonable choice.

My BBC career very nearly didn't happen at all though because I left my digs in Barrow before I had heard anything from the BBC and was all set to start a new job in Newcastle. Weeks went by before an old house-mate spotted an envelope in the hallway, with my name and a BBC logo on its front. He had the foresight to forward the letter to my parents' address – and sure enough it was the offer of a six-month contract from the BBC. Bingo! I was off to London and a huge turning point, not just in my career but in my life as well. Thank you, Chris Rider, for having bothered to forward that letter on to me.

My first week at the BBC culminated in working on that Saturday's edition of *Match of the Day*. In those days, BBC sports production teams were broadly split into two groups, one servicing *Grandstand* and the other looking after *Sportsnight* and *Match of the Day*. To my delight I was attached to the latter programme coupling.

Mind you, it had been touch and go whether there was to be a *Match of the Day* programme at all in the 1979/80 season. In November of the previous year, a national newspaper broke the story that ITV had made an exclusive bid for all Football League rights. The size of the offer was believed to be £5million – more than three times what the two main broadcasters were paying between them – and had delivered their prize. "Snatch of the Day" – a famous headline that was revisited when ITV Sport, under my own stewardship in 2000, had landed a similar deal for Premiership highlights, briefly bringing to an end *Match of the Day*'s Saturday-evening residency.

In the late 1970s ITV was determined to break the BBC's solid stranglehold on Saturday evening. LWT's Director of Programmes,

Michael Grade, had followed up his high-profile capture of light-entertainment king, Bruce Forsyth, with an assault on another BBC Saturday-evening "building-block", *Match of the Day*.

The BBC was caught on the hop but its game-saver came in the shape of the Office of Fair Trading, which intervened in the proposed deal and called for the new contract to be scrapped. It did not feel that having all the league football with one broadcaster was in the public interest.

A compromise four-year deal was struck with the two broadcasters alternating between Saturday evenings and Sunday afternoons. The BBC retained Saturday evening for the first year of the new contract.

So, on Saturday, October 6th 1979, I turned up for my first stint on *Match of the Day* juggling a combination of fear and anticipation as I wandered along the corridors of the BBC's famous Television Centre. My new colleagues were very welcoming and gave me a decent bit of advice straight away. "Go to the canteen and have a bit of lunch. You'll find it's a long day – and you won't leave work until after midnight."

Which is why I found myself standing in the canteen queue waiting to pay for my egg and chips, with that great *Carry On* star, Hattie Jacques, immediately ahead of me. I just managed to stop myself proclaiming "Oh, Matron!" before sitting down at the nearest table with a remarkable trio of fellow diners – Hattie, who had found an empty seat, Johnny Rotten of the Sex Pistols and a Space Alien, or at least a guy dressed up as one. He was whacking down a plate of mince and potatoes before going back to tackle the Time Lord, Dr Who, in a studio close to *Match of the Day*'s home. I could get used to this, I thought, as I made my way out of the canteen.

I was initially employed by the BBC as an assistant producer (AP) and was part of a London-based team of seven APs that would help put that evening's programme together from the videotape area in the bowels of Television Centre. One person would run the programme's VT operation, three others would each edit down one of the three matches to the appropriate length – the plum job – and the rest of us would help construct opening and closing sequences and pick the bones out of the post-match interviews and compile the news and suchlike.

I was both absolutely in my element and completely out of my depth in equal measure but with the help from experienced and generous *Match of the Day* colleagues like John Watts, Roger Moody and Mike Moss I quickly found my feet.

A particularly important early influence on me was the editor of *Match of the Day*, Mike Murphy, a hugely engaging Londoner, who had come across from LWT with Jimmy Hill when he had moved to the BBC. Murphy was both supportive and direct. "You can knock them red shoes on the head" was his slant on the colourful footwear I was sporting in my early days at the BBC. The offending shoes went in the bin but his guidance and support – and that of the *Sportsnight* editor, and later Controller of BBC Sport, Jonathan Martin, were crucial in helping me settle in to my new world.

One of the early things I had to master was the "video disc". This was a machine, housed in a small basement room, that was able to store 36 seconds of visual material, which could then be inserted back into the event coverage as a slow-motion replay, at the instruction of the outside broadcast (OB) director.

The output of the "disc" was especially used for midweek football matches, as time was tight on those evenings and putting the replays in immediately would save vital minutes of edit time. Also there were fewer replay machines on site in those days.

To be honest working on the disc was "last man in" territory – it was often a no-win situation. You were either rarely used – I once did the "disc" work for four and a half hours of a Test match without once being called upon to deliver a replay, only to miss two requests/demands when I popped to the toilet for a quick pee.

The alternative, when the action demanded it, or the whim of the director decided, was that you could be used non-stop. One request from the boxing was to store three knockdowns and the referee's counts – now, you do the maths! On those occasions, the engineer who sat alongside was a technical soulmate in the operation.

People like John Watts, subsequently an award-winning sports OB director, could store five or six different incidents in that "36 seconds"; he could play it like a piano, and would hop from one incident to the next as the OB director, from an event somewhere nationwide, would feed the disc replays into their coverage.

Me? I could just about store one incident at a time and was invariably late getting it back on cue, thus incurring the wrath of the OB producer. Indeed my first attempt at working on the "disc" in London had me servicing a midweek match in the Midlands being directed by BBC's top gun, Alec Weeks. At this point I'd never met the man but by the end of the first half I'd certainly heard him – very loud and very clear. And it was fair to say, for the first time but not for the last time, he was a little underwhelmed by my performance!

To be fair, I was a little underwhelmed by HIS performance and on the point of slinging my hook, a future BBC career in shreds, until my boss, Jonathan Martin, spotted the impending problem and took the trouble to sit with me for the second half and actually explain what I was supposed to be doing. And how.

One thing that did amaze me in my early days at the BBC was that the commentators at the games chosen for *Match of the Day* would describe the action replays "blind" on the afternoon the matches were played. Goals would be scored and the commentator would recall the build-up from memory. Appropriate pictures would then be laid across those slices of commentary on Saturday evening after the match edit was complete.

It was an early appreciation of the skill involved in the commentary work by the likes of John Motson and Barry Davies, aided a little bit by the fact there weren't a zillion replays expected after every incident as there are in matches covered today. Far too many replays for me, actually – not every shot is worth showing again and not every ball in a cricket match needs repeating. I digress.

A lot of the match directors on *Match of the Day* had worked in VT and so knew the tricks of the trade in editing a full match down to perhaps just 15 minutes. Commentators were thus discouraged from talking over goal-kicks as they would always provide perfect "edit points" for the VT team. A goal-kick at one stage of a half could potentially end up as a passage of play later in the half.

"Logging" the game, as it was termed, became a science in itself. You would watch a match and note down any incident likely to make the final edit but also goal-kicks, free-kicks, corners, close-ups of both players and managers – anything that could provide an "invisible" edit point.

Then with the help of the vastly experienced video-tape editors, the game would be condensed with its best features included. The "sound" joins between each piece of action were as important as their "vision" equivalents in making the whole thing look and sound smooth and continuous.

I loved it all, but in those early days, felt editorially well equipped but technically weak – still am really, but with Mike Murphy's encouragement I was given my first chance to edit a game. It was January, 1980, Bolton Wanderers vs. Brighton. Thankfully for me I was working with a great video-tape editor called Neddy Hughes. He didn't really know his football but boy, did he know his editing. We made the air with our game with just seconds to spare – and it was all down to him. I sort of spoke occasionally, offered an opinion, panicked frequently and got the "teas and coffees" in when the trolley came around. Still the edit of my game hit the screens on cue and thankfully both Peter Ward goals that afternoon were in it.

It was the first game of many that I would edit over the next four years or so – I quickly became trusted to get what was a difficult job done in good time, and also to leave the "good bits" in – the two essential prerequisites for the role. And once I'd gained my confidence, and the confidence of my colleagues, in scaling back a match from 90 minutes to perhaps less than 20, I really looked forward to my Saturday-evening "puzzle" – a brilliant challenge and one that had to be done and dusted by 10pm and those familiar *Match of the Day* opening titles.

Midweek games in the BBC's *Sportsnight* provided different problems. The matches would finish very close to the programme's on-air time and therefore would be edited by two people, each taking a half of the game. Even then games, if cup-ties, could go to extra-time and then the dreaded "cut edit" may come into play – literally cutting the tape with a razor blade and joining it to the next bit (sorry, engineers, for my simplistic technical gobbledegook), or the dreaded "duplex", running a piece of action from one machine and then, on a countdown of ten, running the next bit off another machine.

Those particular edit points tended to be a bit bumpy so it was a good time to engage the programme editor and studio director in "important" conversation on the "bizz" phone to distract them from hearing the clunky edit go through. It was a tactic that was often used – and indeed, they too had no doubt used it on their way up the ladder.

Midweek programmes, like *Sportsnight* and ITV's *Midweek Sports Special*, tested both the production and video and engineering teams to the limit, and sometimes also the actual equipment itself.

I once worked on a *Sportsnight* in which the programme's main contents, two FA Cup semi-final replays, Liverpool vs. Arsenal and West Ham vs. Everton, both went to extra-time. Remember these matches had not been seen live anywhere – and there was just a chance they wouldn't be seen as highlights anywhere, any time soon. Such was the heat in the VT area on the night that one of the tape spools relaying the first half of extra-time of the West Ham vs. Everton clash actually melted on the VT machine that was transmitting it.

Cut back to the *Sportsnight* studio and presenters Harry Carpenter and Jimmy Hill memorably trying to "fill", and crucially not give the final result away while we got things up and running again. All this while a delegation of television executives from Japan were being shown around the studios by a BBC big-wig to see the "world-famous BBC Sport" in action. No wonder nobody slept when they went home on Wednesday evenings!

I was hungry to know more about my new trade and enjoyed being sent out on the OBs themselves on a "watch and learn" basis. It was great to see how the match directors, cameramen and commentators worked as a team. Awe-inspiring actually and I was delighted to be part of it all.

On the final Saturday of the *Match of the Day* series in May 1980, I was asked to compile a closing sequence to reflect the best of the action from the new League Champions, Liverpool. And as the pictures I gathered together hit the screen, a very pleasant surprise awaited me. As the names on the closing credits rolled through there was a new name on them for the first time ... BRIAN BARWICK.

I suppose I went on to get hundreds of programme closing credits and slowly my name went up one set and down another until I was the final name on the credits. But I'm sure, like many of my contemporaries, the first time your name was "up in lights" was very special and was also a way of your colleagues saying – "well done mate, you're in". Followed, of course, by a quick phone home to the folks and a "Did you see ..."

CHAPTER 13

CHARLTON, FINNEY ... AND ICKE!

On a hot sunny afternoon in August 1980, a big decision was about to be taken in the BBC Sport offices in Kensington House, Shepherds Bush – and I was in the hush-hush meeting that was discussing the pressing matter.

Behind closed doors television executives, both senior and junior, engaged in a couple of hours of heavy debate, tinged with conflicting and contrasting views. It was finally decided that as *Match of the Day* was to move to Sunday afternoon Jimmy Hill and his co-presenter, Bob Wilson, would leave their suits and ties at home and broadcast the programmes in shirtsleeves or jumpers. Yes, groundbreaking and profound stuff!

As, indeed, was the new rhythm of football broadcasting with ITV's regions now taking the late-Saturday-evening slot and BBC broadcasting its highlights around Sunday teatime.

In truth it was an arrangement that didn't work for either broadcaster. For some ITV regions, the Saturday-evening slot proved a real challenge to meet. It over-stretched their resources, and was a real old-fashioned "kick, bollock, scramble" to get the programmes on the air. While for the BBC, despite the ingenuity of the presentation and production team, showing highlights of games that had finished a good 24 hours earlier just lost some of the programme's sparkle. After all, its "signature" on-air time of 10 o'clock on a Saturday night had become part of the programme's DNA.

Over the term of the four-year contract ITV's appetite for the late-Saturday-evening slot lessened considerably and its programmes were getting scheduled later and later – and for the BBC its ratings too were slipping, jumpers or no jumpers.

What both broadcasters were itching for was some live league football – an idea still being fiercely resisted by the game's authorities. This despite the fact the sport was losing a little of its lustre, not least with the worrying rise of hooliganism in and around the club grounds on match-day, and the inevitable damaging headlines that followed disturbing incidents up and down the country.

The uneasy relationship between the game and its broadcasters rolled on, one side believing that television was getting the game on the cheap and the other believing the game was benefiting from the level of exposure it enjoyed across the two main channels.

Sponsorship was moving assiduously into the sport, and those companies who were investing their cash in football were keen on getting a return on it – and thus it seemed to be time for football and its broadcasters to find an acceptable level of appeasement. Some movement on the "live" match proposition, and equally some movement on things like shirt sponsorship on the other, seemed a logical bridgehead to a common position. Mind you this is football we are talking about!

While my senior colleagues at the BBC were wrestling with all those weighty issues I was having the time of my life working my ticket as an assistant producer.

As well as *Match of the Day* and *Sportsnight*, I was part of the team working on the 1980 Moscow Olympics, the European Football Championships of the same year and also playing my part in the Corporation's showpiece occasion, the BBC's *Sports Review of the Year*.

Actually my early role on that evening was restricted to looking after the *Radio Times* prize-winners, two couples whose voting coupon had been drawn out of the hat to come to London on an all-expenses-paid weekend trip and join the VIP audience at the live broadcast of the big Sunday-evening event.

I was joined in this "arduous" duty by my partner in crime, Roger Moody. We met the winning couples at the swish hotel in west London, whisked them off for a pre-show slap-up meal, sat them down in the audience for the show, let them enjoy the spectacle before making sure they had an autograph book to die for as we swept them around the room at the post-show party.

All fine and dandy, other than on one memorable occasion when the couple I was looking after were a Welsh publican and his wife. A rather large and cheerful soul, our prize-winner certainly enjoyed our pre-programme hospitality, so much so that under the heat of the studio lights as the programme got under way, he slipped into a sound sleep, punctuated with the occasional loud snore followed by a sharp dig in the ribs from yours truly.

As was the custom, we whisked our couple around the room after the show to make sure they had their autographs and photographs, and then made sure they had got back to their hotel safely. Job done, so I thought no more of it until several days later when I received an unexpected call from the hotel asking me when our Welsh prize-winners were due to check out as they were still there – and still thoroughly enjoying the BBC's hospitality!

In 1981, I was tasked with producing a half-hour film for *Sportsnight* to reflect the 100th FA Cup Final. I worked on this project with John Motson, as always a mine of information. We both thoroughly enjoyed meeting the Rt Hon. Lord Kinnaird, a very jolly man and grandson of Arthur Kinnaird, one of the game's early greats. The witty descendant said of his famous ancestor that "hacking he liked and hacking he did!" Hacking in football then sounded just short of full-on physical assault.

Kinnaird would play in nine of the first 12 Cup Finals, collecting five winner's medals. He was undoubtedly the first superstar of his day – although his long red beard would have put David Beckham's tightly trimmed equivalent to shame.

Perhaps the real star performer in our short film was the trophy that Lord Kinnaird brought with him to show us. It was the "second" FA Cup, the one that replaced the original that had been stolen from a Birmingham sports shop window in 1895 and was presented to his grandfather by the Football Association in 1911 in recognition of 21 years' service.

That beautiful polished trophy looked stunning on camera, and eight years ago was bought at auction by West Ham United co-owner, David Gold, for close to half a million pounds.

As part of the *Sportsnight* film we also went with FA officials to a London West End store to choose the ribbons for the FA Cup – white for Tottenham Hotspur and sky blue for Manchester City. Then I helped take the FA Cup and its wooden trophy case out of the strong-room and push it up a ramp and into a security van for its short trip from Lancaster Gate to Wembley. All good pictures and the type of unique and unusual television access that would all help as part of the build-up for the big match in Cup Final *Grandstand* – and the head-to-head rivalry with ITV.

I graduated to producer of BBC's *Football Focus*, working with Arsenal's former goalkeeper, presenter Bob Wilson. I would spend more than 20 years alongside Bob at both the BBC and ITV, and an early task involved us going up to interview the legendary Preston and England star, Tom Finney, for a "Christmas special" for *Focus*. We spent the afternoon at the "Preston Plumber's" home and captured some wonderful stuff on film.

As we made our goodbyes and got into Bob's car to make the journey back to London I momentarily put the precious cans of film on the vehicle's roof before we set off.

Four hours later, we were back at Bob's house. Well, we were, Bob and I, but there was no sign of the film. Not anywhere. A mad panic ensued before Bob took a phone call from a 60-year-old gentleman from the north-west of England, Tom Finney.

Seemingly, I had forgotten to take the film cans off the roof of the car as we left Tom's home and some five miles into our journey they had rolled off the vehicle and into a gutter at the side of the road.

My bacon was only saved because the "gaffer-tape" used to bundle the cans together had TOM FINNEY written on it in large letters. Some kindly soul had spotted the cans, spotted the name and had taken the precious cargo to the local police station. After all, Tom was local "royalty" and the film cans were sent back round to Tom's house in a heartbeat. Phew!

I had developed a relationship with the World Cup, since having first watched it on the BBC in 1962; 20 years on in 1982 I found myself part of the BBC's team out in Spain to cover the tournament.

What a thrill. And despite the early disappointment of being moved from the production team based with the England party (which included my old mate Steve Coppell) I was pleased to be heading up the BBC operation with Northern Ireland in Valencia.

This brought me in direct opposition to that wily ITV producer, Paul Doherty, and his reporter, Elton Welsby. Formidable rivals on the same beat but I had something special up my sleeve (no, not a microphone, Paul!). I had David Icke as my BBC on-screen side-kick.

Yes, the David Icke who left broadcasting in the mid-1980s to pursue a career in, well, extolling the virtues and values of the colour turquoise, whilst being deeply and disturbingly critical of by whom – and how – the world was being run and what was going to happen next on the planet's ultimate "Big Match".

I sensed there was something special about him when he walked *across* the swimming pool to meet me as I arrived at our waterside hotel in Valencia! He was different.

In the middle of the night, in the room next to mine, I could hear him bashing away at the typewriter for hours on end.

When we met up for breakfast the following morning I would inquire what he had been typing. He would reply sombrely, "The script for today's film."

"But we haven't even filmed it yet," I would counter. "In fact, I don't know what it will be about yet. Haven't given it thought."

"Don't worry, the words WILL fit." And then accompanied by a portentous long stare Ickey was off to get his cornflakes.

The 1982 World Cup was a perfect scenario for the British broadcasters as three UK teams had qualified for the tournament. For Scotland it was business as usual, for England and Northern Ireland it was back to the old routine.

In Northern Ireland's case it was their first Finals appearance since 1958, while England were back at the sharp end of international football, having failed to reach either of the 1974 or 1978 tournaments held in West Germany and Argentina.

In those tournaments the broadcasters got firmly behind Scotland, who got close to getting to the knock-out stages in West Germany and were the only unbeaten side in the competition. In Argentina they just fell short of turning around a couple of poor group-stage results, despite beating Holland 3–2 in their final game, capped by a wonderful Archie Gemmill goal. David Coleman's commentary on the goal was equally memorable.

Argentina went on to win that World Cup, and in a flurry of ticker-tape and with the BBC's "Argentine Melody" still ringing out, two of their stars, Ossie Ardiles and Ricky Villa, came over to England to ply their trade at Tottenham Hotspur – and memorably so. Villa would score an FA Cup Final goal in 1981 that has been described by John Motson as the best-ever – praise indeed.

In Spain, the broadcasters had a minimum of nine UK-related group games – and, in fact, ultimately had 13 matches in all as both England and Northern Ireland progressed to the second group stage of the competition.

Perhaps, surprisingly, the two broadcasters did not swamp their schedules with games from a tournament that had increased its entrants from 16 to 24. The BBC, pointing to other television sport commitments including Wimbledon, actually did fewer live matches, 13, down from the 18 it had carried in the two previous tournaments.

Neither broadcaster carried the opening ceremony or opening match, which featured holders Argentina in action against Belgium. The Falklands War was in its last throes and it was deemed indelicate to those serving their country in that theatre of war to carry such an occasion in those circumstances. Although not everybody agreed with that position, as this letter to the *Radio Times* suggests.

"What kind of coverage of the World Cup is it that totally omits the activities of the world champions Argentina. That the BBC and ITV should lend themselves to such deliberate suppression is shameful regardless of the rights and wrongs of the Falklands War."

The split of UK teams' first-round matches saw ITV pragmatically going for volume, and commercial return, over potential quality – five matches, including two England games against the BBC's four games.

The BBC had England's first match, an attractive tie against France in Bilbao, and was rewarded with what was then the quickest goal in World Cup history from Manchester United's Bryan Robson.

It also had two Scotland games, against the Soviet Union and prior to that a glamorous match-up with Brazil. Against all the odds, Scotland led in that game for a short time after David Narey crashed home a shot from a distance to open the scoring. Memorably, in co-commentary, the BBC's Jimmy Hill described the net-bursting effort as a "toe-poke", a hugely contentious description which, to this day, the Scotland fans have still to forgive him for. Brazil went on to win the game 4–1.

The final game in the BBC's quartet of first-stage group matches was Spain vs. Northern Ireland, a fixture that could potentially have been a "dead rubber" when selected earlier that year. Especially as hosts Spain were expected to do well and Northern Ireland were considered one of the minnows of the tournament. But, in reality, they were far from that, as Northern Ireland were about to become the talk of the tournament.

In Valencia's Stadia Luis Casanova – now the famous Mestalla, they pulled off an unexpected 1–0 win against the hosts and in front of a frenzied crowd. Gerry Armstrong's decisive strike early in the second half went down in football folklore.

For David Icke and me, sitting on the pitch directly behind the goal in which Armstrong scored, it was a terrific result as while "our team" were still in the tournament, so were we.

At the end of the game, the instructions for post-match interviews were radioed down to me from the BBC's Madrid base. And those instructions were crystal clear. "Get the manager, Billy Bingham, and the goal-scorer, Gerry Armstrong – and get them FIRST."

Which is why I am immortalised in the official FIFA World Cup film of the event, *G'olé!*, belting across the pitch with my ITV equivalent, a lady called Pat Pearson, in pursuit of our Northern Ireland heroes. I was reasonably trim then but Pat was no slouch either. Anyway, let me suggest we managed to get one each – a score draw accompanied by a ticking off from the officials for encroaching on to the pitch. Mind you so were dozens of other media personnel. After all, this was the hosts, Spain, beaten but struggling through and one of the surprise packages of the tournament pulling off a big, unexpected win.

What I also realised very quickly was that although I had played no part in Northern Ireland's marvellous win I was part of their "good news" story and I milked it for all it was worth. You make your own luck, sort of. Every part of the BBC now wanted a part of the "Northern Ireland story" and I was the on-site conduit by which to make it happen.

During the tournament I had travelled the length and breadth of Spain, quite often on the small private plane that the BBC had hired to move its personnel around quickly. The newspapers made mischief of this perceived "extravagance" although it was actually cost-effective. I say "hired"; in truth, to get around Spanish civil aviation regulations the BBC had to "own" the plane – which it essentially did for the duration of the tournament – "buying" it a day before the tournament started and selling it for one pound more than it paid for it just two days after the end of the World Cup.

This form of transport posed no problems for me, really, other than having to handle my reporter, David Icke, who no matter that his future ethereal visions would suggest otherwise, was actually scared of flying. A couple of years later he was the presenter of the Farnborough Air Show – only at the BBC!

Oh, and the pilot of the small aircraft kept a careful eye on my BBC travelling companions, as he was seemingly deeply depressed by a romantic relationship that had broken up shortly before the start of the tournament – so we took it in turns to keep his mind off the subject as he took the controls for another flight.

As well as the plane, the other innovation the BBC had out in Spain was a mobile satellite dish – 22 feet in diameter. This two-ton monster helped the BBC to be light-footed in getting to the stories first and had the ability to broadcast directly from on site. ENG hand-held cameras were also beginning to come into use – but the old TV gag about "here is the new lightweight camera ... oh, and these are the batteries (huge heavy buggers!) that go with it ..." was a truism.

England and Northern Ireland ultimately went out at the second group stage of the competition but I was kept out in Spain for the duration of the tournament and found myself in the company of England and Manchester United legend Bobby Charlton, out there himself as a BBC studio expert.

Indeed on one evening there was a knock on my hotel door and it was Bobby inquiring whether I wanted to join him on a trip to Atlético Madrid's stadium to see the Rolling Stones on the latest leg of their European tour. The Stones, it would seem, had been in touch with him, and invited him along to that night's show. And that is how I ended up with one of this country's iconic football figures, at the front of a packed stadium, and then afterwards back-stage with one of the world's most famous rock bands. It is a memory that hasn't faded.

My World Cup journey ended with sitting behind the goal in Seville watching the epic West Germany vs. France semi-final and then as a "reward" for putting a real shift in for the BBC while in Spain, a ticket for the final in Madrid.

John Motson would commentate on his first World Cup Final for the BBC while, on ITV, Martin Tyler would also make his debut at the microphone at the sport's ultimate showpiece finale.

In a closing twist to the first of four World Cup tournaments I would work on with the BBC, I was billeted in the same hotel as the victorious Italian team as they returned from the Bernabéu Stadium having beaten West Germany 3–1 in the final.

It was absolute mayhem in the hotel but gradually the Italian players and coaching staff edged their way to a large reception room that had been reserved for them. And when they finally shut the doors on the media and an ecstatic set of well-meaning supporters and sat down for a well-earned private celebration dinner there was one extra person at their party. Me.

As the door had shut on the outside feverish world I had been on the "wrong side" of it and ended up *in* the room with the World Cup and stars like Dino Zoff, Paolo Rossi, Marco Tardelli et al. After soaking up the atmosphere for a few minutes I did what all good journalists would, enjoyed a quick glass of vino tinto, made my excuses and left!

CHAPTER 14

BEARING WITNESS

If England were struggling to regain their supremacy at the top of world football – and still are actually – there was a period in the late 1970s and early 1980s when England's club sides were the dominant force in European football.

Between 1977 and 1984, English clubs won seven out of eight tilts at the European Cup – an astonishing haul given that prior to this spell there had been only one English winner of that beautiful trophy.

Liverpool emulated Manchester United's 1968 triumph some nine years later in 1977, and then majestically followed it up with three more wins in a seven-year period.

They were the European masters and under manager Bob Paisley's shrewd tutelage and Joe Fagan's wily leadership found the key to unlocking the door to conquering the continent's senior club competition time and time again.

Less likely were the remarkable successive victories for unfashionable Nottingham Forest who, with Brian Clough and Peter Taylor in managerial harness, feared no one and nothing.

Aston Villa were the other English side to lift "Big Ears" in this heady period. A scrappy close-range Peter Withe goal was enough to secure them an unlikely victory over European giants, Bayern Munich, in 1982.

Now, in these modern days of two UK broadcasters, across free-to-air and subscription television, carrying large-scale and comprehensive live coverage of the UEFA Champions League matches throughout each stage of a respective season's competition, it may seem to younger readers incomprehensible that only the European Cup Final itself was live on television before the competition was re-formatted in the early 1990s.

No "match-choice" then, no choice full-stop. No thumping big live quarter- or semi-final two-legged saga, no live edge-of-the-seat extra-time or penalty shoot-out moments. It was a case of avoiding the results ahead of the highlights of these matches shown in the late-evening midweek homes for sport on BBC and ITV.

Indeed, I am writing this whilst contemplating the outcome of the last 16 matches in the latter stages of the 2013/2014 UEFA Champions League competition and two-legged ties like Manchester City vs. Barcelona and Arsenal vs. Bayern Munich are mouth-watering prospects.

And wherever I go, friends will be posing the same question ahead of those fixtures. "Are you watching the match tonight?"

But more than three decades before that, it was only the climax of the competition that got live television exposure. This was another telling illustration of the suspicious relationship that existed between football and broadcasting – and belied the huge commercial windfall that awaited the sport as both broadcasters and brands wanted to get close to the action to drive their business prospects, and were prepared to pay top dollar for the privilege.

In more commercially innocent times, it was with contractual access through the European Broadcasting Union that the BBC and ITV would alternate live coverage of the European Cup Final and the European Cup Winners' Cup Final.

The BBC took the odd years for the European Cup Final, so in 1977 majored on Liverpool memorably beating Borussia Mönchengladbach in Rome; saw a Trevor Francis header clinch Forest's win over Malmö two years later; had a date in Paris in 1981 as Liverpool narrowly beat the ultimate European masters Real Madrid; four years later, in Brussels, the BBC witnessed first-hand the shameful events at the Heysel Stadium that brought the curtain down on English football's dominance and its participation at the top level of European soccer.

ITV hosted the 1978 European Cup Final between Liverpool and Bruges at Wembley; transmitted Brian Clough's unlikely second European Cup Final win in 1980, this time over Hamburg and Kevin Keegan in Madrid; and two years later were there in Rotterdam for Villa's big night against Bayern Munich.

Shedding his established role as studio presenter of ITV's World Cup coverage to get behind the microphone for these big European occasions was Brian Moore. In 1979, he was also on board the coach to the stadium in Munich with ITV colleague, Michael Grade, as Nottingham Forest travelled to their night of destiny with Swedish champions, Malmö.

Brian Clough, conscious his players were getting quieter and quieter as they approached the ground, offered them the opportunity to take a beer from the two large crates propped up on the back row of the coach. Nobody actually took him up on the offer but a more relaxed mood was set – and the crates were no doubt emptied on the return coach trip to their hotel – to make room for an extra passenger on board – the European Cup.

Barry Davies would be the commentator for the BBC on these big European Finals. He may well have seen them as a something of a consolation prize as his colleague John Motson had got the nod for the FA Cup Final, which was invariably played ahead of the big European showpiece occasion.

I suppose Barry's point was that the FA Cup Final was the domestic climax to the season in those days – and it was also guaranteed that an English club, well two actually, Welsh clubs permitting, would be in the final, something that its European equivalent clearly couldn't promise.

Understandably, this was a regular bone of contention for Davies and his representatives, and when it became my turn to make those kinds of decisions in the 1990s, I too found it no easier to split Motty and Barry. Both superb commentators, experienced master craftsmen but with completely different styles and approaches to the same job.

There was also strong support for each of the men within the Corporation. The difficulty was keeping them both happy, although Barry Davies did enjoy commentating on a wider spread of sports. What BBC Sport knew was that it was blessed with having two outstanding commentators who, along with ITV's Brian Moore, made an extraordinary contribution to the viewers' enjoyment of football on television over many years. And in Motty's case still very much does.

The European Cup Final wins by the English clubs were the high-water mark moments for our national game as Barry Davies reflected perfectly in 1977 when Liverpool's captain jubilantly lifted the European Cup high above his head following his team's famous victory over Borussia Mönchengladbach on a sublime evening in Rome.

"And there it is. The smile of the season from Emlyn Hughes. The performance of the season and the trophy of the season and won by the English champions – Liverpool."

I would suggest the match of the season too, Barry! Old habits.

Liverpool would go on to beat Bruges, Real Madrid and Roma in future European Cup Finals, the latter memorably on penalties in the Eternal City – Grobbelaar's jelly legs were especially celebrated. It was another major victory for Liverpool who were bestriding the game both at home and abroad. Their dominance of English football, with nine Championships in 13 years, made them famous the world over – and *Match of the Day* fixtures on a Saturday evening.

Yet in deep contrast to their success, they were involved in two very different incidents that helped shape the future destiny of the club.

Certainly senior figures at Liverpool had made their concerns known to UEFA about the ageing Heysel Stadium in Brussels which was due to stage the 1985 European Cup Final between Liverpool and Juventus, but sadly to no avail. On the night of the final itself the inadequate safety features and ticket allocation at the ground were a contributory factor when a set of Liverpool fans charged a section of Juventus supporters who were standing close by. A flimsy fence and a small perimeter wall gave way and tragically 39 people – a mixture of Italian and local Belgian people – were crushed to death.

This was a situation that was developing by the moment and on peak-time BBC One. Barry Davies, an experienced and erudite broadcaster, was able to guide the viewers through both the pre-match turmoil which was repeatedly reshown confusingly off tape, and then the match itself which was played, against some people's wishes, essentially to ease security issues but was possibly the most meaningless game of football I and many other people ever saw. Davies's deadpan commentary was spot on.

The actual BBC broadcast of the final itself that evening had got off to a very awkward start as an idea to put presenter Jimmy Hill on the *Wogan Show* that preceded the football, as a clever scheduling bridgehead, backfired. It meant Hill was short of information and unaware of the gravity of the situation in the Heysel Stadium, and was still trading light-hearted banter with his fellow guests when issues of a very serious nature were in play in Brussels.

For Hill, indeed any presenter, it was a very difficult transition to make from humour to human tragedy. Once with Davies, however, the experienced commentator was able to deal with the unfolding story in front of him.

"Heysel, I shall never forget. I went to commentate on what promised to be one of the great European Cup Finals and became the reporter on the spot describing an unfolding and unfathomable tragedy."

*   *   *   *   *

A little more than a fortnight before another football commentator had dealt with a tragic incident that was far removed from his expected weekend brief.

Yorkshire Television's John Helm had gone along to Valley Parade to commentate on what was to be a day of celebration as Bradford

City were presented with the Football League Third Division trophy ahead of their end-of-season game with Lincoln City. A young Gabby Yorath and her family were there to enjoy the occasion as her father, Terry, was part of the successful Bradford City coaching set-up. There was nothing on the game and the local OB unit went there to get some pictures for their programme the following day. What developed was beyond belief.

Helm had always wanted to be a commentator. "I wrote to Kenneth Wolstenholme as a teenager to ask his advice on how to go about it – and still have the letter he sent back to me to this day. I worked my way through local newspapers and then went into broadcasting via local and national radio."

On that day, May 11th 1985, Helm was working from a purpose-built scaffold opposite the main stand when, about 40 minutes into the first half, he was the first to spot something untoward developing four or five rows from the front.

"A throw-in was about to be taken close by and I said to my director 'What is that little glow in the stand?' In fact if somebody had stamped on it there and then it may have prevented the tragedy which followed."

A combination of an old wooden stand, waste paper that had caught alight and a gusty wind meant a small fire turned into an inferno very quickly.

"I just kept commentating on what I was seeing and very soon the fire and smoke was engulfing the stand. I fell back on my skills both as a broadcaster and a journalist – but it was very difficult because I'm a local lad and recognised some of the people struggling to get clear of the danger."

Unbeknown to Helm, ITV's *World of Sport* had been alerted to the fire at Valley Parade and went live to the pictures.

Fifty-six people died in the fire, some because gates at the back of the stand had been locked, and a further 265 were injured. For Helm it remains a painful memory.

"I did a programme later that evening and then had to fulfil a commentary obligation at a speedway event the following day, which was obviously very difficult.

"I kept bursting into tears for six months after the event and I was not myself for a long time."

Thankfully Helm retained his enthusiasm for football and remains a well-loved member of the "commentary family", describing the action from matches all over the world chiefly through his work with UEFA and FIFA, but the day in May 1985 remains a vivid memory. For the club itself there will never be total closure but their inspiring run in the 2012/13 Capital One Cup which took them all the way to the final at Wembley Stadium also gave them the platform to publicly and sensitively remember those lost to the fire.

Four years later, the scenes at Hillsborough at the 1989 FA Cup semi-final between Liverpool and Nottingham Forest provided another stark reminder of how innocent people were victims of yet another stadium disaster that could have been avoided – and whose fight for truth and justice remains as real and raw today as it was nearly 25 years ago.

That day, April 15th, had started out as just a routine day for me when as editor of *Match of the Day* I headed into BBC Television Centre in London to watch that day's action unfold and construct the programme running order for later that evening.

These were the days when neither FA Cup semi-final was live and both matches kicked off at 3pm. Everton and Norwich City were in the other semi, which was played at Villa Park.

Desmond Lynam, who had recently assumed the position as presenter of *Match of the Day*, and Jimmy Hill, the programme's senior pundit, asked whether they could attend one of the matches – and as there were only two games in the show for them to be across I said yes. They plumped to go to Hillsborough.

I settled down to watch the games in the *Match of the Day* office in the company of two guests. Jarvis Astaire and Sir Brian Wolfson were both in senior positions at Wembley Stadium and Astaire was a famous boxing promoter who had supplied fights to the BBC for many years. Sir Brian, like me, was a Scouser and Liverpudlian.

We watched the crowd entering the stadium and they quickly picked up on the uneven distribution of supporters at the Leppings Lane End. "That can't be right," said Sir Brian, "the middle of the terrace is full and the sides still almost empty."

My visitors were experienced stadium people so I took note of their comments and shared their concern. Officials at Liverpool had asked for their fans to be sited at the other end of the ground, which was larger, because when the semi-final of the two same clubs had taken place 12 months earlier, problems of over-crowding had also occurred at the Leppings Lane End.

The match got under way but as we know now, just six minutes into it, proceedings were called to a dramatic halt.

The scenes that followed were the stuff of nightmares as people spilled on to the pitch to escape the crushing going on around them. Fans helped fans, fully realising the desperate situation their fellow spectators were in. Hoardings were ripped up and used as makeshift stretchers. Their selfless efforts on the day have since been matched by the unquenchable search for justice and truth for the 96 people who ultimately lost their lives. And that fight goes on.

Back in London, I alerted *Grandstand* to the developing scenario at Hillsborough. They spoke directly to the scanner at the ground and then went live to the pictures, which were directed carefully and sensitively by a highly experienced producer, John Shrewsbury. He had been alongside Barry Davies at Heysel; now he had John Motson at the microphone, who had to describe what was unfolding in front of him. Another first-class broadcaster, Motson had to be tactful and relay information in good faith, as it was revealed to him – including an erroneous report that a gate had been forced open by the fans, which was simply not the case.

I spoke on the phone to Des Lynam and Jimmy Hill and told them to stay at Hillsborough as long as was necessary to get a true picture of events – which they did before heading back to London.

I also spoke to my BBC bosses. They had a decision to make. Did they leave *Match of the Day* in the schedule or, more likely, replace it with an extended news bulletin, as was the form on these occasions.

I fought hard to retain *Match of the Day's* place in that evening's schedule. Obviously there would be no football in the shortened programme, but I felt that the combination of Desmond Lynam's broadcast authority and his first-hand observations with Jimmy Hill's seniority in football circles, plus John Shrewsbury's on-site pictures that were now being broadcast around the world, and my own news sense and Liverpool background, would tell the on-going story with depth and sincerity.

As well as Des's minute-by-minute account and Jimmy's sagacious views, we were able to bring the latest pictures and feed in some live interviews from the ground itself, which was already beginning to receive bouquet upon bouquet of flowers.

I did hundreds of programmes whilst at the BBC, treated every one of them seriously and whole-heartedly, but this was the one that I was determined to get right. When we came off air, I think we all believed we had done our very best to deliver a contemporaneous, honest and authoritative programme – and then to a man wished we had never had to make the programme in the first place.

CHAPTER 15

"ARE YOU THERE, GEORGE ... GEORGE, GEORGE?"

The 1980s had seen one significant shift in football coverage on the two main channels. After decades of resistance the football authorities finally gave way and gave a green light to live televised football running alongside recorded highlights. The dam was open and live football matches have flooded through it ever since, although the price of the "water rates" has gone through the roof in recent years.

A deal was put in place for the 1983/84 season that allowed the BBC and ITV to screen a limited number of live matches each across the season as well as carrying national highlights programmes.

The £5.2 million two-year deal saw the BBC opt for a Friday-evening transmission for its live matches whilst ITV favoured a Sunday-afternoon place in the schedule.

* * * * *

ITV got off to a decent start to their live coverage with the accomplished presenter Jim Rosenthal fronting the programme and Jimmy Greaves alongside him in the pundit's chair. Brian Moore and Ian St John shared the commentary box as the commercial channel opened its live campaign with Tottenham Hotspur vs. Nottingham Forest at White Hart Lane in October 1983. A good game, a point everybody seemed at super-pains to stress, including an interesting choice of post-match studio guest, Tottenham chairman Douglas Alexiou. It just proved how television was determined to stay close to the game's power-brokers.

Both broadcasters were hit by industrial disputes in the autumn, and the BBC had no editions of *Match of the Day* for four consecutive weeks and wasn't able to transmit its first live match until well into the season.

The Friday-evening slot never really worked for the BBC. The idea was that a combination of a Friday-evening live game coupled with a Saturday-evening highlights show would give a "complete" picture of that weekend's football.

But supporters stayed away from the Friday-evening matches and many blokes who were their potential audience were out enjoying their end-of-working-week "socials".

The BBC's first live match was eventually broadcast in December between Manchester United and Tottenham Hotspur – usually a banker – but it drew a crowd of only 33,000 to Old Trafford, some 10,000 below the Old Trafford average then, and more than 40,000 lower than their average now.

Replacing a peak-time evening game in the schedule if lost to bad weather was also a problem, which is probably why that season's Aston Villa vs. Liverpool clash in January went ahead despite the pitch resembling something more like an ice rink than a grass rectangle.

Mind you, it didn't stop Ian Rush scoring a hat-trick, including a sublime volley. He still remembers that game. "I don't think the match would have been on if it hadn't been live on the telly. To be honest, it was difficult to keep your feet. Mind you, as players our matches being held on a Friday night gave us the bonus of having the rest of the weekend off."

The 1985 FA Cup Final between Manchester United and League Champions, Everton, was the last in which *Grandstand* and *World of Sport* would compete head-on for viewers, as ITV's Saturday-afternoon vehicle would be taken off the air that autumn.

My role at the BBC had moved from assistant producer through to producer of *Football Focus* and now to assistant editor of *Grandstand*. It was in that capacity that I was charged with recommending the studio guests for the big occasions like the FA Cup Final.

Not too tricky an assignment as I was always out and about meeting sports people, unless, of course, you gave yourself a potential problem by suggesting George Best as a Cup Final guest. Now George was a world-class footballer but was a little, shall we say unreliable (OK, a nightmare) when it came to "turning up". To be fair if the great Sir Matt Busby and Manchester United couldn't solve the problem, what chance did I have?

Anyway that is how I found myself on the morning of a 1980s FA Cup Final standing forlornly outside the door of a fashionable apartment block in Chelsea cursing my luck.

I rang the bell of one particular flat several times – with no answer. And I was beginning to get into a bit of a sweat. Inside the apartment (I hoped) was George Best, as arranged when I called him to make the plans the previous afternoon. He was going to be our star turn, and I had fought both my and his corner when we were deciding our *Grandstand* line-up. What with fellow Ulsterman Norman Whiteside in the Manchester United line-up, and making big news, I thought it was worth the risk.

But that was then – not now, with me standing like a lemon on the great man's doorstep. I went across to the phone box at the corner of the street and nervously made a call, the first of many, to the BBC Wembley production office. "Erm, I'm at George Best's flat now."

"Ah, great. Well done, Brian."

"No, not really, there is no sign of George."

"Oh, brilliant. Now what are we going to do?"

"Leave it with me ..." How quickly I'd turned from saint to sinner.

This routine of ringing his doorbell, cursing my luck, making a trip to the phone box to send the bad news to my colleagues and then being cursed by them, went on for more than an hour. "Career and reputation in shreds," I thought. "Keep my mouth shut next time."

Anyway, one final press on the doorbell and a fleeting move behind the curtains. It was George. Then with a big smile he opened the window and said, "I've been watching you for the last half hour or so. Your nerves must be shot. I'm just putting my jacket on and I'll be with you in a minute."

Kiss him or kill him? No, just get over to that phone box and make the call to the BBC team at Wembley. My relief was shared by them, several times over.

I got George in a fast car to Wembley and an FA Cup Final. In fact something even Sir Matt had never done. And he was an absolute star, charming the BBC team and viewers alike throughout the afternoon. Oh, and then perfectly describing how his fellow Ulsterman, Norman Whiteside, had scored the winning goal.

I suppose the irony of it was that having got George back home safely I was so pleased, relieved actually, with how the day had gone after such an inauspicious start, that it was me that went out and got hammered that night!

As three home nations had qualified for the 1986 World Cup in Mexico both the BBC and ITV looked forward to an action-packed few weeks. In the BBC's presenter's chair now was Desmond Lynam, fast becoming "the most popular man sitting behind a desk" in everyday British life.

The man from Ennis in County Clare, Ireland, had settled with his parents in the south of England as a small boy, and a little later in life a promising career in insurance had been set aside for some local radio exposure before he was to become part of a marvellous stable of national radio broadcasters under the disciplined stewardship of the legendary Angus McKay.

McKay demanded exacting standards from his team of presenters, commentators, reporters and producers, much like Cowgill had honed the skills of many fledgling sports television performers at a similar time.

Certainly the radio was a great place to learn, either as a broadcast home in its own right, as many talented people chose, or as a launching pad into television, or as a bit of both as lots of professional broadcasters would settle for. And, of course, just like its television equivalent BBC Radio would be at all the big events home and abroad.

Lynam had a natural way with his audience, was a sharp journalist with an intelligent news nose, had the ability to turn a well-known gag on its head, and he had a face for radio AND television.

I started working with him at the BBC in the early 1980s and we enjoyed a professional relationship that lasted more than 20 years and a personal friendship that endures to this day.

I found Desmond a real joy to work with – and that is a good job because we were destined to spend hundreds of hours working together on some of the era's biggest television shows – and with some of the largest audiences. I was also involved in his move from the BBC to ITV in a "transfer" some suggested was the biggest television talent switch since Morecambe and Wise had made the same move.

Anyway that was all ahead of us as we settled down to work on the 1986 World Cup. John Rowlinson was editor of the main live programmes which were to be presented from London while I produced a companion daily programme, *World Cup Report*, a teatime show with Bob Wilson and three likely lads, Emlyn Hughes, Andy Gray and Martin O'Neill. A good line-up but not the original one I had planned, or indeed as was published in the special World Cup edition of the *Radio Times*, which along with the equivalent copy of the *TV Times*, still remain sought-after collectibles to this day. Just wish I'd kept my copies!

Martin O'Neill was a late addition to follow the fortunes of the Northern Ireland team. Martin, whom I had got to know when he captained his national side during the previous World Cup in Spain, had got us out of a tight corner when George Best finally did to me what he had done to many before me. He pulled out of our team at the last moment. Ah well, if it was good enough for Sir Matt, it was good enough for me.

O'Neill was a quirky rather nervous performer but his style won him friends and a potential broadcasting future. Emlyn performed like he played, spraying verbal tackles and passes with no safety net, whilst Andy Gray showed the sort of promise that would give him a long career at Sky before his alleged misdemeanours sent him packing.

ITV had Brian Moore hosting their World Cup coverage back in London, with Brian Clough and Kevin Keegan, among others, with him, while the commercial channel also exploited the popularity of Saint and Greavsie, now firmly established as sports television favourites. Their double-act had survived the end of ITV's *World of Sport* and their popularity and profile continued to grow, even having the "honour" of being made into puppets on the smash-hit *Spitting Image*. A bizarre status-symbol of the time.

Some 16 years had passed since Saint had missed out on a trip to the World Cup in Mexico when he was nudged out of first place in the "Find a Commentator Competition". This time Greavsie had, no doubt, flown out in a plush jet plane rather than being bumped left, right and centre in a rally car on his way to Mexico City. No, for this World Cup they were sent out to film a special preview programme.

Mexico City itself was still recovering from a massive earthquake that had devastated the area nine months before. Thousands of people had been killed and buildings had been battered and bruised.

Alec Weeks flew out to see first-hand the damage the earthquake had caused and his report back to senior BBC management was stark and realistic. "Morally, the World Cup should not take place in Mexico. Technically, it will require a miracle. Financially, it will take place. We should cover it fully."

So in late May 1986, the football world arrived in Mexico, and a patched-up Mexico City, and the tournament went ahead. Mexico had itself been a replacement for Colombia, which had been the original choice but whose economy had forced them to duck out.

Weeks's foresight into the potential technical difficulties proved to be an accurate assessment. In the wider scheme of things that Mexico had suffered it was not important but the world's broadcasters had arrived in Mexico and now they were keen to get sound and pictures sent to their home destination.

There were huge problems. Essentially equipment, which had been paid for by overseas broadcasters, hadn't been properly tested – and for the opening ceremony and first match of the 1986 World Cup between Italy and Bulgaria in the Azteca Stadium, less than half of the commentary positions were in working order for the broadcasters. The following day, only one of 69 positions in Guadalajara was operational. ITV had to do their commentary on this match, Brazil vs. Spain, "off-tube" from their London studios.

These sorts of problems went on for several days until a posse of senior engineers, "The Magnificent Eight", as it were, from the ranks of the world's biggest broadcasters stormed the International Control Room in Mexico City and took things into their own hands – wires, plugs and circuits – and finally it all got sorted out.

Technical traumas and tummy bugs were the stuff of Mexico '86 but so was some fantastic football. England started poorly – a defeat against Portugal, a draw against Morocco – before they, and especially their key striker, Gary Lineker, came good. His hat-trick against Poland finally launched England's World Cup campaign and set him on the road to fame and fortune – and crate-loads of potato crisps.

A last-16 win against Paraguay put England in the quarter-finals against Argentina. Four years on from the end of the Falklands War this sporting clash would contain the work of the devil and the gift of a genius. All rolled up in one man, Maradona.

His "Hand of God" goal remains one of the most controversial goals ever scored in a major football match. In lifting the ball over the outcoming England goalkeeper, Peter Shilton, by using an outstretched hand, he put his team ahead, sent those watching back in Argentina wild with delight, whilst sending viewers in England similarly wild – but this time with anger.

BBC's commentator for the match, Barry Davies, generously admits he didn't spot Maradona's handball at the time. But much more importantly for England's sake, neither did the referee and linesmen. The goal stood.

And a few minutes later, the tie was taken further away from England with a goal of utter brilliance by the Argentinean pocket dynamo. The best goal ever scored? Well, right up there. In a way it was diminished in my eyes by the goal that had preceded it. The two goals didn't belong in the same match.

England got a goal back as John Barnes and Gary Lineker combined brilliantly and then went mighty close again just before the end. But like 16 years earlier, England's journey ended at the quarter-final stage.

Time for Bobby Robson's England party to return. Gary Lineker won the tournament's Golden Boot and earned a place on the BBC pundits' panel for the final itself alongside Lawrie McMenemy and Terry Venables. Argentina, almost a one-man team, went on to win an entertaining final against West Germany. John Motson and Brian Moore, who had travelled out for the final, did the commentary honours on their respective channels.

In time for the following season, Venables would take Lineker to Barcelona and the multi-talented lad from Leicester would subsequently prove he could be accomplished both in the box, and on the box, at the very highest level. His future television career at the BBC and elsewhere has shown him in the finest light.

CHAPTER 16

"YOU'LL BE HUMMING IT SOON!"

"It's up for grabs now!" Brian Moore's famous ITV commentary line perfectly captured the unforgettable climax to the final League Championship clinched in the 1980s.

In the final moments of the final game of the season, the destiny of the title was decided. In 2012, something similar would happen at the Etihad Stadium, but in 1989, the two teams playing each other on that May evening were the two teams actually vying for Championship glory.

As Michael Thomas broke through Liverpool's defence to score the stunning injury-time goal at Anfield which cost the home side another "double", there may have been one man even happier than the legions of Arsenal followers on Merseyside who greeted the winner with mass hysteria – well, two perhaps.

First, there was Arsenal fanatic, Nick Hornby, who was able to turn that evening of high drama into the climax of a groundbreaking book, *Fever Pitch*, that would become a best-seller and more. And also a certain senior TV executive present that night at Anfield, who had seen his hunch come up big time.

Greg Dyke had taken over as Chairman of ITV Sport in the late 1980s when he returned to London Weekend Television, his spiritual home, as their Director of Programmes, after successful spells at both TV-am and TVS.

Dyke was a future inspirational Director-General at the BBC and is now Chairman of the Football Association. But during his time at

ITV he made key changes in the sporting output of the commercial giant and played a huge part in creating the football jigsaw, or financial juggernaut, that the game has now become.

Dyke made a few early decisions that got some viewers' backs up, like taking wrestling off the air. He felt – and he was almost certainly right – that the "sport" was past its sell-by date and it wasn't until American television turned it into big arena entertainment that it gathered a new audience – and a new broadcast home.

Dyke's policy for ITV Sport was to major on big live events – events that could do big numbers for his channel, especially at the weekend, and, of course, one sport, above all others, was capable of doing that.

Dyke was a football fan, still is, and whether it is England, Brentford or Manchester United, he has always shown an interest in the round-ball game. He even got a run-out at Wembley, in a pre-FA Cup Final celebrity match in 1987, playing for the David Frost XI against a side put together by Jimmy Tarbuck. Dyke put in a decent performance whilst another future BBC Director-General, John Birt, actually scored the game's stunning goal.

Anyway Dyke's post-match satisfaction at Anfield was not fuelled by his regard for Manchester United. Close ally and Arsenal director David Dein had invited him into the visitors' dressing-room to witness the celebrations first-hand, and Dyke's gamble of buying expensive live league football for the commercial channel had paid off – and in front of a Friday-evening audience on ITV of 11 million viewers – all on the edge of their seats.

Including ITV's match director, John Watts. He takes up the story. "In the old days of ITV, the camera crews were provided by the regional companies where the games were being played. Granada normally provided excellent crews as it was a region with top-class clubs. However when I arrived to cover the title-decider between Liverpool and Arsenal, I was more than a little worried that none of my regular camera crew were there – apparently they were rostered off on a Friday! I was faced with covering the biggest game in Football League history with a predominantly non-football crew. It was a tough night, and although many of them didn't know the players, they were good operators and we survived an unforgettably dramatic evening intact."

In a bid to stave off the potentially damaging influence of a new broadcasting player, British Satellite Broadcasting, BSB, but also to back his view that "big and live" was best, Greg Dyke, helped by that super-connected ITV executive, Trevor East, had entered into a four-year deal with the Football League which guaranteed the commercial channel 21 live matches a season at a cost of £11 million a year. Big money, with a significant edge towards the big clubs, but they had got off to a flyer.

Most editions of *The Match*, as they had named their new show, were staged on Sunday afternoon, and were fronted by Elton Welsby, a presenter who had cut his teeth at Granada TV. A cute decision not to schedule any matches until the clocks had gone back meant the games were real "winter-warmers" as the season progressed.

In a double-whammy, having mopped up the highlights rights as well, which they seldom used, ITV had essentially closed the BBC's weekly *Match of the Day* programme down as well.

The BBC, in turn, had struck up an arrangement with BSB to cover the Football Association's portfolio, which of course included the FA Cup and England internationals.

For the BBC that essentially meant concentrating on the FA Cup – and so it was a case of dusting itself down, moving on and waiting for January to get among the sport's big names.

New times, new contracts called for new blood. So I found myself promoted to the post of BBC's Editor, Football and one of my first moves was to persuade Desmond Lynam that he should split his duties between the "big" *Grandstand* programmes and major events he was synonymous with, and to become the Corporation's regular football presenter.

Needing a fresh challenge, he agreed and thus moved into a chair that had been kept warm by Jimmy Hill for the previous 15 years. Jimmy would move from centre-forward to inside-right and become the channel's senior pundit.

We were off and running. *Match of the Day – The Road to Wembley* was born and we maximised the value of each weekend with a Saturday-evening highlights programme and a live Sunday-afternoon cup-tie.

Every show needs a bit of luck, and our choice of Sutton United vs. 1987 FA Cup-winners Coventry City as our main highlights match in the third round came up trumps when the non-league side created the shock of the round, beating the Midlanders 2–1. Mind you they got thumped 8–0 in the next round by Norwich City.

The first season's FA Cup football was obviously totally overshadowed by the events at Hillsborough on April 15th 1989 but when Liverpool eventually resumed playing football it was fitting that the FA Cup Final was played out between them and their Merseyside neighbours, Everton, who were and still are so supportive of their rivals from across Stanley Park.

The following season, the BBC's *Match of the Day – The Road to Wembley* featured a significant live game in the FA Cup's third round between Nottingham Forest and Manchester United. This is the game that some suggest could have drawn an early close to Alex Ferguson's managerial career at Manchester United. A poor run of results had left him vulnerable, although he still had the support of key United people. Mark Robins scored a vital second-half winner, then Fergie's team went on a cup-run that took them all the way to Wembley and the Scotsman to untold football glory – and a knighthood.

Mind you, not before the best FA Cup semi-final double-header in the history of the competition had been played out on a beautiful early April afternoon in 1990. Both semi-finals were to be broadcast live and with BSB still a fledgling broadcaster, both were on the BBC. I was on-site at Maine Road for coverage of the late-afternoon game between Manchester United and near-neighbours, Oldham Athletic.

Des Lynam, who had presented the Grand National from Aintree the previous day, and Jimmy Hill were there with me on a hot sunny day in Manchester.

Indeed there was a wonderful cameo ahead of our programme when Des and Jimmy kept alternately popping in and out of the makeshift studio at one end of the stadium. Every time Des came out for a bit of fresh air all the fans close by cheered and every time Jimmy came out to do the same they playfully booed. It was like one of those weather-forecast tableaus, where a model lady comes out with a broad smile to suggest a sunny day lies ahead of us and then later comes out with a frown and an umbrella if rain threatens!

Anyway, the sun was shining too at Villa Park, where Crystal Palace and Liverpool played out a thumping good cup-tie with the south Londoners coming out 4–3 winners after extra-time. My old university pal, Steve Coppell, whose Palace had lost 9–0 to the Reds earlier that season, was brilliantly caught live on camera jumping for joy as the winner from Alan Pardew hit the net.

With a 4–3 score down the road, to my professional delight and personal angst, we accepted that "our" match at Maine Road would be an anti-climax after all that Midlands excitement. But, as the action unfolded it turned out to be nothing of the sort. A sparkling, incident-packed 3–3 draw. Two semi-finals, 13 goals, both live on the BBC and a live replay to follow. You get those lucky days – but not many of them! As one of the newspapers the following day proclaimed: "Thanks to the FA Cup ... and thanks to the BBC!"

To top the Corporation's bumper weekend, Nick Faldo won back-to-back US Masters titles in a play-off win over Ray Floyd.

As the summer beckoned so did the World Cup. Italia '90 would be a memorable tournament, a competition in which England started slowly but went mighty close to winning. Gazza introduced himself to the world; Jack Charlton's Ireland team and their wonderful travelling support brought character, colour and wit to proceedings; audience figures on both channels were colossal; going to the pub to watch the match became a new habit; and the BBC turned an operatic icon into a worldwide music phenomenon.

I was editor of Italia '90 for the BBC, working with my colleague, executive producer Jim Reside, and along with the 1992 Barcelona Olympics, it remains my favourite event to have worked on whilst at the Corporation.

It was big-time television; most major matches were played in peak-time, and the BBC had a strong team both in London and in Italy. ITV too had a good team, which included stadium presentation out in Italy with Elton Welsby while back in London Nick Owen fronted many key shows.

The choice of whether to link major event programmes from on-site or back at "base" is often a tough decision and one broadcasters make for a variety of reasons. Not unreasonably cost is one of the key factors, as is the ability to replicate a quality of broadcasting that viewers get used to on a week-by-week basis. Also time-zones come into play, especially with regard to the size of the audience – it can depend on whether it is a fixed location i.e. an Olympics, or a multi-location event like a World Cup. Sometimes being based in the UK helps retain and reflect properly the country's "take" on an event or a tournament. You can very quickly lose that perspective when working abroad.

How often have you heard a broadcaster at an overseas event cheerily say "Good morning, and welcome to ..." as you are heading off to bed for a decent night's sleep?

In 1990, the BBC based its presentation in London with Desmond Lynam and Bob Wilson, and a small army of personnel, including commentators, reporters, cameramen and engineers who were spread across Italy.

To be honest the BBC got off to an unexpected flyer, when our choice of signature tune for the coverage of the tournament became a national talking point.

Des and I, like many of the BBC team, put great store by the choice of event television opening music. Choosing the "music" for a big event was a fun part of the business. Subjective, sure, but fun all the same. Sometimes a choice was made for you, heaven-sent, like Freddie Mercury and Montserrat Caballé's stunning "Barcelona" for the 1992 Summer Olympics. Opening music can so quickly establish an emotional foothold with the viewer, mark out a point of difference from broadcasting rivals, and Italia '90 and "Nessun Dorma" probably produced the best-ever example of that.

Des and I had discussed how football and opera (and glorious food and wine) seemed kindred spirits in Italian life and thought our opening title sequence should somehow reflect that. Rose, Des's elegant partner, suggested the idea of using a recording of a famous Italian tenor, Luciano Pavarotti. This was pre-Wikipedia, so I had to nod sagely and then dig around to find out a bit more about him.

Anyway, we listened to a tape of his music and hit on the idea of using "Nessun Dorma", an aria from *Turandot* by Puccini (I write that like I'm an expert! If only.)

It brilliantly fitted the bill. After its first playing on our opening programme, Des raised that famous wry eyebrow and said, "You'll be humming it soon!" and he was right. I knew we were on to something special when a couple of days into the tournament I heard our milkman whistling the tune and then making a real effort at singing the final note at a pitch that only dogs and cats could hear.

And yet, "Nessun Dorma" nearly didn't make it on to the BBC screens. A couple of days before the tournament I took a call from a rather superior character at Decca Classical Records on whose label Pavarotti had recorded the track. He explained to me that his company were having second thoughts about whether it was the right use of one of their most valued artistes and such a famous piece of music.

"Too late, mate," I said. "We've spent a lot of money on a fantastic set of titles and the music fits beautifully. It is going to be at the front of peak-time shows with massive audiences. I'm sure you will have a huge hit on your hands. And I think, in a few weeks' time, you'll be ringing us up to say thank you." It was and he did.

With England, Scotland and the Republic of Ireland in the tournament there was lots for both broadcasters to go for – with the added ingredient that England and Ireland were in the same group. Their match, the first for both teams, was live on ITV and ended all-square.

In fact the group was not blessed with sparkling football but both England and Ireland got through, edging Holland out of the tournament. Scotland disastrously lost to Costa Rica in their opening game, steadied the ship with a win over Sweden and then narrowly lost to Brazil in their final group match – they were on their way home.

By now the nation was warming to the tournament, especially the on- and off-field antics of Paul Gascoigne. He was perhaps a new name to a lot of the wider television audience, who every four years made a date with the World Cup, but he was a special talent. On the field he drove England forward, and at training and at the team's base in Sardinia he was the life and soul of the party. Innocent times.

Ireland won a penalty shoot-out against Romania to reach the last eight and "Saint" Jack was taking on legendary status in his "adopted" country. His brother Bobby looked on with a warm smile on the BBC.

A last-gasp goal from England's David Platt clinched a hard-fought win over Belgium after extra-time. Indeed, all three of England's knock-out matches went to extra-time. Bingo! For the broadcasters, an audience always builds through an evening – and the peak audience for a penalty shoot-out tops the lot.

England had qualified to play Cameroon in the quarter-final and the BBC decided to send Des Lynam out to Italy to front their quarter-final coverage from the stadium in Naples.

The in-vision positions in the Italian stadiums were fairly unprotected. There was noise and distractions aplenty. The previous evening in the Olympic Stadium in Rome, Des had guided the BBC viewers through Ireland's narrow defeat to Italy. Now it was Naples, England vs. Cameroon, peak-time on a Sunday evening, head-to-head with ITV. Big stuff.

High up and at the back of the stadium, Des prepared diligently for the broadcast despite the noise and general match-day distractions, including the irritation of having to shift his in-vision position close to on-air time.

As the titles ran, Des seemed ready and yet when his face filled the screen, he suddenly stumbled for his opening words. I instinctively realised something was amiss and tried to prompt him on the talk-back from the studio gallery in London, but to no avail. Des briefly had a "mare". He later agonised over it, partially because he had set himself such high standards. Me, I was upset *for* him not *with* him, but felt that as he had been setting the industry new standards over the previous few years, it was a case of just "learn from it and move on". Des, with admirable self-deprecation, would later cutely coin a phrase "See Naples and dry."

More importantly, England dramatically beat Cameroon in extra-time and had qualified for the semi-final of the World Cup. Des flew back to present the semi-final from the London studio. England vs. West Germany. By now the country was white-hot with excitement and anticipation.

What a match-up, peak-time Wednesday evening, England vs. West Germany, again a BBC–ITV head-to-head. John Motson and Trevor Brooking vs. Brian Moore and Ron Atkinson in the commentary box for this huge occasion. A colossal audience would tune in across both channels, the lion's share as always on the BBC. As a television professional these were the occasions you thrived on even if the nerves would occasionally rattle through your system prior to the off. You felt you were at the centre of something very important and indeed you were. I remember sitting outdoors in the "doughnut" – as they called the BBC Television Centre – collecting my thoughts ahead of the big World Cup semi-final night, only to be continually distracted by everybody rushing home to watch the match or wishing me luck.

West Germany went ahead through Andy Brehme, England pulled level through Lineker late in the game. Gazza over-stretched in a tackle and was yellow-carded. It meant even if England won he was out of the final. And he knew it. Tears welled up in Gazza's eyes, and later they would flow freely, a memorable image reshown many times since. So too was the camera shot that caught Gary Lineker, looking through and beyond Gazza, fingers pointing to his eyes, and mouthing the words "Have a word with him" to the England bench. We would have done, Gary – millions of us.

England would lose on penalties, Stuart Pearce and Chris Waddle vitally missing spot-kicks for England. You could feel the nation's balloon being pricked – and Des Lynam's closing words reflected the mood. "If you are going to have a few drinks tonight to drown your sorrows, do it safe, not aggressively. Be proud of England's performance in playing so well."

Both broadcasting teams felt deflated at the end of that evening. If we weren't privileged to play in an actual World Cup, living and breathing the tournament by televising it was a very good second best. And if we weren't able to win a World Cup Final for England ourselves, televising it would have been the ultimate second best. I appreciated BBC's Head of Sport, Jonathan Martin, coming in both to congratulate us on the show and commiserate with us over England's exit.

It wasn't to be, but Italia '90 did monster business for both the BBC and ITV, put football back at the heart of the nation, and England's heart-stopping journey to the closing stages of the tournament guaranteed "None Shall Sleep". Puccini was right.

CHAPTER 17

A BLANK SHEET

In May 2014, Manchester City claimed their second Premier League title in three years. Whilst enthusiatically welcomed by the Etihad Stadium crowd, it couldn't match the extraordinary final-day events of 2012.

Trailing to QPR as their final match of the season went into injury-time, City needed to score twice. If not, their local rivals, Manchester United, whose match at Sunderland was about to finish, would themselves be crowned champions. That would have been the ultimate double-whammy for the long-suffering City fans.

QPR themselves had survived their own final-day trauma as results elsewhere had unexpectedly guaranteed them their Premier League status. And so to injury-time.

City's Bosnian striker Edin Dzeko pulled City level in the match with a close-range header from a corner – and with the dying embers of a remarkable season now glowing brightly, the home side were about to pull off the impossible.

City's former wayward talent, Italian Mario Balotelli, controlled both the ball, and his instincts, and laid a pass into the path of Argentine Sergio Aguero who guided the ball into the net amidst remarkable scenes of hysteria from the club's delirious at the Etihad Stadium. A goal crafted by players from across the globe had sent half of Manchester into ecstasy.

It was the 20th campaign of the Premier League era and certainly one of the competition's finest. And as City's Blue Moon rose high in the sky there was one man appropriately on duty to call it home.

Sky Sports' Martin Tyler had commentated on the first goal scored in their first live match back in August 1992 – Teddy Sheringham's winner for Nottingham Forest against Liverpool. Now, 20 years on, it was Manchester City and their own personal crock of gold at the end of the rainbow.

"Balotelli ... Aguerroooooo ... !!! ... I swear you'll never see anything like this ever again. Watch it and drink it in!"

Barney Francis, Sky Sport's Managing Director, described it to me as "an incredible sporting moment, brilliantly captured with an incredible piece of story-telling from Martin Tyler".

Tyler's words had summed up the moment perfectly as the world's richest league, with its international cast of players and plutocrats, had delivered a pure Hollywood moment – when for all the politics, pounds and pursuit of power, the simplicity of the right pass to the right man at the right time had crowned a wonderful season.

Such a moment must even have surpassed the wildest ambitions of those men back in the early 1990s who were instrumental in turning football on its head and taking the game into a new orbit.

In 1991, football's power-brokers, Arsenal's David Dein, Tottenham Hotspur's Irving Scholar, Manchester United's Martin Edwards, Liverpool's Noel White and Everton's Philip Carter, had gathered for dinner at the invitation of ITV's Greg Dyke. Whatever the starter, the main course was the reshaping of English league football.

This time a break-away was on the menu as the "the big five" wanted more control of their destiny and a greater share of football's television loot. The rest is history, although with one very significant twist. When it became clear that the new FA Premier League would become a reality from August 1992, the destination of its television rights then came into play.

Dyke felt confident, with some justification, that his spadework in helping create the new opportunity, and his growing relationship with the top clubs, would steer him and his company successfully across the line. However the UK broadcast landscape was changing quickly and nowhere more so than in sports television. And football, a little weary of the BBC/ITV carefully crafted domination of the game's airwaves, now had choices.

Technological advances in broadcasting had seen two new players in the UK marketplace, British Satellite Broadcasting (BSB) and Australian media tycoon Rupert Murdoch's Sky. The man in the street was faced with an interesting choice: the "squarial", the dish, or neither.

From its early days it seemed clear that only one "new" system could flourish and in November 1990, BSB and Sky merged to create BSkyB. Five months later Sky Sports was launched.

Sky Sports needed a marquee product to help send it into space and the new FA Premier League seemed to be the perfect fit.

At a historic meeting of the Premier League clubs, BSkyB won a crucial and tight vote for the destiny of the new competition's live television rights over ITV, who had felt justified in believing it had already all but sealed the deal. An important figure on that day was a certain Alan Sugar.

Lord Sugar, as he is now, had bought Tottenham Hotspur from Irving Scholar, and the man who owned the electronics giants, Amstrad, and supplied dishes to BSkyB, sided with the Murdoch empire.

*   *   *   *   *

In fact, Sugar's famous telephone call, made outside the meeting room where the Premier League clubs were discussing the TV rights issue, was a game-changer. He was heard to say, "You've got to blow them out of the water." The guys on the other end of the line, presumably BSkyB, did just that – and have been doing similar ever since.

Sky's inauspicious start to their football life had included coverage of the little-known Zenith Data Systems Cup (albeit with a thumping 6–6 first-round draw between penalty shoot-out winners Tranmere Rovers and Newcastle United) and that other "biggie", the Autoglass Trophy.

Those early days were about to become twinkling memories as Murdoch's organisation was now in full swing when a five-year £304 million deal with the newly formed Premier League was sealed.

The rest is history – albeit recent history. Sky and the Premier League have grown together. They have been an arm's length partnership that has developed a sporting competition that has redefined the boundaries of richness and results.

Of course, other broadcast organisations have also been part of, and played their part in, the two-decade journey but at its core, the key business relationship between the Premier League and its chief domestic broadcasting partner BSkyB has been the platform for the extraordinary change in fame and fortune for those clubs who have shared the financial uplift from competing in this country's elite league.

Of course, the journey has not been without its bumps in the road, and for some people the Premier League represents as much about what is wrong with the game as what is right with it. But the competition, with its blend of top domestic players and overseas stars; with its influx of gifted foreign coaches and foreign owners; its state-of-the-art stadiums; and international broadcast appeal, make it a success story of some magnitude. And there is no sign of its appeal, and its financial drawing power – domestic and international – losing any of its energy.

Against that are the fixture list and kick-off times being something of a moveable feast – a traditional Saturday-afternoon 3pm kick-off is a thing of the past and the admission prices to see some games and teams are prohibitive.

Back in 1992, what we broadcasters were coming to terms with was a whole new ball game and where we all fitted in.

The BBC won the rights for Premiership highlights, and so the regular Saturday-night *Match of the Day* programme was restored to an enthusiastic audience. Along with two feature matches the programme could now also show all the goals from the other games played on the afternoon. For the record, Brian Deane scored the first-ever goal in the

Premier League, and luckily it was on one of our two featured matches in the season's opening programme.

Of course, the activity at Sky Sports was full-on. Having secured the "live" contract they now had to bring it to air. And they knew the pressure on their performance would be enormous. Experienced Australian television sports executive Dave Hill was a gregarious inspirational television man, and still very much is as the Global President of Fox Sports in the USA. He may not have been an expert on association football, but he was a brave innovator and inspired people to experiment with ways of putting sport on the air, and to go the extra yard in doing it.

Hill looked to the likes of Vic Wakeling, who had been part of the set-up at BSB, and Scottish TV sports executive Andy Melvin to steer the coverage through its early days. Melvin was a hard task-master but was instrumental in setting the standards for first, BSB's football coverage and then Sky Sports' soccer output. He tells a wonderful story of going into David Hill's office for an early meeting.

"The day came when David Hill invited me into his office to have our first football production meeting. This is where he was to hand down the tablets of stone, the way football – according to the great Hill – was to be covered in the future.

"I had built myself up for a fight. This bloody Aussie wasn't going to tell me how to make football programmes. I'll show him.

"Now, Hilly is one for great theatricals. He loves a drama, adores a performance ... as long as he is always the star of the show.

"'Right,' he said. 'This is for you.' And with a sweeping gesture fit for Olivier, he produced a piece of paper and handed it to me. It was blank.

"'Just make it bloody good,' he said.

"That's leadership. That's man management."

Melvin, who retired in the summer of 2013, was very much the senior hands-on production executive of Sky Sport's football – and a right tough nut who demanded high standards. And, with the talented ex-ITV man Tony Mills in the match scanner, directing the cameras, the Sky team soon became the team to beat. In football coverage terms the BBC and ITV had helped set standards for the rest of the broadcast world. Now Sky Sports, with the frequency and quality of its live coverage, would raise that bar even higher.

Wakeling would be an instrumental figure in the next two decades of UK sports coverage. His tenacity and single-minded focus, matched with Murdoch's deep pockets, put Sky Sports way ahead of the game across a range of sports including live coverage of overseas Test cricket and golf – big early wins. But, as a man with a background in newspapers and regional television, it was his respect for the sports he was now clearly influencing that kept him ahead of the game – including football.

"Vic had been both a newspaper and television man, but at heart, he was also a football man and throughout his time at Sky he maintained that regard for the sport and understood intuitively when decisions had to be made how they would impact on the game and those who followed it," recalls Martin Tyler.

By having more "time and space" than terrestrial rivals they were able to create a different scale of coverage. In football, for example, they were able to start the build-up to their live matches a full two hours before the kick-off (with no time for a dissertation on chrysanthemums!) and the game could be dissected at length after it had finished. On terrestrial television getting on and off the air tight to the kick-off and close to the final whistle had been a bane for us working on the coverage and the viewers who wanted more of it.

Richard Keys, late of TV-am, arrived as Sky Sports' football presenter. Keys quickly and assuredly settled into a position he would hold for nearly 20 years before he and his long-time studio partner, Andy Gray, parted company with the satellite broadcaster in double-quick time in 2011.

Gray, whom I'd used in the BBC's 1986 World Cup coverage, developed a strong rapport with the Sky audience in its early days.

He had interesting things to say about football and was not fazed by illustrating his points by personally driving his own analysis with the latest technological gizmos and gimmicks. The experienced Melvin was instrumental in persuading Gray that his future lay in analysing the Premier League rather than in the aggro of trying to manage or coach a club in it. Sky Sports got the nod over Aston Villa.

"When we were just starting out Andy Gray and I were once discussing football tactics whilst waiting for a flight, we were using different coloured empty bottles and moving them into different tactical shapes around a table. At the end of it all I said we should be making a show along these lines – and sure enough we did. It was part of the 'blank page' if you like."

With Martin Tyler and Ian Darke in the commentary box, Sky set out to turn their expensive rights into top-quality television.

Of course, the two preferred slots for their live matches, 4pm on a Sunday afternoon and Monday-evening football, with its presenter's bright jackets, cheerleaders and fireworks, aggravated supporters who had realised the traditional 3pm Saturday-afternoon kick-off was now under full-frontal assault.

And the games that had been moved were still being watched on television by precious few compared to the numbers that had been able to see live matches on terrestrial television under the previous arrangements with the BBC and ITV.

"In the early days when we were going up to matches in the north on the train, we would look out of the windows and go through some towns and see some dishes and say 'good on you' and then we would go miles and miles without seeing a single dish. I remember doing that a lot in the early days to see what kind of impact we were making," remembers Martin Tyler.

It was a weakness that Sky's opponents, like us at the BBC, tried to exploit publicly and privately. Inevitably, the habit did catch on though – and Tyler believes one of the key reasons was the pursuit of excellence that each member of Sky's football team tried to bring to the broadcasts.

*   *   *   *   *

"We tried to have the best people in the business doing our games, from every perspective. Pretty soon we became very good at it and we had no excuse NOT to be very good at it. We had the pick of people like the soundmen and cameramen. We had lots of games to hone our performance. Everything was there for us. And it still is what we are about. The whole shebang is staffed by people who are crazy about football, love it, and I think over time that has got through the consciousness of the people who watch us."

As a television professional and rival to Sky's output for many years I had to accept that the satellite broadcaster's ambition to take match coverage to another level was going to test the established order of things.

Each game had 15 cameras from the start and the quality of the sound effects, the upgrading of the graphics and even the innovation of the clock in the corner of the screen tested our system – and our patience. The graphic showing the running time in the match and the current score was a winner.

The score clock in the corner was a fantastically simple innovation, the brainchild of David Hill, but one, as the man in charge of the BBC's football output, I resisted as long as possible.

I, like others, convinced myself it covered too much of the screen. I was wrong. It was a simple, clever, unobtrusive addition and aid to the viewer and only my professional prejudice delayed its arrival on BBC screens. Now you can't do without it.

Mind you in those days at the BBC it was almost sacrilege to admit to even owning a Sky subscription – to me this was a rather King Canute attitude. I did own one, although I had to whisper the fact behind my hand, and could see that we at BBC Television Centre had new and very serious opposition on our hands.

Of course, we were excited about our own programming and the return of *Match of the Day*. We made our own changes at the BBC, not least by introducing a new face to our team of studio experts. Liverpool's classy defender, Alan Hansen, who had enjoyed a glittering trophy-laden career at Anfield, had retired from the game and was looking for his next professional challenge.

He did a little bit of radio work for the BBC and television work for Sky and then I contacted him to see if he wished to take the business seriously and come on board as a regular member of the BBC football team. He talked it over with his family and friends and agreed to go forward with us.

Hansen had been an international at five different sports for Scotland in his youth, and his football career had been outstanding. We now had to convert that natural sporting ability into broadcasting.

As editor of *Match of the Day* I took him under my wing and explained to him what I looked for in a pundit. I told him as he settled into his new weekly role on the Saturday-evening show, in his early weeks I would watch the same match in the afternoon as he would and then discuss potential points of analysis which he could illustrate later with video-tape excerpts.

I explained to him that whilst I had watched a thousand football matches he had played in a thousand, and it was that experience I wanted him to bring to the screen. I wanted him to show me something in his analysis on *Match of the Day* that I wouldn't have spotted whilst watching the same game together earlier. Not actually rocket-science but just a sensible piece of advice to get things under way for the articulate Scotsman. Soon he was flying solo – and his accomplished career in broadcasting has been longer and more lucrative than his first one in football itself. And his accomplished BBC broadcasting career, which he brought to an end after the 2014 World Cup, had been longer and more lucrative than his first one in football.

He was even able to roll with the punches when he famously declared in 1995 "You can't win anything with kids" in response to an underwhelming performance early in the season from a youthful Manchester United. They did win something of course, the double! And have not stopped winning or reminding him since. Hansen had to hold his hands up.

The type of advice I gave Hansen in his early days I have often repeated since to other ex-professional sportsmen and sportswomen going into the broadcasting business. Too often they are given little or no advice or fail to seek out advice when they start out in what is essentially a completely different business to the one they have excelled in, a new business that they are not experts in. They need to think about what they want to say and how they want to say it – and these days also become au fait with the technical side of the business so they can be proactive in using visual aids to augment their analysis. Pundits should read the newspapers and study the internet, understand more clearly how issues are perceived and reported on – widen their perspective on the sport they played. And not 'hit every ball for six".

Otherwise, they end up the "latest" voice in their sport, not necessarily one of the best. Once the currency of their name runs out so too does their broadcasting career. It happens all too often.

"BRIAN, I'VE GOT PELE IN THE BACK OF THE CAR!"

While Sky Sports had started to change our perception of how football was covered, the early years of the Premier League still provided wonderful content for *Match of the Day*.

It was a great time to be editor of football's most famous programme and my Saturday working routine was part-work, part-fun as along with a tremendous team in London and a vastly experienced team of directors, commentators and camera crews out on the road we put together some belting shows.

My working day would start by watching *Football Focus*, making sure I was across all the latest football news and action. Then it was into the car and over to White City and the famous BBC TV Centre. The seven-floor circular building, which opened in June 1960, was the home of some of the BBC's greatest programmes and the studios at the weekend would often be buzzing. My destination when arriving at Television Centre was Room 2143 – an undistinguished windowless room with a few tables and chairs, but built into the far wall was a framework holding a number of television monitors and from about 2pm every Saturday they would come alive with pictures from all the grounds around the country hosting Premier League matches.

Desmond Lynam would bowl up, as would pundits Alan Hansen, Trevor Brooking or Gary Lineker. After an exchange of news about Big Berthas and small bunkers – golfing chat was an ever-present – attention would turn to the matches that were ahead of us.

Each pundit would be allocated a match to watch and Des and I would pick another two. The other games would be watched in tandem with our main selections and on many an afternoon, the evening's programme was turned on its head as one of the non-main selections punched its weight further up the running order.

Then, of course, there was the sweep, with everybody chipping in two pounds and making score predictions. The sweep became a key part of the afternoon's entertainment – as did the wine gums, dolly mixtures, sherbet bon-bons and liquorice all-sorts.

The next couple of hours were sheer heaven. Goals went in all over the place and cheers and boos followed as somebody nudged ahead of somebody else in the sweep. In a way the "London" end's work on *Match of the Day* was still ahead of us.

The afternoon was the business of the commentators, match directors, outside broadcast crews and stage managers who would combine their collective skills to deliver first-class coverage of the matches in front of them.

Behind the microphone were commentators like John Motson, Barry Davies, Clive Tyldesley, Jon Champion, the late Tony Gubba and Gerald Sinstadt.

Motson and Davies were part of the bricks and mortar of the show. The salt and pepper of the programme – brilliant exponents of a broadcasting art they made look and sound simple. And they were very different in style; Motty, the Roundhead, Barry the Cavalier. If there was a war between them, it was a civil war. Both naturally wanted the best matches, both could handle the best matches, but unlike on radio where a commentary double-hander plus expert was the norm, on television it was either commentator solo, or with an ex-footballer.

In a rather superior monograph on football on television published in 1974 by the British Film Institute, the craft of football commentary is dissected: "visual images by themselves are notoriously ambiguous and as Roland Barthes (a famous French-born structuralist and post-structuralist on the theory of culture) has pointed out, it is very rare for them to exist without some form of linguistic assistance".

But had Barthes ever had to describe a dull nil–nil draw in fading light on a freezing January afternoon from a gantry at the top of a rickety old stand only accessed by a ladder with a rung or two missing? Players' numbers totally obliterated by the stripes on their shirts and from the clinging mud on the pitch, and a huge stanchion masking the penalty area. Oh, and no loo! Motty and Barry had, and on many occasions no doubt. And, as pointed out earlier, in the 1970s and early 1980s they had both mastered the art of describing the detailed action again after a major goal or incident without the aid of a visual replay, which would be "painted" into the highlights package over their words later on in the production process.

Motson recalls: "The video-disc machine was used on horse racing and suchlike on a Saturday afternoon for *Grandstand* so the commentators on *Match of the Day* duty had to work without that aid. It was a really tricky thing to do. You had to remember the sequence of passes and suchlike before a goal had been scored and lay down the commentary without the aid of pictures, and also keep it to a length that was right for the edit that would be shown later that night on *Match of the Day*. And you obviously had to repeat that exercise several times in each half. Not easy."

The BBC was spoilt for choice, and often Motson's or Davies's day was spoilt by that choice.

Selecting a match commentator was never a perfect science and when doing the monthly rota it was always a matter of skill, judgement, pragmatism and then "get the hell out of town" because once distributed to the commentators you knew the phone calls would follow – and I could guess the order without fail based on my deliberations. I often think that they all looked at their colleagues' games before their own. I don't think. I know.

Bottom-line for me was that for a period the sheer experience, quality, and difference in broadcasting style, made the Motson–Davies bridgehead one that was impossible to breach by other broadcasters. Others had one outstanding "player", the BBC had a twin strike-force. They worked through a glorious period in BBC Sport, and whilst Motson eventually focused solely on football, Davies spread his commentary skills across a range of sports.

I may not have enjoyed having to shuffle the monthly rota much but I knew how lucky we were to have them both on board.

And they still are intrinsically linked. At the funeral of their long-term colleague and friend, Tony Gubba, in early 2013, Motty delivered a touching eulogy to his old mate, scooped up his papers and returned to his pew. When Barry got up to the lectern to give a bible reading he found his notes, which he had diligently left there ahead the service, had vanished. A brief, if hectic search, revealed them to have been scooped up by the departing Motty. The handover of the precious words had a touch of the Sunshine Boys about it – and Tony would, no doubt, have looked down and smiled.

The art of football commentary has changed over time. Then, with highlights football being the norm, one voice could carry the broadcast. Now, with the proliferation of live football, two voices are usually employed. It seems to have subtly changed the role. Niall Sloane, ITV's Controller of Sport, thinks it has.

"I think the commentator's role has changed a lot in the last 15 years. More live television with more considered expert opinion from co-commentators is turning the commentary into something more of a conversation rather than a strict description of what is happening. Drawing that balance sometimes has been hard and a new generation of commentators will also increasingly have to factor in the social media aspect. But primarily I want my commentator to have done their research and to understand what is unfolding. They then need to deliver that to the viewer in non-technical terms."

*   *   *   *   *

Spending a day with the *Match of the Day* team has become a regular request from newspapers and magazines down the years, and the BBC would try and accommodate those requests as much as possible. In my time as editor of *Match of the Day*, some reporters would want to go out on the road and see the match directors like John Shrewsbury, Alan Griffiths, Chris Lewis and the late Martin Webster "punch" the buttons while others wanted to see how the studio-end worked.

In one edition of the football magazine *Four Four Two* in November 1995, they wanted to see both ends of the operation and went to an outside broadcast at Everton and also to the studios at White City.

When we had members of the press in with us, everybody was a little more reserved, even the "what had happened in the week stories" became a little more mundane. Our visitors, however, were afforded all the luxuries – a "go" in the sweep, a bag of wine gums and a chance to go on the coffee run. However, they were there to get a story and rarely left without one.

On this November afternoon, reporter Paul Simpson sat and watched as the afternoon's activities settled down into their normal pattern, with the matches capturing our attention as goals flew in everywhere. Part of Vivien Kent, our studio producer's job was to feed the scores and scorers up to *Grandstand*, and also at the end of the afternoon to liaise down the talk-back with the match OBs to get the interviews for *Match of the Day*.

Vivien is now happily embroiled in the academic world and the field of anthropology and has travelled all over Africa to pursue her research projects. Back in the 1990s she was an intelligent toughie who could handle herself in what was then more predominantly a "man's world".

From the final whistle and full-time to the OBs standing down, perhaps 45 minutes later, it was always a bit of a trial of strength between the "London end" and the guys on the road at the outside broadcasts. One part of the team thought their day's work was complete while the other's had barely started.

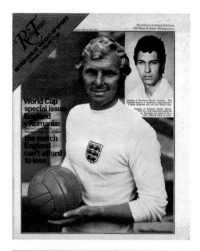

Top left and right: You pays your money and you takes your choice. The 1970 World Cup tournament is promoted in contrasting fashion by the *Radio Times* and *TV Times*.

Above: The famous 1970 ITV World Cup panel – Bob McNab, Paddy Crerand, Derek 'The Doog' Dougan and Malcom 'Big Mal' Allison, with Brian Moore and Jimmy Hill posing the questions – the panel were a smash hit with the viewers.

Left: Rome, 1977 and the BBC team celebrate Liverpool's first European Cup Final win with the Reds' Ray Kennedy (front right) and the magnificent trophy itself.

Left: The 1980s proved to be a challenging time for football and John Helm (pictured) commentated from Valley Parade on the day of the tragic Bradford City stadium fire.

Below and bottom: Two astonishing moments that help define why live televised football is simply so compelling: from 1989 (Arsenal) and 2012 (Manchester City) respectively.

"It's up for grabs now!"

"Agueroooo!!!"

Above: 'Nessun Dorma' – Pavarotti's spellbinding rendition of Puccini's aria from *Turandot* set the mood for BBC's Italia '90 coverage just perfectly.

Below: Up for it! Gazza in typically boisterous mood ahead of an appearance for Lazio on Channel 4's innovative *Football Italia*.

Above left and right: Thumbs up if you can get me an interview with Kinnear! Joe, Roy… any Kinnear. The story unravels in Chapter 19.

Below: "Do I not like that!" – Graham Taylor and his England colleagues provided the subject matter for a remarkable documentary on their fateful qualification journey for the 1994 World Cup.

Above: The goal that launched Michael Owen's career – England v Argentina in the 1998 World Cup. And an ITV audience that peaked at over 27 million also saw David Beckham sent off and England ultimately crashing out on penalties.

Below: Sky television commentator Martin Tyler does his last minute 'homework' in the familiar surroundings of the commentary box.

Left: More than 40 years on from his first commentary on *Match of the Day*, John Motson, 'Motty' remains one of the most respected and much loved figures in the history of televised football in this country.

Below: 'This is the one I came for!' Desmond Lynam alongside the European Cup ahead of the transmission of another big night of top-class Champions League action on ITV.

Above: ITV's *The Premiership* presentation team. There was no room on the photo shoot for the Tactics Truck!

Below: He has scored in the box and on the box. Gary Lineker making a big impression at the BBC's new home in Salford.

Above: Sky Sport's line-up of top-rated football experts. Jamie Carragher (second left) and Gary Neville (second right) take centre stage alongside Jamie Redknapp (far left) and Graeme Souness (far right).

Below: New boys BT Sport get things underway with presenter Jake Humphrey (far left) to the fore and expert summarisers (left to right) Michael Owen, Steve McManaman and David James.

Anyway, Viv would write down interview requests barked out by me and Des, and relay them to the match scanners parked outside the stadiums as soon as possible after the final whistle. It was always a little chaotic. On this occasion Joe Kinnear's Wimbledon had beaten Liverpool so one of the shouts that went out to Viv was, "get Kinnear and Vinnie Jones".

Football faces of the day were popping up all over the screens – and one of the production team read out loud from Viv's note as she had written it down. "Get me an interview with ROY Kinnear and Vinnie Jones." The room collapsed in laughter as her aide memoire was repeated back again.

The mood in the room was now uproarious and the hysteria continued when the reporter at the ground said he wouldn't be able to get Vinnie Jones but he would be able to get Kinnear. Seemingly the dead satirical comedian, Roy, not necessarily the recent controversial ex-Newcastle United Director of Football, Joe.

I looked at the *Four Four Two* reporter and said out of the side of my mouth, "I take it you've just got your headline."

"Yes," he said, trying not to choke on a wine gum, and boy, had he: six weeks later the magazine hit the news-stands and the feature on *Match of the Day* was preceded by a huge double-page headline screaming "GET ME AN INTERVIEW WITH ROY KINNEAR". Brilliant.

*　　*　　*　　*　　*

Despite Sky Sports Premier League output now gathering pace and a growing audience, *Match of the Day* still punched its weight and carried editorial authority and opinion.

Certainly Sir Alex Ferguson thought so. The legendary Manchester United manager had finally ended the Old Trafford club's wait for a league championship by landing the first Premier League title in 1993, followed by a second and then continuing onwards and upwards.

He, and other managers, would regularly be in touch with the BBC *Match of the Day* office – well, me actually – querying their club's position in the previous weekend's programme running order, a line said in commentary, or an opinion expressed in analysis. Certainly Ferguson felt that with me in charge of the programme and Alan Hansen as a studio expert and Mark Lawrenson shortly to follow suit, he was faced with a Liverpool-biased BBC team.

Somehow (!) that view got leaked to a national newspaper and, lo and behold, every member of the programme's management, presentation, punditry and commentary team were asked by the paper which team they supported. Strangely enough for a football show everybody did have their allegiances and were happy to reveal them (except for Barry Davies) but like me, the BBC team kept those allegiances well in check when carrying out their professional duties on a Saturday afternoon and evening.

Still, it all made life a little livelier. Of course, it didn't help that Manchester United didn't win the Team of the Year award during my spell in charge of the BBC's showpiece, *Sports Review of the Year*. The fact that I was only one vote in about a dozen cast for that particular prize didn't seem to count for much when Fergie looked at who was to blame. I was in his sights!

Later, long after I had left the Corporation, Fergie would refuse to cooperate with the BBC by denying them interviews following the broadcast of a documentary which aimed unsubstantiated observations at one of his sons and the football business.

Me? I made my peace with the Scottish managerial maestro when I joined ITV, who had built up a very good relationship with him, and then later when I was at the Football Association I found him generous with his time and thoughts if I contacted him on any wider football issue.

* * * * *

Alan Hansen, Gary Lineker, Trevor Brooking, Jimmy Hill and Terry Venables regularly kept Des Lynam company as the BBC football output's pundits in the early 1990s, but on one Saturday evening even they had to take a back seat when a last-minute guest entered TC5, the studio from which *Match of the Day* was broadcast.

It was early summer 1995, and Tony Gubba was in the presenter's seat for a programme that was carrying action from the Umbro Cup, a rehearsal tournament ahead of the following year's European Championships, which were to be held in England.

About half an hour before the show was due to go on air, the studio gallery rang and when I picked it up I heard a familiar voice. "Hi Brian, it's Peter Kenyon from Umbro here. Listen, I'm at the Hammersmith Broadway and I've got Pele in the back of the car. Do you fancy putting him on the show tonight?"

Now that's Peter Kenyon, as in Manchester United and Chelsea and Pelé, as in ...

And that's how, 20 minutes later, for me, the world's greatest-ever player walked on to the *Match of the Day* set and teamed up live in the studio with Gary Lineker and Jimmy Hill.

Big-hearted Jimmy, bless him, got Pele to sign dozens of scripts for his many and varied charity outlets, and the nation watched him do it – as "the chin" didn't realise he was on a wide camera two-shot when he was shovelling the yellow-tinged pages two-by-two under the great Brazilian's nose.

I also cherished the moment when I heard Jimmy say live on air when discussing a football point, "I'm glad Pele agrees with me." And Pele no doubt did, Jim!

* * * * *

If Pele is one of the truly genuine candidates for the title of the world's greatest-ever footballer, then the Argentinean pocket-battleship Diego Maradona is definitely breasting the tape with him.

Obviously his "Hand of God" goal colours some of our judgement but undoubtedly he had the touch of a genius when playing at the top of his game and he was certainly doing that when he helped his Italian club side, Napoli, to the Serie A title in the late 1980s.

Italian football was in vogue in the 1990s, and filled with the world's top stars, from Van Basten to Gullit, from Batistuta to Baggio, and Careca to Gazza. A smart move by Neil Duncanson of independent producers, Chrysalis Sport, meant UK viewers were about to see the world's best players in action every weekend – in a rather unlikely broadcast home, Channel Four.

Duncanson had filmed a Channel Four coaching series with Paul Gascoigne following his starring role at Italia '90. He followed it up with a documentary for ITV tracking Gazza's return from the serious self-inflicted injury in the 1991 FA Cup Final between Tottenham Hotspur and Nottingham Forest, just weeks before he had been scheduled to join his new team-mates at Lazio.

Gascoigne bemoaned the fact that nobody in the UK would see him play for Lazio. The Serie A broadcast contract with Sky Sports had run its course and, of course, they now had the FA Premier League with which to fill their boots, so they were open to offers.

Duncanson sold the idea to Channel Four's sports boss, Mike Miller, who then sold it to Channel Four supremo, Michael Grade. He loved the idea and while Sky were trumpeting their acquisition of the Premier League, he cunningly hit back with an advertising campaign for Channel Four based around the message "the world's premier league, free, live and exclusive".

The big stumbling block of gaining the FA's permission to show overseas matches live had been surmounted and *Football Italia* went to air. A live match on Sunday at 1pm, highlights on a Monday night and, of course, *Gazetta Italia*, presented by the adroit James Richardson, on Saturday mornings.

The first live match shown in a league noted for its low-scoring fixtures was a 3–3 draw between Sampdoria and Lazio, and despite Paul Gascoigne being out injured, it pulled in an audience of more than three million viewers.

With Richardson presenting, the likes of Ray Wilkins and Peter Brackley adding the commentary, and the "voice" of the show being no less than the great Kenneth Wolstenholme, Channel Four's Italian football scene was a smash-hit. They enjoyed three or four seasons of broadcasting success before the combination of English Premier League taking a grip on the home audience and the Italian FA rearranging the games to feature the better ones on Sunday evening, meant the Italian football bonanza had a slow and graceful slide into retirement. It was on Channel Four for a decade though. Not bad for an inspired hunch.

Duncanson would further make his name as executive producer of *The Impossible Job*, a documentary on England manager Graham Taylor's experiences during the 1994 World Cup qualifying campaign.

What, no doubt, started out as a film to witness first-hand managerial triumph and glory, ended up a banana skin of a show for the likeable England boss who on camera portrayed all the unique stresses and strains of being in charge of the national team. It was painfully compelling stuff and a coup for Crystal Palace fan Duncanson:

"It took nearly two years to film and I didn't tell the Chrysalis bosses we hadn't sold it. We knew we were getting priceless stuff. ITV famously said they would only buy it if England qualified for the World Cup. In the end, the head of documentaries at Channel Four didn't fancy it – and I cajoled the then Head of Programmes, John Willis, a Spurs fan, to come and see it. He watched in total silence, then turned to me and asked 'How much do you want?'"

The camera shots of Graham Taylor on the touch-line for the Holland vs. England match in Rotterdam as he saw the country's World Cup qualification chances go up in smoke were torturously memorable. As indeed was the phrase he delivered as his nerves were shredded: "Do I not like that!"

Chapter 18

The problem for Taylor was that the viewers did – in their millions. It became one of the most talked-about sporting documentaries ever made. Duncanson's persistence had paid off. "I still get on with Graham and he tells me he still gets asked about the film to this day."

In writing this chapter I thought I would watch a couple of minutes of the film to refresh my memory. Fifty minutes later I had watched the whole thing again – in total silence.

CHAPTER 19

REPENT YE NOT!

In late March 2013, England faced San Marino in a World Cup qualifying Group H game. A comfortable 5–0 home win for England at Wembley the previous October was duly followed up with an even more emphatic margin of victory – 8–0 – in the return fixture.

The Republic of San Marino lies on the Italian peninsula. It has a population of around 31,000 and a dreadful international football team.

As I am writing this, the team is ranked equal last in the FIFA rankings and has won only one of its 116 matches – and that was in a friendly against those other soccer "power-houses", Liechtenstein.

England's latest hammering of the plucky students, business consultants, accountants and gym owners of San Marino was live on ITV. And as presenter, Adrian Chiles, brought his agreeable quirkiness to the one-way traffic in San Marino, over on BBC they were having a right old song and dance.

The famous BBC Television Centre in London's White City, opened more than half a century ago, was finally closing its doors. The very building where so many of the nation's favourite programmes had been dreamt up, planned, produced and delivered was marking its last night.

This was the home of *Dr. Who*; *Only Fools and Horses*; *Dad's Army*; *Monty Python*; *The Generation Game*; *Grandstand*; *Multi-Coloured Swap Shop*; *Blue Peter*; *The Two Ronnies*; *Top of the Pops*; *The Morecambe and Wise Show*; *Wogan*; the *BBC News*; *Fawlty Towers*; *Parkinson*; *Strictly*

Come Dancing; oh, and a certain football programme called *Match of the Day*.

The list is endless; the building was alive with television creativity and vitality for more than half a century. And, bringing it all a lot closer to home, a couple of decades ago it was also witness to an unusual touch of television sporting controversy – and the unlikely San Marino were at the centre of it all.

Twenty years ago in November 1993, San Marino faced England on the night of the final round of World Cup qualifying group matches and the implications of the result between the two teams took on a very unusual complexion.

And that evening's experiences gave me my first taste of being the unlikely subject matter on both the front and back pages of the national newspapers. As would be the case many times subsequently, the problem was England – and on this occasion what I ended up doing with them.

A bit of context – England had made a pig's ear of qualification for the 1994 World Cup which was to be staged in the USA. Norway (who would go on to win the group) had taken three points off us – a draw at Wembley and a convincing home win.

Holland had matched Norway's results against us, including a crucial 2–0 victory over England in Rotterdam. A match that was later enshrined in a memorable documentary which captured manager Graham Taylor's touch-line histrionics, including his famous "Oh, do I not like that!"

Anyway, England needed a miracle in their last match against San Marino, who played in the Stadio Renato Dall'Ara in nearby Bologna.

One of football's smallest nations stood between England and their unlikely qualification for the Finals in the USA. Or, not quite.

England needed to beat San Marino by seven goals – perfectly do-able but they still needed Poland to beat Holland on the same night. Less likely, because the Poles were already eliminated and Holland, inspired by their win over England, were in no mood to make any unwarranted mistakes.

Thus the big BBC One peak-time programme, introduced by Desmond Lynam, and broadcast live from BBC Television Centre, was primed to cover England's death or glory night. But there was one significant twist: Wales – who hadn't qualified for the World Cup since 1958 – had got themselves in a strong position going into their final night's action.

This was a strong Wales side – Neville Southall, Dean Saunders, Ian Rush, Gary Speed and Ryan Giggs were in the line-up. Their match with Romania would be in the National Stadium, Cardiff Arms Park. Despite all the history and tradition that went before them, it was the round ball not the oval ball that was making all the headlines going into the game.

Wales needed to win by two clear goals to be certain of qualification but other permutations also existed for it to be a successful night for the would-be Welsh heroes.

Put simply, Wales needed to at least beat Romania at Welsh rugby's spiritual home to have a chance of qualifying for the World Cup ahead of their East European rivals. It was a genuine shoot-out and they had a genuine chance – and it was live on BBC Wales.

This gave me, as Editor of the BBC's football coverage, an opportunity, a problem and the odd sleepless night. Back of a fag packet maths told me that there could come a stage in the evening when England could no longer realistically qualify for the World Cup but Wales could.

Now, England playing live on television was always a ratings sensation back then – as it still is nowadays. So the theory that you would actually leave an England match while live on air to go and broadcast pictures from another game elsewhere – and expect nobody to notice, or have view about it – was to live on the naive side of life.

These days it would be the stuff of the ubiquitous radio phone-in, a social media meltdown, an internet frenzy – and with my head on a stick probably.

Anyway, ahead of the big night, I spoke to senior colleagues at the BBC about the likelihood of my calling for the "Big Switch" some time during the evening. They all nodded sagely, understood the logic, supported it and then made a mental note to be out of the country on that night!

Me, I played the scenario over and over in my head – not for the first or the last time when it came to England affairs – and constructed a programme running order that expected to cover San Marino vs. England from start to finish UNLESS ...

And so on Wednesday, November 17th, the huge early-evening audience was greeted to a set of opening titles dripping in irony, featuring Elmer Bernstein's marvellous *Great Escape* theme and close-ups of the England players who would have to seemingly tunnel under the barbed wire of Bologna to reach next summer in the States.

After all, this was a struggling England side with the inexperienced Andy Sinton and Stuart Ripley in its ranks. Although it was seasoned international, Stuart Pearce, whose inexplicable mistake gave San Marino, the ultimate team of no-hopers, an early lead in the match.

Well, a lead in 8.3 seconds to be exact. A misplaced back-pass by Pearce gave Davide Gualtieri a chance to score the fastest goal in World Cup history. The crowd of barely 2,000 people in a stadium capable of housing 45,000 celebrated the moment – and still are to this day.

The BBC's commentary team of John Motson and Trevor Brooking were trying to make sense of it in Bologna, whilst in the studio back in London, Des Lynam and his trusty side-kicks, Jimmy Hill and Terry Venables, were in shock. As I'm sure was the rest of the nation.

In the studio gallery, I was keeping an eye on another television screen that was bringing in pictures from the game in Poland and was not surprised to see Holland on top and in charge. Things looked bleak for England.

It was 22 minutes before Paul Ince got things on level terms for England, but Holland were ahead in Poland. By half-time, England were 3–1 up but Holland were not to be denied their place in the United States. They would go on to win their match 3–1 but well before that I had made the call I was dreading.

Taking England off the air, without the safety net of BBC Two – the Corporation always used the second channel to provide alternative entertainment to football on these nights – or a modern 'red button' service, was just this side of heresy and not a career-enhancing move. But do it, I did.

England were now winning 4–1, but Holland led in Poland, and in Cardiff, Wales were drawing 1–1 with Romania, Saunders scoring in the 61st minute to equalise Gheorghe Hagi's first-half goal.

In the studio gallery my attention was now totally focused on Wales's gallant fight for qualification.

Saunders's equaliser was quickly followed by the late Gary Speed taking a tumble in the penalty area after a tug from Romania's Dan Petrescu. PENALTY!

I grabbed the microphone linking our London BBC studio with Bologna.

"Motty, stop talking, we're leaving you in five seconds, Barry stand by, we're coming to you in three, two, one ..."

The pictures and sound from Cardiff were now on the BBC One screens in both Wales AND England. This was going to be the moment a brilliantly brave editorial decision by yours truly would bear fruit and capture Wales's moment of glory.

The ball was placed on the penalty spot.

*   *   *   *   *

Twenty-eighth in the FIFA rankings, with hundreds of telegrams wishing them well including those from the Prime Minister, John Major, Princess Diana and the Welsh rugby union team, Wales, under the leadership of Terry Yorath, were on the verge of a historic achievement.

And we were live on BBC One with the pictures. Brilliant move.

Wales missed the penalty.

Swindon's Paul Bodin, a spot-kick expert, hit the bar. In both football and rugby that was no score. The massive crowd in Cardiff Arms Park groaned and so did I, whilst selfishly cursing my luck.

Having made the call to switch to the Wales game, I couldn't go back to the match in Bologna – and every time I looked up at the pictures coming into the studio from Italy, England seemed to be scoring.

Not for the first or the last time in my career I felt the cold wind of leadership. It can be a lonely old place on occasions.

Wales still only needed one goal to qualify. "Come on Wales! Come ON Wales!"

They couldn't get it.

Indeed, they actually lost the game to an 83rd-minute winner from Florin Raducioiu. England's three goals in ten minutes had coincided with my cue to Motty that we were leaving them – but Holland were now ahead and playing out time in Poland.

Final whistles all around. England and Wales had failed to make it to the World Cup Finals in the USA. This was just three years after Bobby Robson's men had provided gigantic viewing figures with their unforgettable journey to the semi-finals in Italia '90 – but more of that later.

The studio debate led by Des, with Jimmy and Terry, reflected on England's disappointing campaign; raised the old chestnut of whether the game was more centred on club football than international football; and discussed that if Graham Taylor went – he did – who should be the next man in the England hot seat.

That man was sitting in the studio – Terry Venables – although I'm sure the irrepressible Jimmy Hill would, no doubt, have made a serious case for his own elevation. In fact, off camera and at a post-match dinner I seem to remember he did!

The studio discussion itself rounded off a disappointing night and the closing title music ended the evening's proceedings – and it wasn't the *Great Escape* theme!

Mind you I was about to need a great escape myself.

My switch from the England match to go live to the game in Cardiff had seemingly not won universal public approval. In short, the BBC switchboard was in meltdown.

By the time I got to the BBC Television Centre reception area, I was advised by a burly security guard to leave by a side-entrance as national newspaper reporters were being sent over to White City to speak to "the person who'd had the audacity to switch off England".

Wild estimates of the number of viewers' calls were flying about – I stopped listening at 20,000!

I had a few beers – which seemed an appropriate course of action to take – and went through the whole thing again in my head. Everyone around me was telling me I'd made the right call but none of them was carrying the can.

Mind you, in later years I would end up having tougher nights on "England" duty.

Two days later the furore had still not settled down – Graham Taylor was getting it on the back pages. I was getting it on the front.

The Times declared gravely: "Man who switched off England unrepentant." Its story said that there were so many calls of complaint coming through on the night of the game that the switchboard had "given up the ghost" before 9pm under the volume of calls.

The piece did emphasise that I had taken the decision in the full knowledge of my senior BBC colleagues, including the Head of Sport, Jonathan Martin, who helpfully acknowledged he was 100 per cent behind my decision.

A BBC spokesman insisted that "Mr Barwick had no regrets. We are sorry if we disappointed some viewers but 70 minutes into the England game it was clear that the miracle many had hoped for was not going to happen." And, of course, it didn't.

The Times piece went on, "The BBC refused to comment on the number of calls but one, at least, was not about football. Mary Whitehouse was objecting to sex scenes in *The Buddha of Suburbia*"!

Good old Mary. Not averse to taking the flak herself.

The debate raged on into the following week and the *Daily Mail* published a faux vote of thanks to "the man who pulled the plug on England".

"Dear Brian Barwick," wrote columnist Neil Wilson, "please accept my sincere thanks for the greatest service you performed in the nation's cause when you pulled the plug on England's football team.

"At the very least you deserve recognition in the New Year's Honours ... a plaque should be attached to the walls of Broadcasting House celebrating the moment when a man from the BBC cried, 'Enough, no more!'"

He did also make the point that a fledgling *Sky Sports* had been forced to stick with the England match and that the number of actual calls complaining had been in their hundreds not thousands.

Other columnists joined the debate. The orange-skinned television protagonist, Robert Kilroy-Silk, used his *Daily Express* column to beat up the England side by throwing praise my way for being "very brave" in sparing the public from any more torture watching the national team.

All very cute, and in some ways quite reassuring. But the piece I took most comfort from was written by Sir Paul Fox in the *Daily Telegraph*, a television grandee who had helped pioneer some of the small screen's most famous sporting brands – *Grandstand*, *Sportsview* and *Sports Review of the Year* among them. His take on it:

"Finally, were the BBC right or wrong to leave the England match with San Marino? It is worth recalling what it was like in Bologna; an eerie atmosphere, the game had gone flat, England were playing badly and the Dutch had gone ahead in Poland. At that moment it looked as though Wales would reach the final stages of the World Cup. Drawing 1–1 with Romania, they had been awarded a penalty.

"What would you have done? Stayed with the boredom of Bologna or go to the cauldron of Cardiff? I would have done exactly the same as Brian Barwick, the editor responsible for calling the change. The decision was the correct one."

Bravo, Sir Paul. The cheque is in the post.

Viewing figures on the night suggested that the audience were not all reaching for their phones – nearly 13 million people watched Bodin's missed spot-kick, a million above the average for the rest of the evening's proceedings.

Anyway, things moved on, another sporting crisis or controversy was always just around the corner. But it was still a reminder to me of how the public, the press, and all matters concerning the England team were lively bedfellows and the way we approached an "England" night was always going to be television big-time.

Oh, and also it is best to get a good night's sleep before the day of the broadcast.

CHAPTER 20

A DALLAS HIT AND A CHICAGO MISS

The climb to the two top floors of the innocuous-looking red-brick building on a steamy afternoon in a bustling American city had taken just five minutes – and nearly thirty-one years to make.

The building my BBC World Cup colleagues and I were walking around was a museum based in the former Texas School Book Depository on Dealey Plaza, Dallas. And as visitors we were retracing the story of the assassination of President John F. Kennedy back on November 22nd 1963.

It remains one of those unforgettable moments of contemporary history and as a nine-year-old boy I remember the news breaking live on television. Now we were able to actually look out of the window presumed to be the one from where the man who shot Kennedy, Lee Harvey Oswald, had actually fired his rifle.

Standing in the footsteps of history was a genuinely remarkable moment and even we, a group of well-travelled media men, recognised the greater significance of this particular visit.

A fascinating by-product of covering a global sport such as football for British television is that it has given people like me the chance to travel the world, several times over, and bring places that would have stayed just pictures in books to real life. I have worked in the USA, Brazil, Argentina, China, Japan, South Korea, South Africa, Morocco, Singapore, Malaysia, Australia and New Zealand as well as virtually every country in Europe during my time in broadcasting and sport.

I have always tried to make time to "see" the country and culture as well as do the job I've been sent out to do – and that afternoon in Dallas a week ahead of the start of the 1994 World Cup was a perfect example.

A group of BBC colleagues, including Desmond Lynam, Tony Gubba and Gerald Sinstadt, visited the site of Kennedy's assassination and drank in the drama of the moment. We also went behind the famous grassy knoll where it has been suggested other marksmen fired gunshots from and left unconvinced, like many others, of the single-sniper argument.

I always felt taking the World Cup to the USA would be a challenge. In essence, FIFA were just "renting the hall" as the American public were still pretty ambivalent about the sport – and would remain so even after the staging of the 15th FIFA World Cup there in June 1994.

Attending one match I asked an American police officer what he had thought of the previous night's game and he hit me with "Well, the game was tied and it went into over-time before the thing was settled with a penalty shoot-up." Yes, sort of.

No England, Scotland, Northern Ireland or Wales. The BBC and ITV had to home in on Jack Charlton's Republic of Ireland side, which had qualified for the Finals for the second successive tournament. Des and I had flown out to the USA to get a feel of the pre-tournament atmosphere. With no England in the mix, he was then going to present Wimbledon for the first fortnight and pick up the reins from Bob Wilson in the closing stages.

En route home we had stopped off in Florida to see the Irish team, captained by Andy Townsend, later to be an ITV Sport colleague. We were also invited to Jack Charlton's room, where we shared a laugh and a few glasses of draught Guinness from the keg especially set up in his room for visitors.

Whilst in Dallas we had joined our ITV counterparts at a broadcast forum and had a drink with their World Cup presenter, Matt Lorenzo.

He looked and sounded a little isolated from his colleagues and the tournament would prove a tough one for him.

The BBC had decided to link the World Cup from London given there was no England side, the time difference and the Wimbledon fortnight. Conversely ITV had decided to present from the States but their decision to do it from a windowless studio in Dallas, the "Dallas bunker" as it become known, proved to be a bad one. There was one big country out there but it was rarely seen on ITV.

The Opening Ceremony at Soldier Field, Chicago, ahead of the opening game between Germany and Bolivia had produced one of those classic much-visited YouTube moments as American soul diva, Diana Ross, stepped forward to take a penalty into an empty goal. She missed. The ball slipped apologetically wide of the posts which then magically split apart – the expected consequence of Ross's penalty crossing the line BETWEEN them. It was a clear case of "Ain't No Cross Bar High Enough, Ain't No Goal-Posts Wide Enough ..." Roberto Baggio would do a cover version later in the final itself.

The Irish got off to a flyer by beating Italy 1–0 in New Jersey and made it to the knock-out phase before coming up short against the Dutch.

Maradona had left the tournament in disgrace, after testing positive for drugs. It was a big story and at the BBC, controller Alan Yentob asked whether, along with all the other World Cup programming we were producing, we could put together a peak-time half-hour documentary for the following evening. We worked all through the night and Bob Wilson came in and impressively dubbed a soundtrack to it in one hit with just minutes to spare. Good piece of telly that.

This was a strange World Cup really. Both the BBC and ITV essentially changed main presenters mid-tournament, Desmond Lynam, Wimbledon duties complete, taking over from Bob Wilson, and clever wordsmith Tony Francis relieving Matt Lorenzo of some of his presentation duties.

It was also the World Cup that saw a changing of the commentary guard at the BBC with Barry Davies being chosen ahead of John Motson for the World Cup Final.

It made front-page news. Motson had done the three previous World Cup Finals and sixteen successive FA Cup Finals, and always got the nod over Davies when selection for the year's top game came around. This time the decision went the other way.

I was heavily involved in making the call – I knew it would hurt Motty, but I felt it was Barry's turn. I knew it was the right decision. I subsequently picked Barry for the following two FA Cup Finals as well.

I am sure there was elation in the Davies household back in the UK when he relayed news of the decision, whilst Motty's 49th birthday, the day he was told, was probably one of the most miserable birthdays he'd ever had.

This was a no-win, no-lose situation. In Motty and Barry, the BBC had two completely capable professionals. People tried to split them on style – they were different – but splitting them on quality was much tougher. And I still feel as lead live commentators on the BBC they have never been matched or replaced.

Des Lynam and I flew out to Los Angeles a couple of days before the final and we had a special treat on the eve of the match when we were invited by Pavarotti's record company to the Three Tenors' concert in the LA Dodgers Stadium, a reprise of their unforgettable pre-final event in Rome four years before.

I thought our seats would be pretty decent and wasn't disappointed as we passed rows and rows of Hollywood 'A' listers before sitting about four or five rows from the front.

As we, and our guests, Terry Venables and his wife, waited for the concert to start we were aware of a queue of people forming, and then walking along the front row of the auditorium, stopping mid-centre, staring at the people directly in front of them, and then moving on. Being curious, Des and I joined the queue, stopped mid-centre and stared, at three elderly men sitting quietly in the "best seats". Frank Sinatra, Bob Hope and Gene Kelly looked up as we passed them and I'm sure I heard Ol' Blue Eyes whisper to the other two, "Hey, Bob, who's that guy with Brian Barwick, he looks kinda familiar?" OK, perhaps not, back to the story!

Whilst England hadn't qualified for the tournament finals, we did play a major role in the final as the man who directed the global television coverage of the climax of the tournament, a rerun of the 1970 World Cup Final, Brazil vs. Italy, was English.

Teddy Ayling was a vastly experienced British OB director and had covered many huge sporting occasions, including five FA Cup Finals and twelve League Cup Finals, during his time at ITV Sport. In 1994, he went to work on the World Cup as a freelance match director and ended up emulating Alec Weeks as an Englishman who would bring football's biggest showpiece occasion to the world. Teddy takes up the story of how he got from Wembley to the Rose Bowl in Pasadena, just outside Los Angeles, California.

"I joined LWT and became a Trainee Director, Sport in 1977. Four days after joining the department, my mentor, Bob Gardam, took me to Wembley to watch him direct a schoolboys' international between England and West Germany. At half-time, he said he was going for a pee, leaving me to do the report into *World of Sport*. The next time I saw him was through the lens of camera three, whereupon he started out on a tour of all the cameras and reappeared at the end of the match to ask, 'Everything all right, heart?'

"In the 1994 World Cup, I was a member of a team of directors selected by rights-holding broadcasters and put together by EBU International headed by Manolo Romero. I was nominated by ITV and although I had actually left them before the World Cup I was kept on. I was allocated Palo Alto in San Francisco and the Rose Bowl in Los Angeles. In theory that represented 25% of the competition, but there was a proviso that after the quarter-finals, directors would be allocated on merit.

"My English crew consisted of five cameramen, George Gardiner, Mike Patterson, Ian Hembury, James Ramsay and Brian Parker, who remarkably had also been a cameraman at the 1966 World Cup Final at Wembley, with Jim Ramsey as VTR producer and Carole Chessun as vision mixer.

They worked to the top of their game throughout the tournament and the American crew who worked with them were also fantastic. They included a senior VTR operator who used to work NAKED. Not a pretty sight, and after the World Cup they moved on to the women's beach volleyball at Venice Beach. Rough life eh? Mind you I suspect he had to put his pants on for that one!

"Obviously on the day of the final there was a great deal of pressure on me, especially as we were in America where they didn't seem to do anything without shouting. Two things stand out in the build-up to the game. Firstly, a man from Colombian television interviewing me live asked, 'How would it feel if you missed the only goal of the game?' I told him the thought had never occurred to me. Well, it hadn't until that point! However, the second thing stopped me having any nerves about the game. The closing ceremony was to happen on the pitch BEFORE the game and we had to cover it. A Whitney Houston/Kenny Gee pop concert was not what I really wanted 90 minutes before the World Cup Final, but it did take my mind off it.

"As far as the match goes, I was able to give the UK commentators a feed of my talkback. It wasn't supposed to happen, for reasons of fairness to all, but I used the excuse that I wanted confirmation on close-calls to enable me to cut up the right close-ups. But despite being offered every facility to cover the game I could do nothing about a 0–0 draw which was ultimately won on penalties by Brazil."

Ayling's CV since that World Cup Final reads like an A to Z of top-class sport but amongst it all is the fact he was a man who directed a World Cup Final and a pop concert to a huge global TV audience – all on the same afternoon.

The 1994 World Cup was to prove a watershed moment for several television performers but perhaps most noticeably for Bob Wilson. He had been frustrated that despite anchoring the early stages of the tournament well for the BBC he had been moved aside when Des Lynam was free from working at SW19.

ITV felt they had an urgent need for an experienced football presenter following their troubles in the USA and ITV's Trevor East's persuasive tones helped take "Willo" from the BBC to ITV. I tried to persuade him to stick around at the BBC but actually felt he was right to make the move and enjoy the mantle of being "number one" – something his celebrated football career at Arsenal had afforded him every Saturday afternoon. Bob and I would meet up again as professionals sooner than either of us thought, and that would prove more of a rollercoaster ride.

While the BBC and ITV enjoyed their terrestrial tug-of-war at World Cups and European Championships, courtesy of a Listed Events legislation that would ultimately include the whole of those tournament's final stages, Sky Sports had to sit on the sidelines and watch. The television home of live Premier League football, and much more, they were no doubt frustrated by that legislative exclusion but they were making giant steps in terms of establishing themselves with the public during the "regular" season.

The action itself helped, especially when matches like Liverpool vs. Newcastle United in April 1996 came along. This was the season when Kevin Keegan's Newcastle team seemed destined to topple Manchester United's early supremacy in the Premier League. This game at Anfield, however, was a confidence-sapper for the Geordies as they finished on the wrong end of a seven-goal thriller.

Martin Tyler, who seems to have been at the microphone for all of Sky Sports' biggest football moments, has no hesitation in naming this one as the best Premier League match he has commentated on.

"That game between Liverpool and Newcastle United was a very special evening's viewing. The matched ebbed and flowed, and Anfield was at its noisiest. I remember we all finished the broadcast and knew we had been part of something very special. In fact we all stopped off at a pub on Queen's Drive on the way out of Liverpool to celebrate."

Two months later it was Euro '96 and the first time since 1966 that England had hosted a major international football tournament. Once again it was the BBC and ITV who went head-to-head and it was an event that really lit up the summer.

The BBC's coverage was masterminded by Niall Sloane, who was now the Corporation's Head of Football. A Manchester United fan, with a great working knowledge of both the game and broadcasting, he made some clever moves for Euro '96 including hiring the Dutch legend, Ruud Gullit, who had skippered his national side to European Championship victory in 1988. He was a big hit with the viewers, of both sexes, and his phrase "sexy football" became one of the motifs of the tournament.

As well as Des and Ruud in great form, Euro '96 would see the introduction of Gary Lineker as a mainstream football presenter. His football credentials were peerless, but aided by careful and caring guidance from his agent Jon Holmes, Gary had set his post-playing sights on being a television sports presenter. He had scored goals on *Match of the Day* and would later become the face of the programme and indeed BBC Sport's main man.

I admired Lineker's diligence and attitude from the off and wanted to help him. He was keen to learn and I asked him to come in on Friday afternoons after training and shadow a BBC Two programme called *Friday Sportstime*, then presented by Helen Rollason, who would sadly later lose her battle with cancer. Once the programme was over we would do a mock run-through of the programme again with Gary, this time, in the hot-seat. He would deliver the links, interview "stand-ins" and occasionally we would "fall off the air" to see how he would react.

A natural goal-scorer, not a natural presenter, but he would work at the craft and ultimately perfect it. With professionals like Sloane around him, Lineker was able to flourish – and indeed in Euro '96 he flew "solo" as a presenter in a big tournament for the first time. We were travelling on the BBC team coach between venues when he introduced his first show and a cheer went up as he got those important first few words out – and was off and running.

Along with some great and stirring football in Euro '96 there was a great and stirring song, "Three Lions", written by the Lightning Seeds' Ian Broudie and sung by soccer-mad comedy duo, David Baddiel and Frank Skinner. Their late-Friday-night BBC Two *Fantasy Football League* show had become cult viewing, a clever twist on established football formats but with inherently a fan's eye-view of the game. And at times it was bloody funny, with "Statto" commentator Angus Loughran in his dressing gown, the late Jeff Astle singing the programme out with an out-of-tune classic, and "Phoenix from the Flames" re-creations of famous old matches.

It was a refreshingly different show – and now its two stars, Baddiel a Chelsea fan and Skinner a West Bromwich Albion supporter, had a smash-hit record on their hands as well.

I had actually replaced Hansen and Lineker with them on one late-season edition of *Match of the Day*. They were in awe of being on the famous show but still showed their comic cutting edge when holding up scorecards for Everton's Anders Limpar's "dive" inside the penalty box during their analysis of the Merseyside team's relegation-survival match with Wimbledon.

The best game in Euro '96 was England's demolition of Holland by four goals to one. S.A.S. – Shearer and Sheringham – took the Dutch to the cleaners, with Paul Gascoigne also in sparkling form. It was ITV's exclusive match and they were chuffed to bits to have landed such a wonderful England performance and in the heart of peak-time too.

Ahead of the England games, the BBC and ITV would toss a coin to establish which broadcaster would handle the instant post-match interview. At one such toss, Ray Stubbs, the BBC's England reporter, called correctly against an ITV team member to secure the interview berth.

In the heat of the battle and with everybody working their nuts off, these seemingly inconsequential incidents took on a ridiculous level of importance, which may explain why ITV's likeable England reporter, Gary Newbon, stormed in and demanded a re-toss.

"That shouldn't have gone ahead without me," he said. "Everybody knows I am the official ITV tosser!" Well you said it Gary! He was even presented with a T-shirt, with the self-same message printed on it, in case he forgot it.

A penalty shoot-out win over Spain included a penalty kick from Stuart Pearce six years on from missing a vital one against West Germany in Italy. This time Pearce scored – and his resultant celebration remained, like Gazza's "guzzling" celebration after scoring against Scotland, one of the images of the tournament.

And so, to England vs. Germany at Wembley again. The two giants, head-to-head again. Oh, and England and Germany as well. At the end of coverage of the other Euro '96 semi-final between France and the Czech Republic, Desmond Lynam looked ahead to the evening's big match. "I'd be surprised if you didn't watch it on the BBC," said Des, with wry eyebrow suitably cocked. "Frankly I'd be disappointed."

This time, as before, the viewers voted with their remote control and voted for the BBC with suave Des and the team. The match itself went to penalties and once again England came up the wrong side of the shoot-out. England's penalty shoot-out failures would be a depressingly familiar summer routine, repeated more often than a *Top Gear* episode on Dave.

The UK television audience for the match was huge: during the penalty shoot-out the combined audience was gauged to be 26.2 million, with a remarkable 19.8 million of them tuned to the BBC. The average viewing figure across the match was 17.4 million for the BBC and 6.2 million on ITV.

Football had come home, had really crackled and fizzed, but had then left our shores with the trophy.

CHAPTER 21

AN UNEXPECTED TURN OF EVENTS

Whilst the English national side would continue into the next decade and beyond to try to land a major trophy, the English club game was enjoying a popularity spurt – or at least the top of it was.

The money raised from Sky Television's determination to stay ahead of the new broadcasting game meant football's top table was being well fed and watered – and increasingly with dishes of a continental flavour. Players were being drawn from all over the world to play in the FA Premier League. England was fast replacing Italy as the destination point for the travelling star.

Foreign players arrived on these shores in search of a new football experience, and a hefty pay packet. They were a mixed bag: some old lags looking for a final big pay cheque, some cheap and cheerful sorts who would ensure equivalently talented English players kept the bench warm and some absolutely world-class stars.

Eric Cantona and Peter Schmeichel at Manchester United, Dennis Bergkamp at Arsenal, Jürgen Klinsmann at Spurs, Zola and Vialli at Chelsea – just some of the names that lit up the Premier League every weekend in its early life. They added colour, skill, controversy, breadth and beauty to the English game and the crowds and television viewers responded positively to their arrival.

Still, there was room as well for some good young English talent to emerge amongst the continental fare. Indeed, there were two new players, as English as fish and chips, and pie and mash, coming along who would make a huge impact on the game – both here and the world over.

David Beckham would start the 1996/97 season in a simply astonishing way. Already a league and FA Cup-winner with Manchester United, he hadn't made England's Euro '96 squad, but the gently spoken Eastender, who would become a soap opera all of his own, scored a goal on the opening day of the season that would have graced any game, any time.

Beckham scored from *inside* his own half in the champions' opening fixture away at Crystal Palace. This wasn't a goalkeeper's punt from his own penalty area that catches the wind or a heavy bounce to beat his rival at the other end. This was a look-up, spot where the 'keeper is standing, and launch a shot that defied logic. Beckham, until then just another player in a galaxy of stars at Old Trafford, had put down a serious marker. The rest is sporting and celebrity history.

Fast forward to the end of the same season and Liverpool were trailing 2–0 in their penultimate game, a midweek fixture away against Wimbledon. With less than 20 minutes to go, the Reds introduced a slight, 17-year-old striker called Michael Owen to a waiting football world. Within a few minutes he had scored his first senior goal – a typical Michael Owen goal, involving speed of thought, speed of foot and a cool finish. Those there, like me, took note.

Within 15 months, Beckham and Owen would both play key parts, albeit in very different ways, in a match that would create television history – and allow me a small professional landmark of my own.

The 1997/98 season had seen a new broadcast pattern in the football business with ITV adding FA Cup and England internationals to its investment in the UEFA Champions League which was finally maturing into a solid peak-time product. But Sky had really been the winner in the latest round of pitch and toss. They critically secured first choice of the live FA Cup and live coverage of England.

The BBC now had its *Match of the Day* brand to house both Premier League and FA Cup highlights. The oldest cup competition in the world was now scheduled in a rather unwieldy way for the viewers across three channels.

Channel Five were also now on the scene and would spend the next decade or so skirting around the edges of the big stuff by niftily purchasing the rights to UEFA's secondary competitions and making "male-skewed" decent Thursday nights out of them. The new channel had made an extraordinary debut in big-time football when purchasing the rights to a World Cup qualifier between Poland and England, played in May 1997, and giving the match a two-and-a-half-hour build-up.

The studio set was modelled on a sports bar, and one of the presenters was a former topless model, Gail McKenna. She joined Dominik Diamond, radio broadcaster Jeremy Nicholas, and racing expert Brough Scott in a team line-up as incongruous as Graham Taylor's England selection against Sweden in Euro '92. The programme took a critical hammering but had done its commercial job by bringing in a huge audience for the new kid on the block.

By the early autumn of 1997 I was getting itchy feet at the BBC. I had been there 18 years, loved just about every minute of it, excepting that first traumatic 45 minutes in the video-disc, but was now being courted by other broadcasters. I had risen to the Corporation's Head of Sport in their Production Division and had been narrowly pipped when running for the vacant BBC One Controller post.

That near-miss alerted ITV, who under the new dynamic management duo of Richard Eyre and David Liddiment were looking to go places with a team of senior players they were to hand-pick from both inside and outside ITV. My name was logged against the Controller Sport job.

Liddiment, whom I had got to know during his brief spell in BBC Light Entertainment, called me and we arranged to meet in a local Thameside pub. He was late, about an hour late, but that 60 minutes had almost clinched the deal in his absence because as I awaited his arrival I was glued to the television in the corner of the bar on which a football match was being transmitted.

No ordinary match, it was Newcastle United vs. Barcelona in the group stages of the UEFA Champions League on ITV. The game is best remembered for Colombian Faustino Asprilla's fabulous hat-trick, complete with celebratory somersaults, in Newcastle's dramatic 3–2 win over the Catalan giants, Rivaldo et al. The atmosphere in the stadium was pumped up and it looked like big-time telly. I found myself thinking I wouldn't mind a bit of that. A few pints later, David and I had put the rudiments of a deal together and when the commercial company also offered me the extra role of Director of ITV "New" – their first new channel offering since 1955 – they had me hooked. ITV "New" was to become ITV2 – we would launch in late 1998, by which time ITV Sport had enjoyed the biggest year in its history.

One of my early long lunches was with one of ITV Sport's senior executives, Jeff Farmer. A former national newspaper journalist, Jeff was a wise soul and became a great mate during my time at ITV. He told me over the second bottle of red that he was off to the World Cup draw in France the following week and would keep things bubbling along until I joined him a couple of months later.

I actually watched the World Cup draw itself in the same pub with Scotsman Bob Patience, the man behind the *Saint and Greavsie* show, who sadly died in March 2013. He kept shaking his head and saying "I canna believe we are here watching this in the pub and in a few months you'll be in charge of a huge chunk of it." It was a bit incongruous but there you have it – that's gardening leave for you. Actually my loyal assistant Marianne, who had decided to follow me to ITV, went one better. She spent her free time travelling across New Zealand and met her future husband, Mark, who works in the Belgian diplomatic service. They are now the parents of three lovely daughters. All of this, because of Tino Asprilla's hat-trick – well sort of!

*　　*　　*　　*　　*

The broadcasters' meeting to split the matches between BBC and ITV after the draw for the recent 2014 World Cup Finals in Brazil seemed a relatively friendly affair. All sorted out in a day, albeit a long day, with both sides seemingly happy with their lot. It was a very civilised and professional affair by all accounts, and certainly very different when compared to the many "battles" down the decades when trying to "split" the matches between two arch rivals. Many of those meetings were the stuff of legend (or bar talk at least!).

On many previous occasions, following a World Cup or European Championship draw, BBC and ITV would have a meeting prior to returning to the UK to see if they could find an equitable split of matches. Each broadcaster had made a quick call back to base to see if the channel chiefs or schedulers had any preferences now that the completed draw had brought the competition to life.

Nothing was ever resolved at the first meeting but it set certain hardy annual positions. The BBC would want to do every England match but was happy to go head-to-head with ITV; it would also want the best Scotland match, the best non-England quarter-final, the best semi-final etc. ITV would demand its fair share of the best matches based on the fact it had paid half of the UK rights costs. It too would want its share of England matches, but it wanted them exclusively. It would also want some certainty in its choices because it would be selling valuable commercial air-time ahead of the tournament.

The first couple of meetings would invariably involve a bit of posturing and feather-ruffling. Away from the sharp end of the negotiations, the sports executives waiting to book facilities would be going bonkers. "We are going to miss all the bloody deadlines." Whilst somewhere else channel chiefs would make discreet phone calls between the organisations to try and use the football choices to secure other scheduling favours. "If I let you have Peru versus Bulgaria will you go easy on our *Badger Watch* during April?"

My former BBC boss, Jonathan Martin, told me he used to clear the kitchen floor and cut up paper strips with the names of the teams on and work out how the whole tournament would be scheduled. And being a clever bloke he invariably got it right – unless his beloved pet dog returned to "Chez Martin" after a long walk in a muddy field, slipped across the kitchen floor and sent England out of the quarter-finals. Who needs a fortune-telling octopus!

There was always a ceremonial signing off of the broadcast schedule and then at an appointed time the respective PR departments would spin away to their hearts' content.

Of course, it didn't always go according to plan because the odd result would go an unexpected way and throw the likely match schedule. And such a thing happened in 1998 and ITV ended up the big winners.

My trip out to France ahead of the tournament to join my ITV colleagues already there proved a little embarrassing as I seemed to catch the plane with all the BBC World Cup team on board. Des and I shared a joke but even that was a little strained. Odd moment really.

ITV's theme music was that classic hit "Rendez-Vous" from king of the laser light concert, Frenchman Jean Michel Jarre. He came over to London to re-record a shortened version of the track with dance fusion band, Apollo 440. Rick Waumsley, a senior executive on ITV's World Cup coverage and I went to watch them in action in the recording studio.

JMJ (as we got to call him!) tried it a few times and came out to discuss it with the lads from Apollo 440, and then, showing great courtesy, with the two of us. Rick, a keen musician, discussed crotchets and quavers; I just ripped a page from a memo pad on the mixing desk and drew a straight line going upwards. "Qu'est-ce que?" asked the puzzled Frenchman. "Le fin de la musique ... we need it upbeat." I just about left off "mate" at the end of the sentence.

Anyway, the multi-award-winning musician gave it one withering look and with an exaggerated Gallic shrug wandered back into the studio. Within a minute he had delivered the perfect cut-down of his famous track and as he reached the climax, he waved the piece of paper with one hand and delivered a big upbeat finish on the keyboards with the other. I slipped out of the studio quietly.

Before the matches had been split between the broadcasters, Des Lynam had written a letter to the senior management of the BBC imploring them to get tough with ITV in the tournament share-out. Noble of Des to do that, and eagerly supported by the BBC World Cup team, but bigger "games" were always in play. In the deliberations, ITV had secured a live England group game, against Romania, and then their last-16 match if they got through to the knock-out stages. All things pointed to that match being between England and Croatia in Bordeaux. That over, the BBC planned to drive the England bus forward into the latter stages and claim huge audiences. Unfortunately their plans came asunder when England surprisingly lost to Romania in the second Group G game. A win over Colombia secured them a safe passage but in SECOND place in the group. This set up a last-16 tie between England and Group H winners, Argentina, in St Etienne, in peak time on a Tuesday evening ... exclusively on ITV.

England vs. Argentina, 12 years on from Diego Maradona's "Hand of God" goal, turned into a footballing classic. Michael Owen scored a wonder goal, the match switched from end to end, David Beckham got sent off for an act of petulance, the match went into extra-time. Sol Campbell scored what looked like a perfectly good goal only to see it rubbed out, and then, as would often prove the case, a penalty shoot-out defeat saw us dumped out of the tournament in the most dramatic fashion possible. This time Paul Ince and David Batty were the twelve-yard fall guys.

It was a piece of pure sporting theatre, an edge-of-the-seat drama played out in four halves (and a penalty shoot-out). It completely emptied the streets and pitched the nation's emotions left, right and centre. At its peak the match attracted an audience of more than 27 million viewers, with an average of 23.8 million. These were simply huge viewing figures. The highest audience figure on ITV that year – indeed one of the biggest audience figures on ITV any year!

At ITV we had mixed emotions, disappointed as we were, of course, by England's early exit from the World Cup at the hands of yet another penalty shoot-out disaster and against one of our most famous foes. The following morning, however, we got the viewing figures and simply couldn't take them in. They were off the scale. Our press release following the publication of the audience figures sensitively reflected both sides of that emotionally epic evening's viewing.

Meanwhile over at the BBC's elegant World Cup headquarters on top of the French Automobile Club offices on the Place de la Concorde in Paris, there was the sound of teeth gnashing and heads banging. Through no fault of their own, the BBC team knew the World Cup had changed overnight from a national obsession to a major football tournament – as was always the case when the home sides gradually exited the tournament one by one. That has never changed. When England leave the tournament, it's like pricking a balloon. Certainly for the "general" viewers, who found themselves caught up in the hype and hysteria of the whole thing despite not watching football from one World Cup to the next.

The rest of the tournament still did really impressive viewing figures, and the BBC delivered it in exceptional style from its studio in Paris. But without England, the television audiences were more in line with a good *EastEnders* or *Coronation Street* plot-line than a Royal Wedding.

In 1998, the World Cup Final between Brazil and France in Paris marked the end of the BBC and ITV careers of two great mates, and two iconic television football men, Jimmy Hill and Brian Moore.

Jimmy would carry on his career at Sky as a presenter and pundit on the *Sunday Supplement*, a weekly round-table debate with top national newspaper football writers, while Brian would settle for a quieter life.

Jimmy didn't want any great song and dance made of his last appearance as part of the BBC team. "I'm not retiring" was his position, so sadly the BBC was not able to make the type of on-screen farewell his long and remarkable service demanded. These days 18 months on Breakfast Television gets you your own "best bits" loop when you part company. Jimmy's could have lasted for hours.

"Mooro" settled down for his last commentary knowing he had made a lasting impression on the British public and also that in the tough television world of dog-eat-dog he was universally liked. When we held a farewell function for him a couple of months later the "industry" turned up for him, whatever team strip they wore in their day job.

I was privileged to host that event for Brian and also made sure I was in the commentary area close by him when he put the microphone down after his final commentary. I had only worked with him for seven months but our paths had crossed many times over the previous 20 years.

On the day of the World Cup Final itself, I had started my day in the Northamptonshire countryside at Silverstone, like tens of thousands of others, including colleagues, Jim Rosenthal, ITV's Formula One presenter, who had also worked on the channel's football coverage in France, and master technician, Roger Philcox. We were at Silverstone for ITV's coverage of the British Grand Prix – another of the channel's five-star sports contracts of the time.

As soon as the programme had ended the three of us were hurtled across the old wartime airfield as pillion riders to a helicopter that was on stand-by to get us across to an airfield in Oxfordshire, where a small plane was ready to take us across the Channel to Le Bourget Airport just outside Paris.

I must admit, as I sipped a glass of ice-cold champagne mid-flight, with my shoes off, I did think back to my old maths teacher who had said if I didn't buck my ideas up I'd end up on the road to nowhere. Or, as it turned out, on a private plane to Paris. "Another glass of champagne before we land, sir?" "Yes, I could probably handle it ..."

When we landed in the outskirts of Paris a car picked us up and ferried us swiftly to the Stade de France where the final was being held. Thankfully the roads were absolutely deserted because everybody was indoors to watch France in the final. We made it to our seats just in time to soak up the back-end of the pre-match atmosphere and wish "Mooro" well. Close by was his friend and colleague, BBC's John Motson, and Guy Mowbray, at 26, a young man commentating for Eurosport. He would eventually take up the mantle of BBC's World Cup Final commentator in 2010.

The big story for all the commentators to chew on pre-match emerged when the team-sheets showed Brazilian superstar, Ronaldo, who had only really played in patches in the tournament, had been left out of the side. But no, a later team-sheet showed Ronaldo was now back in the line-up. The sniff was that the Brazilian commercial sponsors had made their displeasure at Ronaldo's absence clearly known and suddenly a troublesome left ankle injury had been passed fit.

It mattered little in the end as France steamed into a two-goal lead by half-time, courtesy of two Zinedine Zidane headers. During the interval, I hurtled off to a stadium loo for a pee. Fine, other than when I came to leave the lavatory I suddenly realised it didn't have a handle on the INSIDE of the door. I was well and truly locked in. I could hear a range of international voices excitedly talking about the first half. I shouted, but to no avail. I was just another voice. As time passed, the number of voices got fewer and fewer, and quieter and quieter, until I could hear nobody. I guessed the second half was just about to start. Without me.

It was at this point I could hear my old biology teacher saying that if I didn't buck my ideas up one day I would find myself locked in a football stadium lavatory during the second half of a World Cup Final ...

Motorbike, helicopter, jet plane, chauffeured car, best seat in the house and now locked in the loo. I was trying to work out an excuse to my colleagues as to why I hadn't showed for the second half – "The commercial sponsors didn't want me ..." – when I heard a man whistling outside the locked toilet door. I shouted in my best French, "Aidez-moi!" And to my eternal delight, the guy, who turned out to be a stadium cleaner, used a "master key" to release me from my half-time hell.

I know just how the Count of Monte Cristo must have felt after his long stay in the dungeons finally came to a close. I wandered back to my seat in the commentary area. During a break in play Brian Moore looked across at me and mouthed, "Where have you been?" I just looked back and mouthed, "Checking out that Ronaldo story." He nodded and got back to describing the action, including the final French goal, made and scored by Arsenal, Vieira to Petit – 3–0. I settled back and watched the rest of the final in silence, knowing that at half-time, life had just put me back in my place. C'est la vie.

CHAPTER 22

"DES OFF TO ITV. BLOODY HELL!"

Anybody who has watched football for any length of time instinctively knows when a match has run its course. When whatever the score currently is, will, in fact, end up the final score. When the elastic in a game has snapped and the players are treading in treacle.

Oh, and then there is the UEFA Champions League Final between Bayern Munich and Manchester United on a balmy – and barmy – night at Barcelona's Nou Camp Stadium on May 26th 1999. Remember it?

Mario Basler put the Germans ahead six minutes into the match. The next 80 minutes or so were sterile, and the match was apparently running down its own clock. Bayern had two late chances to finish United off but fluffed their lines. The game just started to turn United's way but time was running out – and fast.

Then we entered injury-time, three minutes of it displayed on the illuminated board, and football folklore took over.

Dwight Yorke and Andy Cole had been Sir Alex Ferguson's first-choice strikers for the match but substitutes Teddy Sheringham and Ole Gunnar Solskjaer were now both on the pitch and were destined for injury-time glory.

"Can Manchester United score, they ALWAYS score."

Thirty-six seconds into injury-time, Sheringham turned the ball into the net from close range following a corner from David Beckham. "SHERINGHAM!" United were dramatically level.

"NAME on the TROPHY!" The game was now very much swinging United's way.

Gary Neville forced another corner just 98 seconds on from United's equaliser. Beckham sent it over again.

"Is THIS their moment?"

This time it was the other substitute striker, Ole Gunnar Solskjaer, who scored a typical poacher's goal – a simply priceless poacher's goal, again from close range. "AND SOLSKJAER HAS DONE IT!" Cue hysteria in the Nou Camp.

"Manchester United have reached the PROMISED LAND!"

ITV's senior football commentator Clive Tyldlesley's description of those unforgettable few minutes still resonates when you hear it. His commentary on what lay before him was accurate, evocative, clear and controlled. Sir Alex Ferguson's post-match reaction was understandably a little more earthy – "Football, bloody hell!"

For ITV, and Clive Tyldesley, these were heady days. The 1998/99 season saw 15 of the top 20 sports television audiences come from ITV's live football output with Tyldesley at the microphone.

For the commercial channel it was a deserved moment of exhilaration. It had jumped on board the UEFA Champions League excursion at its embarkation point in 1992, and then waited seven years to enjoy a British club in the final.

ITV had bought into it in 1992 as it had needed Champions League football to keep itself in the game. Over time the channel would become synonymous with broadcasting football from Europe's top table. And even when Sky came on board, watching Champions League football on ITV was still the natural order of things. Clive Tyldesley remembers the formative years.

"The Champions League wasn't too kind to ITV in its early years – Rangers made an impact in the first year but English teams, like Blackburn Rovers, struggled in the competition. In fact they all did, and so when Manchester United got to the final in 1999 and then won it, and in such a dramatic fashion, you felt ITV had earned the right to enjoy the moment. And over the years the viewers have come to expect the Champions League on ITV as part of how they watch their football, and have watched it with us even if they've had a choice of channels. And, we've been able to bring them some very memorable occasions."

Like Istanbul. The Champions League Final of 2005 will go down as one of the greatest games of all time, and perhaps the greatest comeback in a major match. Liverpool, three down and lucky to be only three down to AC Milan in as one-sided a first half as you would ever see, conjured up a comeback that defied belief. Tyldesley again:

"It was an incredible match. Liverpool had a very special 15 minutes or so early in the second half, but AC Milan could have already been out of sight. And also they could have won the game after Liverpool's comeback. If ever there was a game won by one man it was that night. Steven Gerrard popped up in three positions that night – including a stint at full-back – he was totally inspirational and it was fitting he was the man who lifted the trophy."

The idea to turn the European Cup into something more substantial and perhaps less open to an early exit or knock-out surprise was the brainchild of two marketing executives, Klaus Hempel and Jurgen Lenz of TEAM Marketing. UEFA's President Lennart Johansson and General-Secretary Gerhard Aigner also added their support and persuasive tones.

With the standardising of kick-offs in European football's senior competition; the dressing of the stadium; the centre-circle sponsors mat; the "star ball"; all upgrading the level of television coverage, which varied dramatically across Europe. This, coupled with the addition of a classy pre-match anthem, turned an already great competition into one that is perhaps less open to surprises and that chugs along at a moderate speed up to Christmas, but produces massive match-ups in the knock-out stages from February onwards.

Given its entry point is no longer necessarily being a country's football champions, the "race for fourth place" has become a hardy perennial in English football. The "Champions League" title stretches a point, but for UEFA, the competition's season-by-season entrants, and the commercial partners and broadcasters, it has become a top-quality sporting product, played out in peak time, with brilliant multi-camera coverage, and bringing the best footballers in the world to our screens on a regular basis. Players with whom the audience are now hugely familiar.

The format has also given some "security" to those big European football institutions which have recruited the game's biggest stars – not least through some of the income that has flowed into their coffers via the Champions League. An early exit in a two-legged first-round "shock" may be what the purists and romantics call for, and it is something that perhaps would improve their faltering second competition, the Europa League, but in their primary asset, sporting and commercial pragmatism demands a safety net and the group stages provide that.

They still don't guarantee progress as reigning European champions Chelsea and Premier League title-winners Manchester City learnt to their cost in 2012/13. But there is a level of security for those companies investing heavyweight money in commercial and broadcasting contracts. Richard Worth, who had cut his teeth as part of LWT's crack football squad, became one of the most influential executives at the Swiss-based TEAM headquarters.

"It was about bringing a consistency for broadcasters. They were planning their peak-time schedules months ahead and needed some idea of what they would be dealing with in terms of live football. It must be remembered that before the Champions League were able to put all the rights in one 'basket' it was very difficult for a broadcaster to follow the competition from beginning to end. The concept for the Champions League was high class and high quality. We were also very keen on making sure that the actual broadcast coverage was of a high and consistent standard. And we were able to develop long-term partnerships with major broadcasters. Of course it wasn't all straightforward; in the early days, for example, it was a devil of a job to get the newspapers to call the competition the Champions League as they still referred to it as the European Cup. Over time we got there."

ITV would lose their broadcast monopoly of covering the UEFA Champions League when Sky Sports bought their way into owning the lion's share of the contract, but with the matches spread over two separate nights, and over free and pay television, there was room for both broadcasters to manoeuvre. Sky would use the breadth of their service to deliver an enticing proposition where every ball kicked was available to the viewer other than the marquee game ITV would concentrate on. Both broadcasters would benefit from an improved performance by English clubs in the competition and following Manchester United's dramatic win in 1999, Premier League clubs were involved in seven of the subsequent 13 finals, including providing both finalists, Chelsea and Manchester United, in the 2008 final staged in Moscow. That match finished dramatically in a penalty shoot-out with the Reds coming out on top – four years later Chelsea would deliver more spell-binding TV moments with a penalty shoot-out win of their own against Bayern Munich in the German team's own stadium. Penalty shoot-outs might divide football people on their virtues in settling a result but for TV executives they are the bee's knees. The audience always builds to a climax in this sporting game of sudden death.

The final itself has also been staged in England three times in the last 11 years, once at Old Trafford in 2003, and twice at the new Wembley Stadium, in 2011 and 2013. It was also held up in Glasgow in 2002, when Real Madrid's Zinedine Zidane scored one of the greatest goals ever scored in a final, or any other match come to that. Match director, ITV's John Watts:

"For that match, we had 22 cameras in the stadium and the EVS digital replay system which meant we could replay from all 22 cameras. When Zidane hit that wonderful goal, we had 12 great replays; the best was from the reverse low six-yard-box camera which caught the action perfectly. The cameraman, Ronnie Seeth, managed to stop his pan as the ball burst the back of the net, which was a brilliant piece of camerawork."

The Champions League really kicked on and made the other European competitions look second-best. The BBC seriously looked at ways it could join the party but such was the heavyweight overt and on-screen commercialism wrapped around the Champions League that it always seemed a stretch too far when a public-funded state broadcaster with a charter and a licence fee to protect looked at the wider picture.

And the broadcast rights for the Champions League changed hands in a truly significant way in the autumn of 2014 when BT Sport agreed an exclusive headline-grabbing deal with UEFA for a colossal £900 million to wrest away the live rights from Sky Sports and ITV from 2015.

The free-to-air commercial broadcaster, that has been with the competition since its inception, will still transmit highlights but its big midweek live European football "event" would seem to be a thing of the past.

* * * * *

"Will the members of the jury now please retire and consider their verdict."

Along with another 11 men and women, all no doubt good and true, I solemnly got out of my seat in the jury box and left the court-room to reflect on the past two days of evidence, and find the accused guilty or not guilty of the criminal charges laid before us.

This was August 1999 and I was doing my public duty by performing jury service. It is an important part of being a citizen but on this occasion, during the long hours of waiting for my name to be called to be part of a jury panel, it also provided me with plenty of thinking time as I helped play my part in one of television's more spectacular manoeuvres.

David Liddiment, ITV's Director of Programmes, and I had decided it was time the best live peak-time football – the UEFA Champions League – should be anchored by the person universally acknowledged, at that time, as the best presenter on British television.

We had decided to try to get Desmond Lynam to leave the BBC and join ITV.

This was going to be tough. Although Desmond was a good mate of mine, we had always treated business as business and friendship as friendship, and when I had left the BBC to join ITV we were both reconciled to the fact that our "business" days were over.

Perhaps it was the scale of and reaction to Manchester United's victory in May that persuaded Liddiment and me to go for it – and so we set off to see Des at his waterfront home near Brighton.

Des was warmly welcoming but he guessed we hadn't come around for afternoon tea at Sussex by the sea. I talked football content and presentation, David talked about ITV's ambition and money.

We had the Champions League, live football in peak time, which I knew would appeal to him. I also suggested that at ITV he would be "more lightly raced" as any thoroughbred should be. I thought that would resonate with him.

Those were persuasive arguments, as was the size of the reward for coming over to ITV. As became clear when Liddiment revealed "the numbers".

On the way back to London, Liddiment asked me how I thought the meeting had gone. Pretty well, I told him but said I would know more tonight. "If Des phones me tonight I think we're on, if he sleeps on it and rings me in the morning I think he'll say no."

Ironically that night I was out to dinner with Bob Shennan, who had replaced me at BBC TV Sport. A good bloke, and now the mastermind behind BBC's successful Radio Two, Bob and I discussed mutual bits of television business and all the while I was thinking "God, if he only knew what I'd been up to this afternoon."

When I got home that evening, I was just getting ready for bed when my wife, Gerry, casually volunteered, "Oh, by the way, Des phoned whilst you were out." I nearly dropped my toothbrush. We were on.

We hooked up the following day. Des was seemingly up for it and so were we. Only a couple of problems: I was about to go on jury service and Des on holiday with friends, also in the sports broadcast business, to the hills behind San Pedro del Alcántara on the Costa del Sol for a couple of weeks. As it turned out that ultimately worked in our favour. We were both out of the way, as were plenty of other people, enjoying their summer holidays.

*   *   *   *   *

Only once was our surprise nearly sprung, when Des, poolside, awaiting an update phone call from me, had his mobile playfully nicked from him by one of his fellow holiday-makers. Now if I had phoned and they answered the call and recognised the voice on the other end, they may well have put two and two together and hit on a very large FOUR. Des had to get shirty with his holiday mates to get his phone back. They fell out for a few minutes. But our coup was still on course.

Back in London after his holiday, we all met in Desmond's London flat. David Liddiment, Jeff Farmer, Simon Johnson, ITV's lawyer, Jane Morgan, Des's agent, and Des and myself walked through how the following day would go. And then we had some pizzas delivered, as we were all starving.

The next day, two meetings took place, one shortly after the other. Desmond went in to see BBC TV's Managing Director, Will Wyatt, and resigned, citing amongst other things a sense that the BBC had lost the will to fight for the big television sports contracts. It was tough for both men, both long-serving Corporation men and both good eggs.

With that difficult meeting over, Desmond was heading towards ITV Network's offices in Chancery Lane, whilst Jeff Farmer and I had the equally difficult job of telling Bob Wilson of the impending news.

We had brought Bob in, under the auspices of discussing the new season with him, but once we were aware that Des had resigned at the BBC, we were able to reveal that news to Bob. It was a predictably emotional meeting. Bob was furious and, boy, did he let us know it.

Bob, always an underestimated presenter, had done some great work for ITV and the programmes he had fronted had delivered big numbers, record numbers, and he had ploughed on working whilst handling, with typical dignity, the desperate issue of a family illness.

Bob and I had worked together for ages and enjoyed each other's company. But he had told me himself that when he heard I was heading to ITV he knew it would signal the end for him. I suppose this was the day his prophecy came true.

Bob continued to work for ITV for a further four years after Desmond's arrival, and I'm glad to say we eventually got our relationship back in a decent place. I'm sure at this distance he now looks back proudly on having been successful in his two chosen careers, football and television. He was fittingly awarded an OBE for his services to charity, specifically the Willow Foundation, founded in memory of his late daughter, Anna.

Desmond's arrival at the ITV Network Centre was via the goods lift to avoid going past the ITN Newsroom, which would have immediately roused suspicion. Having been spirited into the building and met the ITV senior team, he was the subject of a hastily organised press conference. His leaving the BBC was big news, how big we couldn't have guessed.

The following day's newspapers were absolutely full of it. Some described it as the "football transfer" of the summer, others as the biggest talent move between the BBC and ITV in years. Whatever the headlines, whatever the impact on either organisation, the overwhelming verdict, from men and women, all good and true, both in and out of the broadcast industry, up and down the country, was that the transfer of Desmond Lynam from the BBC to ITV was a good old-fashioned coup.

And the following month, Desmond Lynam started his five-year spell with the type of game that had tempted him to switch "clubs", a Champions League match between Chelsea and AC Milan. He began his first programme on the commercial channel with a typically understated wry remark.

"Good evening," he said. "I had a feeling we'd be meeting again."

CHAPTER 23

THE RIGHT TIME FOR T...?

So there I was standing up in front of the assembled media throng selling a whole new broadcasting concept.

ITV had invested a huge lump of money in buying the rights to Saturday-evening Premier League highlights and they were about to take the plunge and break new ground in how and when the programmes would be scheduled.

Although Sky had paid another enormous sum, £1.1 billion, to maintain their dominance of live Premier League coverage, the sexier story had been the move of the Saturday-evening highlights package from the BBC to ITV. The (temporary) end of *Match of the Day* made front-page news – "Des 1, Gary 0", was how one newspaper saw it – but before the clocks would go back Des would find himself on the wrong end of a similar scoreline.

David Liddiment, ITV's programme boss, was always brave with his schedule and a successful risk-taker. He had always believed that early-evening football followed by a top light-entertainment show was an unbeatable combination.

He, like us, would have preferred a 6pm kick-off for his new football programme, and we believed we could technically deliver it, but Sky and the Premier League denied us that opportunity and a contractual tweak. Still we ploughed on.

It was early August 2001, and our closely guarded secret was about to be revealed. Having added a "Snatch of the Day" to our "Snatch of the Des" we were determined to try and do something different and now was the moment to let the cat out of the bag. However, it would seem it wasn't to be the lucky black cat *Match of the Day* had enjoyed.

I hit the mildly interested set of media observers with my four "Ts" – the new programme's *title*, *theme* music, presentation *team* and the coup de grace – the *time* the show would go on the air.

The Premiership was to be the new show's title, "Beautiful Day" by U2 was to be the theme music, Desmond Lynam would be joined by the evergreen Terry Venables and the lively Ally McCoist to be the top-line studio team, and critically, the programme would go to air at a brand-new time – seven o'clock.

That was the headline that hit the papers the following day. ITV had placed their new prized asset, Premiership highlights, into the very heart of the Saturday-evening schedule. At the press conference I had heard myself say that it was a "pioneering and ambitious move for televised football" and that our main programme was in "position A in the schedule and no longer a late-evening preserve". Well, it was for a few weeks anyway. Perhaps it was the ghost of the ill-fated Blackpool vs. Bolton match from 1960 that wafted its displeasure at a repeat of ITV's earlier experiment at early-Saturday-evening football but certainly something was in the air in the first early weeks of the newly conceived *The Premiership*.

Something in the air – but not clouds actually. And it was a fifth "T" that gave the programme an early bright yellow card. The *temperature* on the opening Saturday was in the high 70s, the sun was high in the sky and people were out in the streets and parks enjoying some lovely English summer weather. And well into the evening. Bah, humbug!

*   *   *   *   *

The opening programme itself was something of a fiasco. It had been so long in preparation – more than a year – that the running order had almost been written on parchment, the new gizmos weren't world-beaters and the commercial breaks drove the viewers nuts. The ITV production team, who would go on to make this programme as appealing in many ways as its more famous BBC predecessor, were guilty of trying too hard. It was often the case at ITV Sport.

Another set of Ts were also in play. The Tactics Truck, essentially "football video analysis on the road", proved underwhelming. Thankfully it didn't sink the career of its talented fledgling pundit, Andy Townsend, who is still an ITV ever-present some 12 years later.

ITV survived the Tactics Truck, and indeed, the "Tic Tacs Ruck", many years later, when an advert was inadvertently inserted into the closing moments of extra-time in a Merseyside derby FA Cup replay. Of course, as luck would have it that's when the only goal of the game went in. I digress.

The first edition of *The Premiership* got slammed by the critics and the public alike, but the second programme was better than the first and so on – even if the weather continued to provide an unlikely gremlin. The last Saturday in August enjoyed temperatures in the high 80s. Yellow was turning to red! I began to think God must have been an avid *Match of the Day* viewer as the following five Saturdays were absolute belters as well.

The programme would continue to settle down and the viewing figures would gradually increase but the early die was cast. Not least by the ITV executives themselves. The ITV "sales-boys" wanted a swift return to the tried and trusted formula of commercially attractive light entertainment on Saturday evenings like *Blind Date*, and the grandees of the ITV companies backed their view.

Just six weeks into its run, ITV Director of Programmes David Liddiment summoned me and Des Lynam to an urgent meeting which ended in raised voices and a new post-10 o'clock on-air time for *The Premiership*.

"Cilla 1, Des 0" crowed the tabloids, as *Blind Date* was restored to its established home. Mind you, it was on the home straight itself.

The Premiership settled back into being a *Match of the Day* with adverts, the running order put the best match first, the programme's running time was increased and the analysis, strong in opinion, became more pundit-led than Pro-zone led. It turned into a very decent watch for the rest of its three seasons.

The Saturday afternoons watching the games coming into the ITV studios were as much fun as they had been at the BBC – similar windowless room, different building but same buzz. In particular, when Ally McCoist would regale us with tales of his previous seven days, including the spell when he was filming a movie with Robert Duvall. But the bottom line was the programme was never going to get a second term.

It did however give ITV an opportunity to make a refreshing call in giving a woman an opportunity to front a mainstream football programme. Gabby Yorath, the daughter of Leeds United's Terry Yorath, was a real find. Gabby, bright and intelligent, with a true fix on football and broadcasting, made an immediate impact when she presented *On the Ball* and, later, filled in for Des on *The Premiership* when he was away. Gabby has gone on to change her surname to Logan – she married Scottish rugby international Kenny Logan – and change channels too, and is now a big hit on BBC Sport. And I'm genuinely pleased for her.

When ITV won the rights to Premier League highlights in 2000, Greg Dyke, then the BBC's Director-General, had fired a red-hot broadside at the Premier League and ITV for spending a fortune on the rights. On the night before the deals were announced I had actually drawn up alongside him at a set of traffic lights near Richmond where we both lived. He didn't spot me but I spotted him and watched him with some amusement as he seemed to be shouting down the phone. For all I know he was ordering his Chinese takeaway but I persuaded myself he was talking to his BBC team and telling them to put together a better bid ahead of the following day's rights auction. I allowed myself the view that we might win the next day. And Greg, in truth, probably enjoyed his prawn balls in oyster sauce.

The following day, ITV's winning bid for Premiership highlights was revealed and Dyke, an ultra-competitive soul, fired salvos in all directions. Twenty-four hours later he was able to celebrate the BBC winning the FA Cup rights, originally the main ITV target – and three years later, in 2003, the Corporation would pay less than ITV's 2000 rights figure to reclaim their prized asset – *Match of the Day*. Such was the pitch and toss of the television football rights market at this time. And it certainly toughened you up.

Another ITV venture, the ITV Sports Channel, a new digital terrestrial service, opened in early August of 2001. It was ITV's companies, Granada and Carlton's attempt at breaking into the wider pay-TV business through their On Digital proposition. One of the areas was sports television and the ITV Sports Channel promised a strong sports mix, including Champions League football, and "groundbreaking" coverage of the Football League and the Worthington Cup. With a bid of £315 million, for three years' worth of rights, it was a significant throw of the dice from the ITV companies hoping to build a credible alternative pay-TV model to BSkyB.

It was a tough ask. Sky, originally a part of the consortium, was dominant in its broadcasting sphere – and fiercely protective of it. The new ITV Sports Channel would be available through both ITV Digital and NTL and a fired-up production team threw themselves into it. A lot of the team had come from Sky Sports themselves and felt they had something to prove to their previous paymasters. Whilst I admired that ambition I did think having 12 cameras at a Worthington Cup first-round match in late summer smacked a little of misplaced enthusiasm.

By the afternoon of the Worthington Cup Final between Blackburn Rovers and Spurs at the Millennium Stadium the following February things were getting critical for the new pay-TV service. I sat with Stuart Prebble, ITV Digital's boss; he was more than a little distracted, not just because football was not necessarily his thing but because he knew he was just days away from pulling a premature plug on the deal with the Football League.

When that course of action was pursued, and a financial cut in fees subsequently offered and rejected, a huge financial burden was faced by the Football League clubs, especially in the lower reaches, many of whom had budgeted for the original contracted sums, and as is the way with football probably already spent the money. ITV Digital collapsed in June 2002.

It was a difficult time for football and ITV. Their relationship was at rock bottom and only over time, aided by those at the respective coalfaces, did it improve.

*　*　*　*　*

The summer of 2002 would see another World Cup and England would be there but not without a scare and a sensation or two. And so, indeed, would the BBC and ITV despite some difficult moments acquiring the rights to the tournament. Negotiations with German media giants, Kirsch, who had bought the global rights from FIFA for the World Cups of both 2002 and 2006, had proved particularly difficult to conclude. Having spent a sum believed to be in the region of £2 billion for the rights themselves they now needed to charge top dollar to get their money back.

The two British broadcasters batted back an original demand for £171 million for the 2002 Finals alone and, with time and Listed Events legislation on their side, sat back and waited for Kirsch to blink first. Which they eventually did, as they hit financial issues themselves, and in a combined deal for both the 2002 and 2006 World Cup Finals the BBC and ITV paid a total sum of around £160 million.

I had left my own indelible mark on the tense negotiations – or, at least on the German company's carpets – when knocking over a huge water-cooler in the reception area of the Kirsch offices near Munich as our consortium of BBC and ITV sports executives made their way into the building for the final set of talks. Water, water everywhere but not a drop to drink.

*　*　*　*　*

On the field, under the guidance of their new coach, Swede Sven-Goran Eriksson, England had recovered from their indifferent start to their 2002 qualifying campaign to produce two memorable pieces of sports broadcasting – a performance from the gods, and a goal, perhaps from the Greek gods.

England's 5–1 win over Germany in Munich was as exceptional as it was unexpected. A hat-trick from Michael Owen, and a goal apiece from his Liverpool team-mates, Steven Gerrard and Emile Heskey, set the country alight and the illuminated scoreboard with the final score emblazoned on it remains an iconic television image.

It was so good, we saw it twice. A suggestion by commentator John Motson was taken up by Greg Dyke and Mark Thompson, the BBC's Director of Television, who persuaded BBC One Controller, Lorraine Heggessey, to re-run the whole game the following evening.

David Beckham's last-gasp equaliser against Greece later that autumn, which gave England guaranteed entry to World Cup 2002, still gets an astonishing 30,000 views a month on the FA's official YouTube channel some 13 years after the event, and is a piece of football magic that remains as evocative now as it was then. John Motson described it to me as "the most iconic goal I ever commentated on".

His fantastic free-kick and the celebration that followed it, all on his home turf at Old Trafford, helped cement the legendary figure he was fast growing into – an old-style matinee idol in a technologically advanced age. His on-screen persona would just grow and grow as his marketability and made-for-TV image was exploited for all manner of goods in all manner of countries. And he was married to a Spice Girl.

If Beckham was the poster boy of the England team then the man who had set the fans alight in Italia '90 and Euro '96, Paul Gascoigne, was slowly running his career down. Recently at Everton, under the fatherly watchful eye of ex-Rangers boss Walter Smith, Gazza was still a potentially attractive proposition as a guest pundit for the World Cup.

Both broadcasters, BBC and ITV, were basing their presentation of the World Cup, which was being played in Japan and South Korea, back in the UK as the time zones worked against the European broadcasters.

Gazza was in demand as both the BBC and ITV fancied using him in their coverage. ITV won his services and every London bus carried his image and the ITV World Cup logo in the build-up to the tournament.

Fellow ITV pundits, Ally McCoist and Andy Townsend, who had both been team-mates of his, at Rangers and Middlesbrough respectively, told me they would chaperone their mate through the four weeks of the tournament and so off we started. It soon became clear that despite trying hard, Gazza struggled commenting live in the studio on individual matches and he was obviously still fighting his demons.

The production team found him a more suitable role meeting and talking to the fans in the London streets. In fact, he nearly caused a riot in one film shoot at Trafalgar Square. When England exited the tournament so did Gazza from ITV's coverage. I was left with the impression that here was a terrific guy, sensitive, intelligent and funny. And troubled.

One man who did make an early impression was Gary Neville. Left out of the England squad through injury, his contribution to ITV's World Cup programmes marked him down as somebody who could have a future in television.

The 2002 World Cup would mark the last of ten in which Barry Davies commentated. As a final test of spirit and identification, Davies's commentary rota found him criss-crossing Japan and Korea, where he fell upon the story of the tournament – the performance of the hosts South Korea. Davies, who had begun his World Cup journey with North Korea in 1966, rounded it off describing South Korea clinching a semi-final place via a penalty shoot-out.

Congratulated by his BBC boss for the extra-long pause in commentary as South Koreans, on and off the pitch, wildly celebrated the decisive penalty, Davies's wry observation was "Ah, I am the world's best commentator when I keep my mouth shut."

*   *   *   *   *

The 2004 European Championships would mark the end of Desmond Lynam's long and distinguished career in live sports broadcasting. The tournament in Portugal was lit up by some outstanding displays by a precocious young talent, Wayne Rooney. England made it through the group stages and were then to face the hosts in the quarter-finals. As the match was live on the BBC, the ITV team had a night out and it was fun seeing Des and Terry climb up more than 100 steps to their seats – and watch the England fans' jaws drop as they sat amongst the supporters during the game itself.

The ITV team travelled across Portugal in a tour bus usually used to transport rock and pop stars across the continent. Instead the "Desmobile", as it was dubbed, carried the likes of Des, Terry, Ally, Andy T and Sir Bobby Robson. And it was just a sheer delight to sit amongst that football brains trust and listen to their theories, thoughts and stories. Sitting and listening to Sir Bobby recall matches and players from his past was just wonderful and he loved to be involved in any board game or such that we used to kill the time. Happy memories.

We had used Bobby as our co-commentator on the opening England group match against France – a huge game as the French were recent World Cup-winners and reigning European Champions. England were leading through a Frank Lampard header before two late goals, one a penalty from Zinedine Zidane, killed the night for the travelling English fans and the near 18 million viewers back home.

Bobby had replaced Ron Atkinson at short notice as "Big Ron" had been forced to leave his long-standing ITV co-commentator role towards the end of the 2003/04 season when he made a racially inappropriate remark about Chelsea's defender, Marcel Desailly, after the conclusion of the Monaco vs. Chelsea Champions League semi-final. Off-mike, off-air but arguably not off-duty, his use of the "N" word was picked up at the fag-end of a Middle East television broadcast of the match. They had stayed on the OB pictures longer than most other broadcasters would and had picked up his words, which were being relayed without permission, as he reflected on the match to his colleagues.

The following day a tabloid newspaper picked up the story, and I was alerted to it and by the end of the day, Ron Atkinson's career with ITV was over.

As ITV's Controller of Sport, and after discussions with senior ITV executives, I had some very difficult telephone conversations with Ron. I also called Clive Tyldesley and asked him to talk to his commentary colleague. It was crystal clear to me that Ron couldn't continue to broadcast on ITV. He was still out in France and deeply upset by the whole incident but by the end of the day, we both agreed that he had to step down from his post – which he subsequently did. His use of the offensive word and his high-profile departure opened the flood-gates to columns and columns of press reaction, some focused on the central story, others on its wider implications. They ran for days.

The 2004 tournament was marked by Desmond Lynam completing a glorious live sports broadcasting career by fronting the final between Greece and hosts Portugal. Before his final programme got under way, the BBC's counterpart, Gary Lineker, made a kind gesture by coming over to wish Des well before both channels' coverage began.

After the final Des and I had a few drinks – well, more than a few drinks – to mark the occasion. And as we reminisced he threw a question my way. "That's me done. What are you going to do next? I reckon you've got one more big job left in you."

Six months later I was the new Chief Executive of the Football Association.

CHAPTER 24

THE OTHER END OF THE LENS

I knew I was about to enter a slightly different world when having just completed a job interview I was asked "How did it go?" by a Sky Sports News reporter as I exited the central London building where I had been quizzed for the previous couple of hours.

The job interview had been the second and final one for the post of Chief Executive of the Football Association. My "no comment" was the first of many I would give to my Sky Sports News inquisitor, Dan Roan, over the next four years.

Soho Square was part of his daily beat and Dan, an earnest young man making his way in a tough business, would regularly whack a microphone in my face and ask for an opinion on something I may, or more likely, may not know had just happened in the wider world of football.

I understood his job and tried to help as often as I could. I think we only fell out once when in the midst of one of the FA's regular searches for the next England coach he tracked me down to a small football club in Surrey where I was on the touch-line watching my 14-year-old son, Joe, playing for his local team in their end-of-season Sunday cup final. I thought that was crossing the line.

When I left the broadcasting business to join the FA I did it in the full knowledge that I was taking up a senior position in an organisation that was incredibly newsworthy. Indeed the reason the CEO's role had been vacated had been because of the media interest in the life and times of some of those people who had been working at that time in Soho Square.

I was determined to be as helpful as possible to my former media colleagues although the sheer volume of requests that came into the FA for access and information meant there had to be some form of news management.

I hadn't left my chosen career in sports broadcasting lightly. First, I felt I'd achieved more than I could have dreamed of, and second, I had really enjoyed my time doing it; being part of respected teams of great professionals at both BBC and ITV. And, of course, we reached every final!

However when the post at the Football Association came up I thought it worth pursuing – and I thought I might actually get it. One of the areas that I felt was important for any incoming new CEO at the FA, at that time, was a sense of how the media – both broadcast and print – worked and how to approach it.

Once behind the desk at the FA, the intensity of media interest in the daily business of the organisation surprised even me. The whole "England" experience, be it team, matches, results, coaches coming and going, was difficult to contain – no, impossible to contain.

The organisation created news – the stuff of television news bulletins and sports programmes, and front- and back-page newspaper stories – and those involved in the decision-making processes became well-known faces to the public. Like those in the office before me, for a time, I became a well-known public figure. Fame it definitely wasn't, celebrity it certainly wasn't, but profile, for good or ill, it was.

In fact, it was during my time at the FA that 24-hour news and sports channels really kicked in, and the new dynamic of social media really kicked off, and the need to fill all available space meant a television camera was pointed in your direction and a question asked on any professional trip you found yourself on. Any excursion out of the building in Soho Square at lunchtime to grab a lungful of fresh air and a cheese and tomato sandwich was invariably followed up by having to spirit up an on-the-spot quote on the latest dastardly deed besetting English football on the way back into the building. And, one lunchtime, having left my entrance pass indoors and unable to get back through the front door of the FA for several minutes, my attempts to attract the attention of those in the building were filmed and replayed numerous times that afternoon on Sky News on what must have been a quiet news day.

All those years behind the camera, liaising with reporters, cameramen, presenters and pundits over what we should ask a manager, player, owner or chairman helped me to deal with it all as equably as possible. But it was still difficult at times.

It helped that I knew so many people "in the business" but only to a degree as I had "crossed over" and was now rightly seen as fair game.

My previous employment history also meant that, whenever I went to FIFA or attended the International Football Board meetings where the game's laws would be discussed, FIFA President Sepp Blatter would say "Hey, here's Brian, Mr Television Man."

As it happens it was my previous expertise in football broadcasting that I brought to bear when we regularly discussed the subject of goal-line technology. I have been a champion of it for years and the over-long wait for its installation in top-class football has been difficult to understand as other less notable sports readily engaged with video technology to resolve contentious issues.

Convinced that their opposition was based on not understanding how efficient, fast and reliable the best systems are, I would explain to my fellow delegates just how swift the process was – instant, actually. Then I would still hear them in the news conferences following the event talk about the indeterminate length of time it would take for a decision to be reached. "And how would the game restart?"

I did say that one day FIFA itself would be mightily embarrassed if an important "goal" was scored in one of its major tournaments, and then not given, even when the ball had clearly crossed the line. During the 2010 World Cup in South Africa, Germany vs. England, Frank Lampard's "goal" was indeed that moment. Now everybody at FIFA seems to be a Mr Television Man. And the Premier League introduced it in 2013.

During my time at the FA we had to sell our television and radio broadcast rights for a new term, 2008–12. This was an interesting spin of the wheel for me: having spent many years buying or trying to buy rights I was now on the other side of the table. And the money was crucial to the welfare of the Association, with the new Wembley Stadium to pay for, Burton – later St Georges – Park, to complete and the game at all levels, all 37,000 clubs, 2,500 leagues of it, in need of financial support.

The BBC and Sky Sports were the incumbent broadcasters, and had done a very good job in helping to restore some of the lost lustre of the FA Cup. In their arrangement the BBC was the senior partner and had the best "picks" when the FA Cup draws were made. This rankled with their pay partner. Also, of course, the FA Cup Final was a listed event, which prevented any pay-TV service from trying to buy the competition outright because its climax had to be resolved on free-to-air television.

The FA's negotiating team hoped there would also be interest elsewhere in the broadcasting business in their prized properties. This was important because if the market just believed the BBC and Sky were a shoo-in for the next term, the rights fees offered from all sides were likely to reflect that. My colleagues at the FA worked hard in bringing other broadcasters to the table. In a novel twist, we actually presented to them rather than the other way round. We explained the range and scope of our rights and tried to tailor each conversation to the people across the table from us.

The interested broadcasters then reversed the process and presented back to us. Standard fare this, broadcasters "selling" their new ideas, innovations and ingenuity. A three-yearly attempt at reinventing the wheel, ahead of trying to hit the right and winning price for the rights. The whole process took a few months.

The eventual winners, after two separate rounds of bidding, were a surprise combination of ITV and Setanta, a new pay-TV broadcaster that had already invested in some of the packages that the Premier League had sold in 2006.

The authorities, the European Commission especially, were keen that one pay broadcaster be prevented from being able to buy the whole "live" element of the Premier League, so six packages were created, with a limit of four for any one broadcaster. Sky paid an enormous £1.3 billion for its four – the cream of the crop – with Setanta picking up the other two.

Michael Grade had been the Chairman of the BBC when the FA rights sales process was being thought through and had moved across to become the Executive Chairman of ITV by the time the whole thing was in its final throes. I thought this might have a significant influence on the FA's negotiating stance, since I felt Lord Grade, as he is now, would see capturing the rights as a positive start to his tenure; and so it proved.

So it was ITV and Setanta, Grade and Trevor East who jointly held the FA Cup aloft for the cameras to mark the start of a new four-year deal worth around £425 million – up from the previous £300 million.

While ITV enjoyed a vintage FA Cup season in 2012/13 with shocks and surprises galore, sadly for the FA, Setanta would disappointingly fail to go the course and distance, and the FA would be significantly hit in the pocket early in the new contract. ITV and newcomers, US sports broadcasting giants, ESPN, would however take up some of the slack. Now from 2014/15 the live FA Cup rights will be split between the BBC and BT Sport. Many observers see the return to the BBC of the country's most famous, if somewhat faltering, domestic cup competition to be the competition's best chance of restoring itself to some of its former glories.

*   *   *   *   *

The level of interest in the England team continued to deliver huge television audiences despite a continued failure to bring home the bacon. Quarter-finalists, and penalty shoot-out losers, again to Portugal, in the 2006

World Cup in Germany and then non-qualifiers for the 2008 European Championships just added to the sense of frustrating under-achievement.

The latter occasion involved a crucial home defeat at the hands of Croatia, a result that cost coach Steve McClaren his job and put all those involved in a harsh light. The live media conference held at the FA with Chairman Geoff Thompson, me and several members of the FA Board the following morning was a tough session. And had every right to be. In my previous jobs I would have expected my reporters to get stuck in and on that morning I wouldn't have been disappointed by their efforts!

During the England vs. Croatia match the television directors had regularly featured me in their coverage as I went through death by a thousand camera cuts. Twelve months later it would be a different story as England, under new coach, Italian Fabio Capello, went out and hammered their new international nemesis Croatia 4–1 in Zagreb. I was caught on camera ignoring all protocols and jigging with delight as Theo Walcott announced himself properly on the international stage with a stunning hat-trick.

The game was live on Setanta and was therefore denied a wider audience and despite strenuous negotiations same-day highlights on a terrestrial broadcaster were not forthcoming. It became a major story, not least because England playing Croatia had become a big deal.

The previous month news of my impending departure from the FA, somewhat ironically, leaked out mid-way through a live television broadcast of an early-season international friendly at Wembley between England and the Czech Republic.

I had agreed to "step down" from my post after nearly four years in office and an announcement was scheduled for the following day. But somebody had got the story – somebody always did – and so when we all went into the hospitality suite at Wembley for a half-time cup of tea my ugly mug was actually on the television screen and was "breaking news"! Some of the old "blazers" nearly had a heart attack!

On arrival at my home we were welcomed by a TV news crew "doorstepping" me, as it is called. That over, I awoke the following morning to more news crews outside our house before I set off to work and an impromptu live media conference on the steps of Soho Square. And then, as is the way with these things, the story quite rightly moved on.

*　　*　　*　　*　　*

Back in "civvies" I still took a huge personal and professional interest in the 2010 World Cup, splitting my time between South Africa and back home. It was interesting to see former Southampton winger, Terry Paine, one of Sir Alf's "boys of '66", turning out as a regular studio pundit for South African TV, now his adopted home.

Once again the tournament gripped the nation. ITV had to survive the acute embarrassment of a technical hitch resulting in Steven Gerrard's opening World Cup goal against USA being missed by the channel's HD customers, and then the sending home of long-time pundit, Robbie Earle, for his part in a ticket scandal that seemingly helped underpin an ambush-marketing scam.

There was huge interest in the performance of the channel's new front-line presenter, Adrian Chiles, who had been a big-money transfer from the BBC in the dual role of co-presenting ITV's new breakfast-time show *Daybreak*, with BBC's *One Show* side-kick Christine Bleakley, and fronting its peak-time football.

The breakfast show proved to be a ratings flop, but Chiles's acerbic presentation style, blessed with the channel's current strong live football offering, has proved something of a hit. Certainly back in the summer of 2010 there was lots of interest in how he would perform on ITV's big World Cup shows. Continuity in this area has never been ITV Sport's strong point, and Chiles was the channel's seventh different World Cup host in seven different tournaments. The West Bromwich Albion season-ticket holder did well, and went to the 2014 World Cup in Brazil as the commercial channel's lead presenter, finally breaking ITV's remarkably destabilising sequence of its World Cup front-men finding themselves casualties of both internal and external broadcast "wars".

The BBC have historically gone for the 'same as last time' approach – and it's proved hugely successful. The Corporation's main presenters, Des Lynam and Gary Lineker, have guided viewers through the ups and downs of eight tournaments from 1986 to 2014. In 2010 in South Africa, the BBC, with Lineker at the helm, proved conclusively the viewers' choice again when the two channels went head-to-head. Lineker's recent tour of duty in Brazil was his fourth as the BBC's main man. He famously did two for England as a player!

Again, in both South Africa, where the final between Holland and Spain drew a combined audience of over 20 million with the BBC running out convincing winners again, and during this past summer in Brazil, there were huge viewing figures for both broadcasters – especially for the England matches. Further proof if any was needed that England's participation in a major football tournament is still gold-dust as far as television ratings are concerned.

It is also further indication that World Cups and European Football Championships will always pull in an audience wider than just the football fan – and that remains a constant pattern in viewing habits. The tournament, and especially England's performances in it, becomes the stuff people are talking about at work, at school, on the bus and on the train. It fills the newspapers and the air-waves. And people who would never normally watch football on the television temporarily get hooked – like the rest of us.

CHAPTER 25

SKYBALL!

In the summer of 2012, Sky Sports secured the rights to show 116 live Premier League matches in each of the next three seasons. The price: a cool £2.3 BILLION.

Richard Scudamore, the hugely successful chief executive of the Premier League, once again was entitled to think "job, very well done", especially with a further £738 million coming from a secondary tranche of live matches on newcomer BT Sport. These numbers are simply stratospheric – and the overseas market is also returning record numbers too.

English football, and especially the weekly diet of English football's top Premier League football, is a television smash hit the world over. What used to be the unlikely sight of the ubiquitous Coca-Cola or McDonald's sign in a completely out-of-the-way place as proof that the world was getting smaller is now a Liverpool, Manchester United, Arsenal or Chelsea shirt worn on the backs of people of every colour and creed across the whole planet. The word "phenomenon" is over-used but without doubt, the Premier League as a broadcasting product is just that. Staggering.

Television pictures from Premier League matches are pumped live across the globe from IMG Media's base near Heathrow, with around 200 countries in receipt. Add previews, reviews, studio debates and news, and you get a sense of the sheer scale of the footprint that the Premier League now has across a football-hungry globe.

Graham Fry, Managing Director of IMG Sports Production, reflects on the growth. "Every year you think it can't get bigger and every year it does."

Through attention to detail; an informed strategy; exploitation of new trends in the communications business; making sure the sport is technically produced to the highest standards for television; plus a healthy dollop of sheer bloody-mindedness and good fortune, Richard Scudamore has guaranteed himself a healthy bonus and a three-yearly lap of honour around the Premier League clubs as the latest set of domestic and international television rights figures are unveiled.

And, of course, the television rights figures and profile of the Premier League have attracted not just some of the best footballers in the world but also some of its richest individuals who want to have their slice of the action.

Oligarchs, tycoons, members of international Royal families all now dine on English football's best cuisine. And their ultra-wealthy footprint straddles the world; from the United States to the Middle East, from Russia to Malaysia, and, perhaps, reassuringly for some, from those a lot closer to home than that. Premier League club owners have now become as well known as some of the players whom they have invested in as part of their portfolio. And so much of this remarkable financial metamorphosis has come through television's box office. The broadcast rights fees associated with the product are on a remarkable upward trajectory – global recession or no global recession – and an estimated £5.5 billion will have been shelled out here and abroad when all deals are concluded for the next one.

Mind you, ever-escalating players' wages, agents taking their over-generous slice of the action, a suspicion of the motives of new club owners – fair or unfair – and transfer fees that occasionally defy logic do mean that the game has to be on high alert against turning off the ordinary man in the street, or the fan with an increasingly expensive seat in the stand. Many see the sport's top table's opulent wealth as a divisive element in English football life, especially as the game seems to drop so steeply off a financial cliff beyond the top division – even with a silky parachute or three.

What cannot be denied, however, is that the top English football product is attractive, exciting, all-action and now truly international. And it has timed its run perfectly to fully exploit the changing communications landscape and breadth of broadcasting in this country and beyond. What Mr Hardaker and his colleagues of the Football League fought so vehemently to keep off the screen 50 years ago is now being professionally sliced and diced to satisfy a voracious and diverse set of commercial demands.

In fact, in the late 1990s the broadcast companies themselves turned from wanting to carry coverage of English clubs doing battle to actually owning part of the war itself. In 1998, Sky famously tried and failed to buy Manchester United, despite offering around £625 million. That purchase was stopped by the UK's Competition Commission who thought it would have "hurt competition in the broadcast industry and the quality of British football". BSkyB chief executive at the time, Kansas-born Mark Booth, got the hell out of town, not least after he had been memorably asked at a press conference to announce the deal, "Who plays left-back for Manchester United?" Sky, and other companies like Granada and NTL, continued to acquire small chunks of football clubs, around 9.9%, as a way of being both "in the game and of the game" – and having a seat at the negotiating table – seemingly both sides of it. "A knee-jerk reaction" offers Trevor East. In the end, although being common practice in other parts of the world, such football club–broadcaster synergy was frowned upon and didn't quite stick here.

Now, it is all about acquiring rights and using an organisation's range of technologies and outputs to get the appropriate return on investment or route to market with subscriptions, commercial revenue, or a new product or service. Televised football has become a conduit for substantial growth in an ever-widening range of digital services, telecom and internet innovations, mobile phone apps, tablets and broadcast platforms.

And, for an Aston Villa fan, maximising the value from a huge investment in the sport's broadcast rights is what Sky Sports managing director, Barney Francis, does on a daily basis. An Economic History graduate from the University of Liverpool, Francis learnt his television trade on the shop-floor.

Now in charge of 50,000 hours of live sport every year across the Sky Sports channels, Francis started his professional life with them as an assistant producer writing scripts and editing packages for *Sports Centre*, before going on to drive their outstanding cricket coverage forward.

Francis, who was just 37 when he landed the top job in June 2009, acknowledges he was taking over from a "giant in broadcasting", Vic Wakeling. "Vic gave me this great six-month handover period and I would choose a different topic every day to talk to him about. We might pick a sport and I would invariably know the players and our production team and suchlike but Vic would ask where the sport fitted into our overall business. A great question."

Under Wakeling, Sky Sports' business grew and grew, and their football output grew, grew and grew. And in so doing, it has left other pretenders to the crown in its wake; the likes of On Digital, Setanta and ESPN have found the competition just too tough. Next contender bouncing into the ring is BT, who bought up ESPN's rights and purchased 38 Premier League games a season in the last round of rights negotiations.

Sky Sports' breadth of programming on the round-ball game is comprehensive. Live Premier League games, essentially three a weekend, have been augmented by blanket coverage of the UEFA Champions League , now the preserve of BT Sport, matches from the Football League, including the dramatic play-off games and the Football League Cup, the Capital One Cup, as it currently is. Scottish football and glorious Spanish football also feature strongly too. Back-to-back live La Liga matches, often featuring the majestic skills of Ronaldo and Messi, Real Madrid and Barcelona, richly round off a weekend of football on Sky.

But it is Sky's symbiotic relationship with the Premier League that has been at the heart of their mutual success and Barney Francis recognises that.

"We have been with the Premier League since the start. We are entwined, and yet Richard Scudamore has rightly said publicly that any notion of an umbilical cord is severed by the rights process and we, at Sky, have to go into battle for what we want and whatever we can get. It is a strong relationship that has endured – and after all it is the sporting league that is more globally in demand than any other."

He is also keen, however, to recognise the value of the other 72 professional clubs who make up the Football League – a wider part of the football constituency and potential television audience and subscriber base.

Francis, it seems to me, has piled a lot of experience into his relatively short career, both in production and now overall management. He has developed his thinking from long-time established sources, like Wakeling, while being totally au fait with how the next generation or two will engage in watching their football on television. His views have genuine modernity about them, including his complete take on the role and impact of social media – a genuine game-changer.

"We always take the view that the event is the most important element of the broadcast – and the 'telling' of the event becomes the second most important component. I want my host to be very professional, knowledgeable and able to get the best views out of the pundits. And at the end of the programme I want the views of the pundit to be ringing in my ears, not those of the presenter.

"And, of course, with social media having more and more outlets we have to be very conscious of them. People are getting their views out much quicker than they were ever able to do. What happens on the pitch is being discussed the world over within seconds of things happening. Trying to pull the wool over people's eyes doesn't matter any more."

And, of course, as well as the live matches and the Super Sundays, Sky have exploited the breadth of their rights with a range of support programming.

I tuned in a while ago to see whether the long-running *Soccer AM* still earns its corn and shortly after the presentation duo of Max Rushden and Helen Chamberlain had guided us through the programme's up and coming delights, a pair of semi-naked men in a bath of beans were being pulled across the studio floor. I knew in an instant I hadn't tuned in to *Football Focus*.

Soccer Saturday has taken the early seeds of David Coleman and his memorable teleprinter routine of many moons ago and successfully developed it into a whole afternoon's viewing. Jeff Stelling is a brilliant ring-master, with a winning combination of dash and detail, to a panel of ex-pros who have got plenty to say, and say it with a smile. Liverpool's Phil Thompson, Arsenal's Paul Merson, Southampton's Matt Le Tissier and Arsenal and Celtic's Charlie Nicholas – "that's the first XI" – swap stories and strategies and plenty of oohs and aahs as the afternoon's matches unfold in their eye-line and in our mind's eye.

As a television concept it shouldn't work but it richly does. In many ways it reminds me of the many hours of fun we had in the BBC TV's Room 2143 or ITV's Premiership basement hideaway as the matches were relayed back to headquarters on a Saturday afternoon – only *Soccer Saturday* shares the experience with a television audience.

I actually tried that style of programme myself twice at ITV – once without even a feed of the matches for the studio guests to look at on a fledgling ITV2, still not a bad programme, and then *Goal Rush* on ITV1 when we had the Premier League rights. It never had a fixed on-air time and invariably looked rushed and incomplete at the business end of the programme when the clarion call of let's get on with the Saturday-evening entertainment schedule seemed the popular commercial television shout – and left us with a lot of late-kick-off captions in our results sequence.

As is so often the case the scheduling space Sky Sports can afford a programme like *Soccer Saturday* helps develop its personality, even if the BBC's *Final Score*, which had Gabby Logan in the presenter's chair in recent times, regularly comes along and beats it up at the box office around a quarter to five. A regular on the BBC team is likeable ex-Spurs favourite, Garth Crooks, whose so-so serious, on-screen persona always makes you think he is about to deliver a very earnest reflection on the splitting of the atom and then ... (long pause for effect)... reveals to an expectant nation ... now on the edge of their seats that ... "Southampton will be happy with that point at Norwich."

The reading of the day's scores has always been part of any results show and, days gone by, when *Final Score* was the climax to a day's edition of *Grandstand* it was wonderful to hear the familiar voice of Len Martin pop up, and you knew by his intonation which way the result had gone. What the viewer at home didn't know was that Len had four different "gears" he could go through when reading the results, depending on how much time we had left in the programme. Bournemouth and Boscombe Athletic could become just "Bournemouth", Tottenham Hotspur, "Spurs" and Wolverhampton Wanderers, "Wolves" at the drop of a hat. It saved many a programme editor's bacon, that trick, including mine. I digress.

Back on Sky, *Goals on Sunday* with Ben Shephard and Chris Kamara has developed a good following and once again benefits from an ever-changing set of guests and a generous slot, whilst the *Sunday Supplement*, a weekly round-table of the noble knights of the nation's back pages, proved to be a gentle broadcast home for the great Jimmy Hill and provided a different type of professional opportunity for the much-missed Brian Woolnough.

And running alongside it all is Sky Sports News. A news, views and results service that has matured from its early days when you felt Alan Partridge could have got a peak-time presentation slot, to it now becoming an accessible, invaluable sports news service which has developed in confidence, competence and content. Perhaps still slightly gauche, when it handles a SERIOUS subject on a Monday evening, say, and completely bonkers when unravelling the last-minute lunacy of the transfer window deadline days, but an entertaining and informative mix of news and action – and a maturing and moving billboard for television sport of all denominations and channels. And those transfer deadline days! Andy Cairns, Sky Sports News boss:

"Deadline day has grown. We knew fans were interested but they seem to love the tension and uncertainty of the day. We share the fans' passion and work hard to be up to the minute and accurate. What doesn't make the air is as important as what does – we have plenty of people trying to manipulate the media so we have to check and attribute every story."

The transfer deadline days give Sky Sports News its most marketable broadcast proposition. There is Scotsman Jim White – dressed in suits seemingly tailored by Gillette they're that sharp – going off entertainingly in all directions, while his colour co-ordinated co-presenter Natalie Sawyer, a Brentford season-ticket holder, remains reassuringly feet fixed on terra firma. It works. But twice a year is enough! Andy Cairns again:

"Jim comes alive – a bundle of nervous energy who has to grip the desk to stop shaking with excitement as stories break and develop. And he's always on the phone chasing new lines of information during the ad breaks. He survives on coffee (one sugar) and large slices of chocolate cake, usually baked by one of our graphic operators.

"Natalie is a calming influence – keeps great notes. Producers can go to Nat if they want to change the pace slightly. Still engaging, but calmer."

Andy Cairns is the man behind the growth in personality and professionalism of the channel, with its revolving-door, round-the-clock approach to its sports news-gathering and presentation teams. Ex-newspaper journalist and BBC TV newsman Cairns justifiably takes pride in his channel's journey:

"Highs for the channel? Some big scoops including Claire Tomlinson breaking the news that Kevin Keegan had resigned as England manager – in the toilet. Breaking the news at 3am that Jose Mourinho had been sacked by Chelsea – great for a rolling news channel, but it also meant we were ahead of the rest in our morning programme.

"But it's not just about the big names and big games. We cover sport at all levels and our 2006 series 'Respect the Ref' where we highlighted the plight of referees at grass roots, the abuse they suffered ... helped inspire the FA's Respect Campaign." It did.

And not before time, its presenters are beginning to migrate across to the main Sky Sports channels with the likes of Ed Chamberlin and David Jones being amongst the key beneficiaries of the fall-out from one of the organisation's most public crises.

The dismissal of Andy Gray and resignation of Richard Keys from their seemingly jobs-for-life slots on Sky's prime asset, its live big-time football output. Keys and Gray had been the faces of the output from the very beginning of Sky Sports' football, and in no small part responsible for its on-air success.

Their departures made big news. A female assistant referee, Sian Massey, had been the subject of some unnecessary sexist remarks by the pair ahead of a Saturday lunchtime game between Wolves and Liverpool in 2011, and that, accompanied by some subsequent allegations of sexist behaviour, set in train the departure of two of the most high-profile and original members of the Sky football cast list. First Gray and then Keys were out on the street looking for new employment. It was as brutal as it was brief.

It was also a severe early test of the new man in charge. Barney Francis had to handle the crisis and move the company forward. He did both.

Keys and Gray have subsequently returned to broadcasting, including award-winning radio shows on TalkSport, and regular slots on Al Jazeera Sports. Andy Gray has also made a return to television coverage in the UK as co-commentator on BT Sport.

Gary Neville was coming to the end of his football career as Andy Gray was coming to the end of his Sky Sports stint. Within months Neville had become their lead expert, with opinions and observations born of a lifelong commitment to the game as a player fresh out, still dripping wet, from the dressing room of one of the world's top clubs. And he was thrown in at the deep end. Early games included "Super Sundays" with Manchester United's 8–2 thumping of Arsenal and then "noisy neighbours", Manchester City's 6–1 win over Neville's former team-mates at Old Trafford. Throw in an early Liverpool vs. Manchester United clash and he had just about handled the set of games that could trip him up.

Neville, though, is refreshingly honest about what he sees, has a modern informed view, and can fall back on his trophy cabinet bursting at the seams for credibility. He is comfortable with the technology he needs to use to illustrate a point and, like Gray before him, drives it all himself. And he calls his brother Philip.

Barney Francis is pleased with his new man.

"We took a leap of faith with Gary and Gary took a leap of faith with us. He has done an outstanding job for us – especially his brilliant work on our *Monday Night Football Show*."

Gary Neville's new team-mate for the 2013/14 season was long-serving Liverpool stalwart, Jamie Carragher, who retired from football at the end of the previous season. Neville and Carragher, once hardened rivals on the pitch, now an intelligent, informed and contemporary pair of pundits off it. Along with Jamie Redknapp and the richly experienced and mature views of Graeme Souness, Sky have a strong line-up of opinion-formers.

Sky faced new pretenders to their crown from the start of the 2013/14 season. This time it was BT Sport that was out to impress and find new ways of making football look and sound different. They have some battle-hardened professionals in their production set-up and at the helm of their coverage is Jake Humphrey, late of BBC's Formula One coverage. As is often the case these days, the rest of the on-screen presentation team and voices in the commentary box have done some of the circuit before. One does get the feeling though that BT Sport are in it for real and for the long-term.

And Sky Sports? When I suggest to Barney Francis they have become part of the "establishment" he rails back in mock horror. "Oh, don't say that. I'd hate to think that we are seen as the establishment." Well, here's my breaking news, after more than two decades of producing top-class coverage, day-in day-out, week-in, week-out, I think they have become just that. Perhaps just the "new" establishment, as it continues to be formed in front of our very own eyes. It is, after all, such a dynamic and fast-moving industry, which never stays the same for long. This is a business in which the goalposts are always moving.

* * * * *

That said, some things will thankfully never change. As every broadcaster has found out down the years, as far back as the fledgling televised football days of 1936, a good game is a good game, and a poor game is a poor game. And perhaps, refreshingly, for all the modern technology, the 30-odd cameras, the brilliant FX mikes, the multiple instant-replay sources, the blimps in the air, super-slick presentation and stylish scene-sets, the outstanding commentaries and the views of experts awash with medals, the quality of the match itself is still the true criterion regarding whether the television programme itself is memorable or not.

And that's why we all still turn on to watch, some 75 years since the first cameras, all three of them, were pointed as players in baggy shorts and boots the size of house-bricks set about their business in flickering black-and-white images.

The game has changed beyond all recognition, as have the ways an eager public consume it. From grainy black-and-white to glorious colour, from 405 lines to 625 lines, from 4 x 3 to widescreen, and HD to 3D, from viewing on the move via apps and tablets to watching on home-movie screens that fill a complete wall. From watching one live match a year to watching one live match at a time, and not having to wait very long for the next one to come along. From being able to see only games from this country to being able to witness live action from all over the world at the touch of a button. From only seeing your club on the telly occasionally to seeing them launch their own dedicated television channels.

*   *   *   *   *

Live televised football remains a wonderful social diversion, either as a singular or collective viewing experience, a slice of unrehearsed drama, a compelling human tale with a genuine back-story, episodic with a different ending every time. Television with its own remarkable history and heritage, momentous images, unforgettable times and enriching words, capturing football's own epic moments, most memorable goals, its greatest players and its larger-than-life characters. Television and football started their relationship with arm's-length suspicion. Now they are friends for life, providing for the viewer a regular reason to watch together, share the glory of victory or the pain of defeat and, perhaps most importantly, provide a good reason to get the beers in!

CHAPTER 26

MORE THAN A MATCH

As the 2014/15 season got underway, there was one celebration that just couldn't be ignored – at least by football nuts. August 2014 marked the 50th anniversary of the start of BBC TV's *Match of the Day*.

Less a programme, more a way of life, *Match of the Day* has played a regular part in millions of people's lives during that half-century. From its instantly recognisable theme tune to its famous presenters, pundits and commentators, the programme has tracked the best and, sometimes, the worst of English football in a virtually unbroken period of televising the national sport.

And if an occasional repositioning of broadcast contracts has meant a brief break in *Match of the Day*'s Saturday evening dominance, the title has been kept alive by switching it to whatever football the BBC has retained during these periods.

But for most people, and for the most part, *Match of the Day* has meant Saturday evening at 10.00pm, or thereabouts. Undoubtedly the most famous brand in televised sport – still.

Of course, things have changed radically since it first was aired on August 22nd 1964, with major *live* football now being the established and expected norm, rather than the special treat it was way back when.

And the BBC have had to sit out on the sidelines as the price of live Premier League football and the UEFA Champions League continues to rocket out of the Corporation's reach.

In truth, given the potency and immediacy of live football across the range of channels, it is something of a minor miracle that a programme of *Match of the Day*'s make-up has actually survived, let alone thrived.

However, that says something about the popularity of the brand, the quality of the product and the strength of the format of the programme. *Match of the Day*, and in more recent times, *Match of the Day 2*, remains a no-frills concentrated look-back at the Premier League action of earlier that day, dissected and analysed by former players and out-of-work managers.

A "highlights" show would be a simplification of how to describe it – but, at heart, it *is* about putting the action first – the goals, the saves, the misses, the tackles, the fouls, the cautions and dismissals, augmented by post-match reaction from the managers and players involved, then a healthy chunk of studio analysis. Then a "Before we leave you let's have a look at the Barclays Premier League" followed by some pertinent images of the day in the closing titles.

A simple but brilliant format – a simply brilliant format.

So, in the closing chapter of this book, let's go back in time and look in more detail at how *Match of the Day* came into being, in the face of some tough resistance from the guardians of the Football League, who saw television as more foe than friend.

Its existence is derived as much from the frustration at not persuading the football authorities in the late 1950s and early 1960s to allow the BBC to cover more live league football, as it did from anybody having an inspired idea.

Also ITV, the Corporation's commercial rivals, were showing a keen interest in televising football, and their regional network, as explained earlier in the book, had shown a spirited enthusiasm for getting weekend soccer highlights into the schedule.

At that time it seemed BBC and ITV seemed to be on a permanent war footing, or certainly their respective sports departments were. This despite the regional nature of ITV's output meaning there was rarely a network "position" taken on sport in the late '50s and early '60's – and for much longer after that.

The BBC's monopoly of big football occasions was gradually being worn away by their hungry young commercial rival. Some key floodlit friendly matches in the late '50s and major competitive matches such as those from the newly-formed European Cup were finding their way more regularly onto the new channel.

For example, the 1956/57 European Cup semi-final second leg between Manchester United and Real Madrid was considered by some to be the first really major sporting event lost to ITV after a bidding war between the channels was won by the ITA companies – £3,000 being the winning figure, a full £1,000 ahead of the BBC's offer – a deal believed to have been concluded by the great Sir Matt Busby himself.

The history of BBC's football coverage in the '50s and early '60s was one of being "live" where and when it could. This meant FA Cup Finals, FA Amateur Cup Finals, England internationals, World Cups, "floodlit" friendlies and junior representative matches.

For the BBC, though, the Corporation's target remained live *league* football – and on a Saturday afternoon, too. The Football League, for their part, had been firmly and unanimously against such a proposition.

An early ITV punt in 1956 for live Saturday evening Football League coverage had been matched by a counter-proposal by the BBC, who also made an exclusive bid for FA Cup matches. Perhaps surprisingly, the League's Management Committee backed the ITV live bid only for the coup to be stopped by the clubs themselves. Neither channel got the nod for live football.

The BBC again tried to get a live batch of mid-week league games in 1957, but once again the clubs weren't having it. Other BBC offers followed on a regular basis but the Football League, now led by the resolute Alan Hardaker, a wartime Royal Naval officer, found them easy to resist.

In 1960, ITV had their short-lived attempt at live Saturday evening football curtailed, as featured earlier in the book, while the BBC, via

Sports Special, had kept up a regular on-screen relationship with league and cup football, with short highlights shot on film.

However, this pioneering BBC show also hit the buffers at the end of the 1962/63 season, partially due to cost. It had earlier only covered half of the 1961/62 season, following more disagreements with the Football League.

That particular contractual impasse had let some minor ITV contractors like Tyne-Tees, Anglia and TWW to do a deal with the Football League to film their local teams' matches – and, in due course, when moving from film to fledging electronic cameras, Anglia and Tyne-Tees were able to create the first *Match of the Day*-style programmes.

Anglia's show – *Match of the Week* – featured Norwich City vs. Derby County on its first programme in September 1962 and was recorded on two Ampex electronic cameras with John Camkin on the microphone. The programme was broadcast at 10.25pm the following evening. BBC Sport's concerns over some of their commercial rivals building a strong "local" following via their football output concentrated minds.

In the autumn of 1963, the stage was set for another crucial round of negotiations, both inside the BBC, and between the Corporation and the football authorities to establish a way forward for the national game on the licence-funded broadcaster. Within a year, *Match of the Day* was born.

An initial idea within the BBC had been to create a *Match of the Week*-style programme, with each BBC region selecting its own key match and then being part of a simultaneous opt-out across the country to carry highlights either on a Saturday evening or Sunday afternoon. This was also seen as a possible way of blooding some new commentary talent ahead of the forthcoming 1966 World Cup.

Other key BBC Sport executives felt that the audience was becoming more sophisticated and demanding and that live football coverage was now becoming the only game in town. They pushed the Corporation to approach the Football League with a proposal based on broadcasting a live second-half from a top match on a Saturday afternoon, one per month.

The matches were to come chiefly from the First Division, and for there to be also some live coverage of the newly-created Football League Cup competition's Final, which was played in midweek, over two-legs, at the two finalists' respective home grounds.

But, as *Doctor Who* began his BBC Saturday tea-time journeys in the Tardis back in November 1963, BBC Sport was finding in the Football League's Secretary, Alan Hardaker, an opponent just as formidable as the "Doctor" would find the Daleks.

I'm not sure Hardaker actually wanted to "exterminate" the prospect of live televised league football but he certainly wasn't going to champion its introduction, that's for sure. Relationships between him and the BBC authorities could best be described as prickly.

Negotiations on a new football position for the BBC took place throughout the early months of 1964 with, you sense, a good deal of suspicion in both directions.

The mood moved from live football to highlights, network highlights, albeit on BBC's new channel, BBC2, with its limited reach. The new channel had opened in April 1964 and was only being broadcast in London in its early stages. The football authorities were contented that the new highlights show would be remain somewhat under the radar on BBC2, rather than potentially over-exposed on the main channel.

BBC2's desire to invite the viewer to "occasionally stretch himself a little further" had not been an overwhelming success in its early months – audiences that could get it didn't completely "get it" and were turning away in significant numbers.

It was against this unpromising backdrop that broadcasting's newest sporting gem was to hit our screens.

A deal had been struck between the BBC and the Football League just a month before the start of the 1964/65 season.

And the outcome? A weekly Saturday evening programme, 55 minutes long, which featured the edited highlights from one pre-selected match, to be broadcast on BBC2 at 6.30pm, or any time after.

The action was covered on three electronic cameras and recorded onto videotape. A fee of £20,000 was agreed for 36 matches – and the programme was off and running. The programme's title – *Match of the Day* – would seem to have been originally used on internal scheduling plans for other sports programming, meaning the daily highlights programme during Wimbledon fortnight, but it was as the title for the BBC's new network football series that it found its way into television history.

Reaction to *Match of the Day*'s first edition, which featured the game between league champions Liverpool against Arsenal at Anfield, was mixed. The following day, *Sunday Citizen* journalist, FW Deards, claimed; "It looks like a proper clanger to me. The real sporting breakthrough on TV will come when pay-TV arrives."

A remarkably prescient view of the future of sports broadcasting if perhaps a little wide of the mark on the potential future of the BBC's new show.

Match of the Day's popularity picked up quickly though not all clubs wanted or welcomed the BBC cameras at their home games. However, the programme was steadily making its mark – and not just on these shores.

Within months of the first programme being broadcast it was being sold and seen in faraway places like Hong Kong, Australia, Rhodesia, New Zealand, Mexico, Saudi Arabia, Liberia, Egypt, Aden, Gibraltar, Malta and Trinidad.

A second season of *Match of the Day* on BBC2 followed at the established time of 10.00pm, the programme now 45 minutes long, and the fee contracted with the Football League was £25,000.

The final key move for the programme came after the 1966 World Cup when, following England's famous victory that summer, the show was moved from BBC2 to BBC1. There was an acknowledgement that the BBC's young "second" channel was losing one of its key building blocks, but *Match of the Day*, both on its own merits, and also as a pro-active response to ITV regional companies proposing to run their own highlights programmes on Sunday afternoons, was on the move.

Match of the Day settled into its familiar BBC1 Saturday evening slot and has become part of football folklore. And part of broadcasting folklore too for the past half-century.

Its current presenter, Gary Lineker, scored goals on the programme for Leicester City, Everton, Tottenham Hotspur and England, before settling for a second career in broadcasting, and now fronts the famous programme in an assured fashion.

The 2014/15 season beckoned a fresh look in the studio as long-time pundit Alan Hansen called time on his role as BBC's senior expert after two decades.

Trademark phrases like "pace and power, touch and technique" and an uncompromising analysis of goals conceded with his forensic-style uncovering of defensive errors, had made him highly watchable and, along with Lineker, one of the BBC's most important "faces" – and top earners.

With his ex-Liverpool defensive partner Mark Lawrenson moving out of his regular TV berth alongside Hansen the previous season, it is a significant changing of the guard at MOTD, as it brands itself.

Hansen looks back fondly on his time on the programme. "It's been a privilege to work on *Match of the Day* – it is an institution.

"*Match of the Day* has a tried and trusted formula and a format that hasn't changed over the years. One of its key strengths is that it has stuck to its principles – the football comes first, the talking after that. The show is always based around the action.

"And, of course, the Premier League has become such an exciting product – the game has become so fast-moving and it remains the league where the bottom team can beat the top team.

"It may sound biased but over the period I have been involved in the programme the outstanding player for me has been Liverpool's Steven Gerrard. Not only for everything has he done in the past but his ability to recently re-invent himself as a footballer."

And what about his famous "you can't win anything with kids" remark'?

"Well, that is something I will be definitely be remembered for. It was a slight re-working of a phrase used to me by the great manager, Bob Paisley when, as a young player in 1978, I was left out of the Liverpool side after a short run of defeats, despite having been told I had been playing well.

"I now look forward to sitting back and watching the programme as a viewer. It has been such an important part of my life."

As befits a programme of its reputation, *Match of the Day* continues to make headlines – and its prominence used to highlight wider Corporation policy and issues.

For example, in early 2014 it was one of the programmes highlighted by BBC's Director of Television, Danny Cohen, in his call to boost diversity across the television service, both on and off the screen.

So, the programme rolls on, still light on technological innovation compared its pay channel rivals, but strong on format and audience reach. And it remains a fact that nobody likes their team to be the last one shown on *Match of the Day* on a regular basis.

Armed with a new contract to broadcast the FA Cup, the BBC moves its famous brand forward confidently into its next 50 years.

As Alan Hansen departs the football broadcasting scene, a fellow long-time Liverpool defender, Jamie Carragher, has just started out on the journey in his new role as a Sky Sports football pundit. With a season under his belt, Carragher explained how he had quickly adapted from player to pundit.

"I'm actually surprised how much I have enjoyed it. I didn't know how I would find it but I am putting a lot of preparation time into it. Certainly for Sky Sports' *Monday Night Football* show I am thinking of ideas, along with the producers, three or four days before the programme goes to air.

"I have also obviously had to get comfortable with the on-screen technology that is so much part of the way Sky covers its football. Once you get used it you do it without thinking.

"But a bit like there's a big difference between taking a penalty in training and taking one in an actual match itself, there is a difference in practising with the technology off air and then using it live on the air.

"I am also building up a good rapport with Gary Neville. A lot of people are amused by the fact we are working together after our respective careers for Liverpool and Manchester United. We don't agree on everything of course, but respect each other's opinion.

"We hope the audience enjoys how we approach our analysis of the action. And, of course, we are invariably talking about players we recently shared the pitch with – and can give that added insight."

Sky Sports still remain firmly in the driving seat in terms of its ownership of the Premier League UK broadcast product but another PL tender document is never too far away, and with it the opportunity it delivers for new players to enter the market and attempt to prise away one of Sky Sports' major calling cards. The Isleworth-based organisation will no doubt continue to fiercely resist those challenges.

Sky has a long-standing relationship with the Premier League and, while its famous acquisition of the competition's original rights wasn't the sole reason BSkyB got a solid foothold in the British broadcasting world, it certainly played a significant part.

Sky Sport's own on-air response to a newcomer like the much-publicised arrival of BT Sport last year has been more subtle than seismic, and, in turn, BT Sport's on-screen football debut more steady than sensational.

For example, Sky have developed a studio-based Saturday early evening programme to house a live Premier League match, live "down the line" interviews with the respective managers, and a studio audience on hand to both watch proceedings and then throw in questions to the pundits.

New boys BT Sport have, on occasion, moved between their gigantic and adaptable studio to on-site and touch-line linking positions for its presenters and pundits, have used screen-in-screen inserts in its live coverage and dressed its on-screen talent in smart casual attire.

Different styles and different approaches but in the end it is still the match selections and the quantity and quality of those matches that defines where the audience spends its time.

In the end, the big "rights wars" have to be played off the pitch and any new on-screen innovations brought in to make a difference must add value for the viewer and subscriber, not just be a technical indulgence introduced to impress a few curious industry watchers.

Of course, gone are the days when everybody watched everything. If you miss one match, you know there is another one just around the corner.

It is good to see broadcasters are now readily screening many different elements of the sport including embracing women's football and supporting its growth, with significant live coverage of both major international tournaments and domestic competitions, and regular news inserts into their sports bulletins.

The amount of live football and football-related programming across the broadcast spectrum is now just incredible. Is there too much? Almost certainly, but it isn't compulsory to watch it all and there is always the "off" switch on the TV remote control.

So, what happens next in the football broadcasting business? As this book has attempted to illustrate, the development of broadcasting and football have at times gone hand-in-hand, at other times been daggers drawn. What is clear now is they have become partners by necessity and design; the top end of the football business demands huge income streams and the broadcasting business can deliver it. And vice versa.

And in this country, leagues and their matches are still sold as "leagues" in the broadcast market and not as individual matches featuring individual clubs – collective bargaining is still seen to be the right route to market for the Premier League, the world's most commercially-successful football product. For some new club owners, this takes some getting used to given their own experiences elsewhere but the remarkable domestic and overseas rights sales results show the current approach is still working.

In this country there is still the Saturday afternoon window preserved for football to be played free of the incursion of live TV match coverage. Some would see this as slightly prosaic, especially as matches played in this slot are offered for live overseas consumption.

Some major clubs grumble that their own games, if not picked by the pay television partners for the established broadcast slots, should be made available to their own supporters to subscribe to watch via club channels or other means. Once again this has been resisted.

The Saturday afternoon window, however, does preserve to some degree the much-diminished but traditional 3 pm kick-off, and, potentially with it, the home gates of individual clubs across the whole football spectrum. However there continues to be ways in which this non-broadcast zone is still regularly breached by those individuals determined to find ways of watching their teams live via overseas stations and satellites, or on-line streaming.

And the football authorities quite rightly continue to rigorously police this situation to protect and retain the full value of their intellectual property and that of their rights holders.

Big live televised football matches, like many other sports, have become the focus for huge in-game betting markets across the globe and, once again, the authorities are fully aware that such a development, while just a source of fun and extra involvement for the vast majority, potentially gives an opportunity to unscrupulous elements scouring the sporting world to corruptly earn a fast buck.

*　*　*　*　*

The English game is now being broadcast all over the globe in any number of time zones, and when Premier League clubs and their stars travel abroad on pre-season tours and so on they are greeted by literally tens of thousands of fans who religiously follow their English team's progress week-by-week on television from thousands of miles away.

It is just the latest phenomenon in a broadcasting story that has taken some remarkable twists and turns – and obviously has plenty more to come.

As the world has seemingly got smaller, the global football business has just got bigger. And, the super-modern broadcasting business that runs alongside it is at the very epicentre of its growth spurt.

It is all a long way away from September 1937 when a team of Arsenal players laughed and joked as they left their Highbury dressing room and took to the famous pitch to demonstrate their football skills and compete against one another. Famous players like Cliff Bastin, Ted Drake, Eddie Hapgood, Wilf Copping and George Swindin were football's first small-screen stars. Arsenal finished the season as League Champions; they had helped create a little bit of broadcasting history.

Witnessing their on-field activities for the first time was a new-fangled piece of technical kit, the television camera, three of them in all, and the players' every move was briefly captured for a tiny audience able to watch it. The *Radio Times* publicised this little piece of broadcasting history thus in its programme listings:

"Football at The Arsenal. A demonstration by members of the Arsenal team at the Arsenal stadium, Highbury, introduced by George F. Allison."

That simple understated programme billing was the first of the thousands that have followed it since informing viewers when and where they can switch on to "watch the match".

The relationship between football and television had got quietly underway – and has never stopped since.

SELECT BIBLIOGRAPHY

Barry Davies
Interesting, Very Interesting:
The Autobiography
Headline Publishing Group
ISBN 978 0 7553 1423 2

Greg Dyke
Inside Story
HarperCollins Publishers
ISBN 0 00 719364 5

Jimmy Hill
The Jimmy Hill Story: My Autobiography
Hodder & Stoughton
ISBN 0-340-71248-1

Geoff Hurst
1966 World Champions
Headline Book Publishing
ISBN 0 7553 1414 X

Gary Imlach
My Father and Other Working Class
Heroes
Yellow Jersey Press
ISBN 0-224-07267-6

Des Lynam
I Should Have been at Work:
My Autobiography
HarperCollins Publishers
ISBN 0 00 720544 9

Cliff Michelmore and Jean Metcalfe
Two-Way Street
Futura Publications
ISBN 0 7088 3598 8

Brian Moore
The Final Score: The Autobiography of
the Voice of Football
Hodder & Stoughton
ISBN 0 340 74830 3

Joe Moran
Armchair Nation: An Intimate History of
Britain in Front of the TV
Profile Books
ISBN 978 1 84668 391 6

John Motson
Motty: Forty Years in the
Commentary Box
Virgin Books
ISBN 978-1-905264-68-1

Compiled by John Motson
Match of the Day:
The Complete Record since 1964
BBC Books
ISBN 0 563 37062 9

Gordon Ross
Television Jubilee: The Story of
25 Years of B.B.C. Television
W.H. Allen London 1961 (no ISBN)

Ian St. John
The Saint: My Autobiography
Hodder & Stoughton
ISBN 0 340 84114 1

Sky Sports Football Yearbook 2012–2013
Headline Publishing Group
ISBN 978 0 7553 6356 8

Giles Smith
Midnight in the Garden of Evel Knievel
Picador
ISBN 0 330 48188 6

Alec Weeks
Under Auntie's Skirts:
The Life and Times of a BBC Sports
Producer
The Book Guild Limited
ISBN 1 85776 962 7

Kenneth Wolstenholme
50 Sporting Years … and It's Still
Not All Over
Robson Books
ISBN 1 86105 278 2

Kenneth Wolstenholme
They Think It's All Over...
Robson Books
ISBN 1 86105 170 0

Edited by David Coleman
Grandstand Sport
Vernon Holding and Partners Limited
(no ISBN)

Edited by Peter Dimmock
Sportsview Book of Soccer 3
Vernon Holding and Partners Limited
(no ISBN)

Kenneth Wolstenholme's Book of
World Soccer
World Distributors (Manchester) Ltd
© 1963 (no ISBN)

Kenneth Wolstenholme's Book of
World Soccer
World Distributors (Manchester) Ltd
© 1968 (no ISBN)

Martin Johnes and Gavin Mellor
The section "...men seized cushions..."
Taken from Academia.edu
1953 FA Cup Final: Modernity and
Tradition in British Culture
ORIGINALLY from John Moynihan,
The *Soccer Syndrome: From the Primeval*
Forties
Macgibbon & Kee, 1966 (no ISBN)

BBC Radio Times

BFI Television Monograph 4
Football on Television

INDEX

Index

Index

Index

Index

Index

ABOUT THE AUTHOR

Brian Barwick has an extensive working knowledge of both the broadcasting and football industries. Born in Liverpool, he watched his first live televised match in 1962, that year's FA Cup final between Burnley and Tottenham Hotspur.

An early career as a regional newspaper journalist was followed by an 18-year stint with BBC TV Sport, including spells as producer of *Football Focus* and editor of *Match of the Day*. He worked on four World Cups, and developed the early television careers of Gary Lineker and Alan Hansen, before leaving the Corporation as its Head of Sport in 1997.

He then spent seven years as ITV's Controller of Sport, and highlights there included a record TV audience for England's classic 1998 World Cup clash with Argentina, unforgettable UEFA Champions League nights, and the transfer of Desmond Lynam from BBC to ITV.

In January 2005, Brian became the Chief Executive of the Football Association and spent nearly four eventful years at the helm of English football.

His autobiography *Anfield Days and Wembley Ways* was published in 2011; he's founded his own media and sports consultancy, and now regularly writes about televised sport across both national and regional newspapers.

In February 2013 he was appointed as the new Chairman of the Rugby Football League.